21ST CENTURY ROSICRUCIANISM

Frater Robert Gordon

Lewis Masonic

First published 2022

ISBN 978 0 85318 624 3

Published by Lewis Masonic Ltd
St Neots Masonic Hall, 166 Great North Road, Eaton Socon, St Neots PE19 8EH

Printed in England

Visit the Lewis Masonic website at www.lewismasonic.co.uk

For El,

the Light that Shines on my Path

TABLE OF CONTENTS

LIST OF ILLUSTRATIONS

LIST OF ILLUSTRATIONS

Untitled by František Urban (c.1910)

INTRODUCTION

This book is about a personal journey, one that readers will be familiar with. No matter how quickly the world changes, or how unstable it can sometimes feel, there is a stillness that lies at the heart of the human experience that calls to every one of us. Hearing that call for the first time, in whatever form it may take, starts one down a path where you evolve from person to Aspirant. Some take the leap from Aspirant to Initiate, whether with an organised group or alone, and even further to Adept if we are graced with the circumstances to both hear and follow such calling.

It often starts as a kind of curiosity. We feel drawn to the mystery of unknown things beneath the surface of mundane lives. Perhaps seeking a greater sense of meaning than professional pursuits can provide, or having reached a point in our lives where a different path is necessary. As one continues, the curiosity becomes deeper and we begin to see it changing our perception of the world. This change often brings with it a passion (sometimes an obsession) before arriving in the realm of spiritual vocation and entirely altering how we interact with the world. Changing the essence of who we are, but not what we have always been.

That you are reading this book means you know that feeling, because you too have heard the call. Perhaps you were drawn in by a sense of intrigue into what lies behind the strange and evocative label *Rosicrucian*. Maybe it's because someone you respect took this path in their own journey. Many of you are years, or even decades, into exploring what that call really means and where it is coming from. Some have found a home within the Rosicrucian tradition as manifest today, through its many orders and groups that have evolved in different directions over the centuries. Some travel this path alone, through various forms of self-initiation and exploration of the hidden mysteries of Nature and Science. In whatever way you are responding to the call in your own life, it brought us together at this point – even if only for a brief moment. It is the same call that has created the circumstances for conversations and collective efforts under the umbrella of Rosicrucianism to occur for at least the past 400 years and in countless other forms, through every generation, since the dawn of humanity.

My own path took me from the curiosity of a child; to the experimentation of a teenager; into the academic study of religious anthropology; initiation into various forms of Freemasonry, Rosicrucianism, Martinism and more; through to a decade-long professional life within the Church of England. There, I managed a wide range of research and events both theological and celebratory at St Paul's Cathedral and Lambeth Palace (some writings from which make up the third section of this book) before arriving into the world of cultural heritage at the Garden Museum nearby (the final resting place of none other than Elias Ashmole). The global shift that then occurred during the pandemic provided an opportunity to reconfigure priorities around family and spirituality, so I'm now grateful to be residing in a more contemplative environment in Italy.

Don't worry. Although this book emerges from my own personal journey it contains little more personal biography. Instead, what it presents are my own attempts to understand how we might reconcile our old esoteric traditions with the hyper-dynamic, politically-fractured and increasingly digital world that we reside in. The papers presented in the second section were delivered at meetings of the *Societas Rosicruciana in Anglia* (SRIA) and *The Order of the Rose and Cross* (ORC) between 2010-2019 and are presented in chronological order; not only because some of them build upon one another directly, but also to show the development of ideas over time. The chapters in the first section (some of which were also presented to such audiences) were written more recently, from the perspective of where I stand today, and aim to tackle the question that had been brewing over the past decade: *what does it mean to live as a Rosicrucian in the 21st century?*

It's worth noting that the papers are presented as they were originally delivered. Outside of minor grammatical changes, additional footnotes and basic proof-editing, I have resisted the desire to change things to be more carefully formulated and in line with my current understanding. The essays in the second and third sections are thus presented as they were given at the time, so that the evolution of the ideas and writing can be seen. There are topics in these papers that I would treat differently today, or perhaps even have a quite different understanding of, but I think it's important not to try and change the past but to show the journey as it occurred. The first section, making up one larger piece on *21st Century Rosicrucianism* and giving this book its title, can therefore be seen as a more recent view of the overall vision and purpose of publishing the book today.

Pseudo-Dionysius has been quoted as saying that *"It is the nature of love to change a man into that which he loves"*[1]. The themes in this book can be encapsulated through seemingly simple words: *Love, Light, Peace* and *Truth.* Unpacking those words, however, takes a lifetime to even scratch the surface of what they describe. But throughout that journey we can keep returning to these simple phrases because, ultimately, what we are talking about is as simple as breathing – even if not always as automatic. It takes time and commitment, there are moments where you feel lost or despondent and, just when you feel you might have a handle on everything, there will be great challenges or readjustments required. Challenges that not only test everything you thought you knew, but make you wonder whether any of it is worth doing at all. But that is part of the path and we know this because we've all lived it in different ways. The inward aspects of our lives can be difficult to discuss openly with one another, but we can be reassured that there is more similarity to be found within them than difference.

Nothing presented in this book requires any secret knowledge to understand or arrive at that could be held back from you by others. We all have access to the same call and the nature of what is to be found there transforms those who are open to hearing it. There is no power held by people or institutions that can act as a barrier to that transformation, even though many might try to delay its potential or even violently disrupt its cause. It is a birthright that we all possess through the fact that we are human and the role that we play as custodians of the bond between material and metaphysical realms. To state that, though, also understates the vast

---

1. Waite, A. E. 1923 (1973), *Lamps of Western Mysticism,* Rudolf Steiner Publications, p156

richness of living symbolism (in artistic, literary and ceremonial form) that can be found within our religious and initiatory traditions. This includes the living symbolism that exists under the name Rosicrucianism and has enabled myself and many others, well before and long after, to evolve from the resonance that they emit and wisdom they help us to receive. Symbolism that connects us into a shared expression of human existence and our relationship to both God and Nature.

We need to find ways to be open with one another about our experiences without need for exaggeration or deceit, so that we might find our confidence bolstered by the affirmations and similar experiences of others. Not in the sense of evangelical testimony, but in a realistic portrayal of the fact that none of us have figured it all out. We are feeling our way through the journey, constantly fighting against our own shortcomings and trying our best to keep heading forward. There is no single person or group that has an answer that suits everyone. Indeed, there is nobody that has sole claim to the answer at all because ultimately it rests in experience and not interpretation. We are all born into different contexts and environments and so our spiritual paths differ accordingly. We all have access to the One universal teacher that transcends and inspires all forms of genuine religious and spiritual expression. You have already been graced with everything needed to speak with and learn from the source that resides both within and without. The ideas presented in this book have sprung from the lessons and experiences I have been grateful to receive. I share them in the hope that they might resonate with yours.

There is little detailed history in this book (and I am certainly not a scholar), but it is important to recognise that, although just one tradition among many bright lamps, there was something peculiar about Rosicrucianism that meant it quickly caught the imagination of an entire continent in the 17th century and spread from there. From this we find not only the original words of the anonymous Rosicrucian founders, but other echoes through time in the contemporary works that sprung from them and others inspired by their vision. Works responsible for both identifying that Light which shone forth from the Rosicrucian movement, while also carrying it forward so that future generations might be guided by its glow.

We are not the source of the Light itself, but we are its motion through time and space. To hand such a lamp over to another is both a great privilege and responsibility. My hope is that by reading this book you will be energised by the idea that Rosicrucianism is a lot more than obscure symbolism put down in old texts. Its truth is not just to be found through the complicated rituals and orations of theurgists operating in worldviews that are difficult to take on board today. These things hold great value, no doubt, and they are worthwhile avenues in order to experience and embody divine wisdom; but they exist mostly in the contexts of the past. Whereas we are, right now, the ones tending to the Rosicrucian flame of today.

Our illustrious forebears broke new ground in exploring the hidden depths of human consciousness and our relationship to things above and below, within and without. It is now our duty to figure out how to apply this impulse once more to our technological age. Many of the areas of psychology and medicine that were being explored centuries ago are now far better understood by modern science. In many ways these parts of the Rosicrucian tradition are no longer as relevant to us today, but that was only part of the story. A functional piece similar to the early material science and proto-chemistry that was being conducted by those labelled alchemists. Embedded within that search to understand the natural world, however, was something more eternal. An impulse driven by an appreciation of the majesty and wonder present within the creative act, emerging from that which encompasses all things that have been, are and can be – the limitless Light and potentiality of God.

For those initiated into Freemasonry there is a call to 'make a daily advancement' in one's knowledge and understanding of that tradition. This sentiment should necessarily be applied to our whole spiritual journey, for it is only through dedicated learning, practice and contemplation that we can hope to achieve the heights of the soul's relationship with its source. In some small way, I hope that this book can provide you with moments of insight and inspiration for your daily advancement as it is the result of my own steps along the same path that we travel together.

Given that the chapters were originally written as separate papers, presented over the course of a decade, I would recommend taking your time reading through them. They will have the most impact if you are able to let the ideas percolate in your heart and mind so that they have time to engage with your own wisdom that you are carrying within. By approaching this book in a more contemplative manner, you might then also find that you wander into the same realisations and deeper understandings that writing each paper provided for myself before writing the next. This process often meant that statements made previously no longer applied, or have a lot more nuance to them than originally stated, but that is all part of the journey.

The beauty of the Rosicrucian path is that it is a path of Love and Light that is open to anybody; regardless of background, education or particular talents. It doesn't require an erudite understanding of Latin or Hebrew, or the ability to memorise large tracts of ritual. You don't need to have a laboratory in your basement to practice medieval alchemy, nor do you need to be able to pull scriptural references from memory. These things can be of great benefit to those able to achieve them, but they are not a prerequisite to calling yourself a Rosicrucian. The only prerequisite is that you seek to better yourself in order to be more capable of doing God's work; and that the manner in which you do so is to *cure the sick, and that gratis*. The beauty of the path is that you quickly realise that by healing others, you are healing yourself; and by healing yourself, you are healing the relationship between Creator and Created so that it might be restored to the glorious majesty brought about by the infinite presence of Love and Hope in the world. Expressed through the miraculous pinpoints of the universe that are formed by the evolution of consciousness.

The aim of this book is to serve as a guiding lamp for those who are treading such a path. My request is that you in turn respect the role we play as custodians of that illuminating lamp and continue to carry it forward for others. Our duty as Rosicrucians is to develop enough self-awareness to have an intuitive understanding of the macrocosmic universe around us and our role in it as microcosmic beings. By doing so, we will better know where we are needed and how we can act as a force for good in a world that sometimes feels like it is consumed by darkness. This is as true and needed in the 21st century as it was in the 17th century and all that happened between. The true secret of Rosicrucianism can be found in the knowledge that we all carry within us the Light needed to dispel darkness, for it is eternal and present at the core of existence itself. We can all kindle the flame that lies at the heart of consciousness and shine brightly.

There are many out there far wiser and more disciplined than I will ever be that have provided us with the materials needed to truly understand what Rosicrucianism was in the past and how it can be practically translated into our lives today. This book isn't an academic text, nor is it one that provides a full view of the Rosicrucian arcanum. What it is, though, is an honest attempt to provide as much as possible an authentic explanation of the joys and heights, as well as the challenges, of living a Rosicrucian life in the 21st century. The papers contained within were written for small groups of people whom I felt comfortable enough to share my experiences with. I hope that you will find some comfort of your own as you read them, because the words are intimate and vulnerable even while they talk of ambitious ideals and the seemingly inaccessible heights of mystical yearning. These papers represent the truth of my spiritual journey to this point and that journey has been a Rosicrucian one. By reading my truth, I hope that it encourages you to live, speak and be with yours to the greatest extent possible. Because when it comes to curing the sicknesses of our modern world, Truth is our greatest companion and most powerful tool.

I've also included throughout the book illustrations from old texts and artists of the past, either specifically referencing Rosicrucian ideas or otherwise by those who were within the Rosicrucian sphere of influence and evolution. Symbolism is a living language that can convey different ideas to words alone and so these illustrations can be useful to deepen our understanding or receive new inspiration. One of the great benefits we now have is access to so many of the texts and artistic efforts that throughout history were rare and difficult to get hold of. Although there are still quite a few important works yet to be translated into English (or at least made readily available), there's little from the early periods of Rosicrucian history that isn't available in some form and I encourage you to take the time to discover with fresh eyes what might lie within them.

Finally, I want to extend my gratitude to you for taking the time to read this book. I've also always been blessed with the support and encouragement of my friends and family (my wife, Elizabeth, in particular, and our children Joshua and Caleb who have taught me so much) and all those close in life that have only rarely looked over with that funny glance that says *'you might be in too deep'*. I am truly grateful for such understanding and acceptance as it allowed me to fully embrace this path and what it was asking me to become. There are also those who I met through various Masonic and Rosicrucian or similar organisations that gave of their time and energy to bring me into contact with the initiatory traditions of today. I am forever humbled by the manner in which so many give so much to one another within such organisations, it has been and always will be an honour to join you in such spiritual companionship.

Even so, to have the support of all those closest to you doesn't fully overcome the apprehension of publishing this material for everyone to see, including many from my former professional life within the Church of England who might feel this is all too fringe for my own good. Yet to any from such a sphere that might be reading this, my thanks also goes out to you. My faith and the ability to see the Light that shone from within, while also recognising it shine in others, was greatly strengthened by my time working within the Church. Although I didn't end up finding my home within its walls, I certainly found many examples of Truth and Peace that brought me directly into contact with that which guides us. Thank you all for your wisdom and compassion; your interest and humble service; your kindness and the love through which you express the call in the manner in which you heard it. I have included my writings from this area of my life in the third section to show how an exoteric version of our esoteric traditions can be shared more openly with the world. You can see from the dates of publication that these were running very much in parallel at the time and so by publishing them together there is an integration that can finally take place before moving to the next stage of my own journey.

I make no claim to lofty heights of spiritual attainment, nor to the summits that can be achieved within the Rosicrucian tradition. There are many others past, present and future that will go much further and more effectively then I ever can. However, what I am offering you with this book is a genuine look at what it means to be a Rosicrucian in the 21st century. Hopefully the thoughts and ideas here resonate with your own experiences and vision for what Rosicrucianism means in an increasingly fractured and disingenuous world. Authenticity is the antidote for many of the poisons that our materialistic, power-obsessed society have been consumed by.

Truth is its voice.

Love is its practice.

All of which combine within the shifting field of our relationships and creative actions to manifest into reality. Bringing forth the Kingdom of Heaven into each potential moment.

May Love, Light, Peace and Truth guide us all,

Frater Robert Gordon

PART I:

21ST CENTURY ROSICRUCIANISM

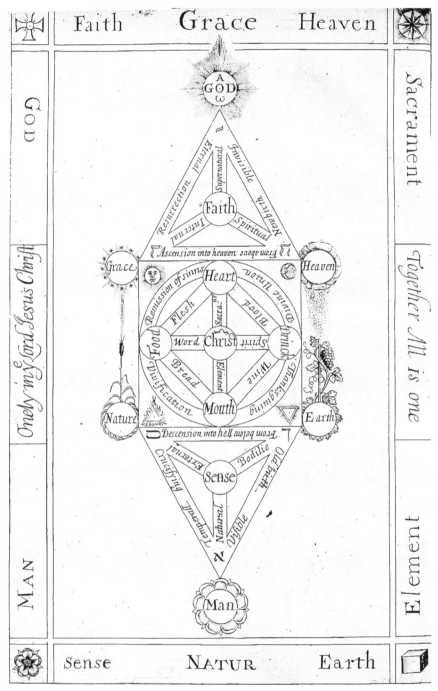

Illustration from *Mysterium Magnum; or an Exposition of the First Book of Moses...*
Jacob Böhme (1654)

21ST CENTURY ROSICRUCIANISM

What does it mean to be a Rosicrucian in the 2020s? We are now 400 years on from the publication of the pamphlets that birthed the Rosicrucian movement and our activity in various orders requires a reconsideration of the context in which Rosicrucianism now operates and its relevance to the world today. We need to consider the modern context for Rosicrucianism in light of its original purpose, while also providing guidance on how individuals can incorporate our teachings into their daily lives.

Combining multiple strands of esoteric thinking (from Paracelsus and Agrippa, to Heinrich Khunrath and Jacob Böhme) with the politics of post-Reformation Europe and a complex relationship with the Papacy, Rosicrucianism burst into European consciousness and spread a message of Universal Christianity, based upon ancient traditions and personal revelations of God, that was revolutionary and radical. It brought alchemy and other occult sciences into the limelight, with a boom in literature following the release of the pamphlets that influenced the religious landscape of the West and provided a progressive vision for society at the time.

Rosicrucianism can be seen throughout the 18th century among the detailed development of ceremonial magic, alchemy and other hermetic sciences encapsulated by Der Orden der Gold- und Rosenkreuzer alongside others such as Martinès de Pasqually, Louis Claude de Saint-Martin (and thus the formation of Martinism) and Cagliostro that were all championing the mission of restoration found in the manifestos. It is a time in which Freemasonry is flourishing with a huge amount of creative output and new degrees, particularly in France and Germany; a time in which Jean-Baptiste Willermoz formulates the modern Rose-Croix degree, influenced heavily by German Rosicrucianism and the Rite of Strict Observance. Influence can also be found in the colonies of the Caribbean (Pasqually spent the last years of his life in what is now Haiti), on the backs of the esotericism of French Masonry that breaks through into North America at the end of the 18th century.

Alongside this boom in esoteric and fraternal orders, it is also a time in which the science of chemistry is rapidly advancing and so the public perception of alchemy becomes degraded and increasingly mocked; albeit matched by a strengthening of the esoteric understanding of alchemical work and its position as a symbolic language of metaphysics and the human soul. Occult practice and mystical theology flourish, walking a path between the institutional Christian and scientific realms of mainstream society, and the influence of occultism during the time of the French Revolution that creates a huge amount of activity in a wide variety of directions. Many of the offshoots that arise are heavily influenced by Rosicrucianism and its combination of Christianity with ancient and more universal understandings of our relationship to the Divine.

The 19th century saw much further progress in connecting Rosicrucianism with its ancient and medieval counterparts. Scholarly understanding of ancient society and their religious traditions developed, combined with a boom in comparative religion as an area of study and social science. It is here that we see the emergence of the Societas Rosicruciania in Anglia (SRIA) and its counterparts, as well as the Hermetic Order of the Golden Dawn, the Rosicrucian Fraternity of Pascal Beverly Randolph, and other culturally significant public expressions such as the series of Salon de la Rose + Croix hosted by Joséphin Péladan. This culminates in the works of Papus, René Guénon, Eliphas Levi, Helena Blavatsky, Arthur Edward Waite and plenty more that close the 19th century with new translations of texts into English, detailed histories and dissemination of textual evidence, and anecdotes of exotic practices and experiences (some fictional) that allowed for different strands of occult traditions to spread quickly and take on new forms.

This textual and organisational boom laid the groundwork for the 20th century and brought Rosicrucianism once again into the public eye with a fervour that matched the excitement of the original manifestos, but now fully accessible to any who wished to engage with the orders touting connection to this illustrious tradition. This had its clearest example in the Ancient Mystical Order Rosae Crucis (AMORC), which had its beginnings around 1915 and saw rapid growth, as well as Rudolf Steiner's Rosicrucian Fellowship, but also through the popularity of other less public and commercial esoteric orders such as the various offshoots of the Golden Dawn – most of which took on a more overtly Rosicrucian character, removing the pseudo-Egyptian influence – and the continued centrality of the Ancient & Accepted Rite's 18th Degree in the landscape of modern Freemasonry.

The occult revival and counterculture of the 1960s and 70s meant that Rosicrucianism became an ongoing fixture throughout the 20th century. Anybody who was interested in generalised forms of spirituality and the New Age movement would have come into contact with Rosicrucian symbolism and mysticism with its heavy influence on Western esotericism. The approach seen here was unashamedly on personal development and attainment; which met both a liberating need as a counterweight to stifling conservatism, but also encouraged some of the excesses of ego seen in the formation of the consumerist mindset and occult symbolism as a fashion statement. Thankfully, the end of the 20th century saw a return to the publication of authentic texts and advanced treatises seen a century earlier; even though in the wider culture the true purpose of such thought had once again gone primarily underground, albeit available in specialist bookstores worldwide.

I put forward this far-too-basic overview of Rosicrucian history to show two things: first, that Rosicrucianism has been part of the backbone of Western esotericism for almost half a millennium; and, secondly, that it has always had a central role in how this undercurrent of thinking and practice emerges periodically into public consciousness. Through periods of extension and retraction, dilution and concentration in almost equal measure, new directions and responses to transformative events in global consciousness have emerged out of the Rosicrucian tradition. It is not alone in doing this, of course, but we should see our tradition as part of the formative elements of Western society and how it creates and adapts to shifting contexts through radical and visionary thinking. Even if it often succumbs to the materialism and commercial drives that surround us in the modern world.

In this way, the first 20 years of this new century has seen a fall back of Rosicrucianism in public consciousness, but an extension of understanding its role in the psycho-spiritual development of the West and increased attention from academics and other scholars of esoteric history and thought. The huge boom of hyper-commercialised spirituality has devolved into watered-down aphorisms and New Age-lite mindfulness, alongside a weaponised form of evangelical Christianity, but a more serious return to detailed esoteric understandings has become increasingly accessible to those who seek it and is starting to take greater root. 21st century esotericism has overcome many of the more commercial pitfalls of the late-20th century, as well as the boom of internet-based groups claiming their own eminence amongst digital cult-like structures, and there is now a landscape of original thought and development in these areas that could be seen as a new revival in advanced magical practice and mystical thinking.

It's important to note at this stage that Rosicrucianism, at its core, has never really been about magical practice (for the most part) and so the more mystical Christian approach taken by the tradition has found itself better established in the 21st century in the more devoted corners of esoteric communities around the world. The centrality of INRI has been restored, aligned with a continued societal move away from institutional forms of Christianity towards deeper and more personal mystical understandings of the Christ Within.

Although the limelight might not be on Rosicrucianism as much today as in the recent or distant past, it still reigns supreme in many ways; harking back to the importance of the manifestos in reviving esotericism throughout Europe and the straddling of exoteric and esoteric spheres that it has long been situated between. Even though the search to join an Invisible College of the Elect is no longer really in the public consciousness (replaced, perhaps, with a more direct neo-paganism and folk-magic witchcraft) the various orders and groups that have inherited the Rosicrucian mantle seem to be entering a new phase of serious endeavour that upholds the legacy of the tradition and its influential nature.

The retraction of the more commercial elements that had come to dominate 20th century Rosicrucianism has provided a great opportunity to redefine and reorient our traditions towards the pressing needs of the 21st century that is already well underway. The purpose of Rosicrucianism today has therefore changed somewhat from what it was aiming to achieve in the past, however there are still clear connections to the impetus behind the initial pamphlets and the esoteric movement they represented. When thinking about the role of Rosicrucianism in the 21st century, we must start by recognising that it isn't just about personal, individual transformation (although many of its practices will achieve this with great effect) but it seeks a wider impact on the direction of society as a whole. Achieving this is incredibly difficult, but ultimately a more fulfilling destiny to pursue and one we should collectively strive to bring to fruition.

So, if Rosicrucianism was trying to provide a context for Universal Christianity, rooted in the esoteric traditions of the past and free from oppressive power structures, what context do we find ourselves in today of equal importance and similar metaphysical distress?

The context we find ourselves in today is one in which the entire basis of the human condition and evolution is shifting into a new phase of existence and agency. We are now at a turning point in which our technology and scientific endeavours will soon be able to direct the path of our future biological and intellectual forms. This covers everything from alterations to our genetics; extension of life-span; adjustments to biochemistry and enhancements to our physical capabilities; through to neural implants that connect us to artificial intelligence and the library of human knowledge in a synthesis with technology previously only dreamed of. If it was 'Free Will' that marked a test of faith in millennia past, we haven't seen anything yet! In many ways, we are approaching the heights of occult transformation and the promises of alchemy in its most physical manner: immortality, omniscience and the power to change shape and form.

This turning point should not be underestimated or merely seen as steady progress towards an unknown future. Rather, it requires a mature and highly developed spiritual component in order to understand the metaphysical, philosophical and emotional gravity of what is occurring around us and what we are increasingly accepting will happen to and within ourselves. As has long been understood, but perhaps not quite in this way, our current physical forms are not the final and only kind of existence that we will inhabit. At this point in human history and evolution we can see the changes that are about to take place and the practical roadmap is starting to be laid out. However, we need to recognise that it is currently one that is primarily dictated by international power structures – whether they be government or corporate – without much consultation, or even seemingly any forethought as to the likely endpoints.

Rosicrucianism is particularly suited to addressing this, as it has done so many times in the past, and challenge the norms of potentially oppressive power structures, as it is primarily concerned with the meeting point between personal agency, collective responsibility and the role of the Divine in all things. The connection to early scientific endeavour gives us a reason to consider and fully incorporate the scientific landscape of today and how we address our role in the cosmos. The balance between scientific and religious pursuits leads us to see that all human progress and so-called advancement has an impact on our metaphysical destiny, as the thought forms that emerge from our capacity to co-create reality have an increasing impact on the material world. Not just in how we forge and combine different elements outside of ourselves, but how we are now able to influence and even completely change the make-up and construction of our own physical, emotional and intellectual forms. This kind of responsibility has never been in the hands of humanity in such an immediate and powerful way and it will rapidly change everything that is to come in the future.

Rosicrucianism, with its emphasis on esoteric science, medicine and our journey through life and death, needs to speak directly into this context of 21st century transhumanism. We should act assertively and brazenly, although often anonymously as before, to ensure that we undermine and counteract the influence of corrupted vested interests. Uplifting the kinds of transformative streams of grace, compassion and beauty that only a conscious connection to the Divine can truly manifest.

The other, closely related, context that we find ourselves in revolves around the rapid growth of public communications and propaganda of all kinds. This has formed an all-encompassing influence on our perception of reality and how we construct personal and shared identity. I have discussed this in more detail in my paper *On the Transformation of Glamour* but, to put it briefly, we find ourselves in an era in which truth is almost entirely eroded in the public sphere (and increasingly our personal lives) as we construct illusory identities and present them to one another aggressively as fact. Truth is an important yardstick by which to measure Rosicrucian success, connected closely to the notion of Light that we are guided by, and is part of the spiritual underpinnings of the source of our shared inspiration. Seeing ourselves, therefore, as guardians of Truth in a digital, post-truth age is an important and necessary role for Rosicrucianism in the 21st century.

This isn't without its dangers, as it is far too easy to mistake personal opinion and desire for Truth. So we need to hold ourselves up to scrutiny and develop a deeper understanding of how opinion is formed in order to find ways to assist humanity in seeing through the fog of advertising, propaganda and hierarchical influence that subverts our creative ability and agency on a daily basis.

Becoming a champion of Truth certainly starts with the timeless advice to *'Know Thyself'* and so it can be seen that the Rosicrucian teachings train us to do exactly this. They provide guidance so that we might understand the philosophical, emotional and metaphysical influences that create the experience of consciousness we label 'I' and recognise that it is through this focal point of ego and material form that we can assist in spreading God's Will and Love to all those we come into contact with.

Understanding and embodying this allows the Adept to then seek a more active role in the wider world, to help direct the course of influencing factors and act against those that seek (whether consciously or not) to undermine humanity and our relationship with God. The Initiate learns and the Adept teaches; and this applies when considering the glamours that surround us as it does for any other aspect of the Rosicrucian path. In the context of the 21st century, this needs to incorporate a view of the global communications and influence networks that we are all participating in, acting as agents of Light and consciously struggling against the corrupting darkness that threatens to distract us from the inspiring spark of the Christ Within. Endeavouring to do so fulfils the obligation to *'cure the sick, and that gratis'*; for it is the dissolution and subversion of Truth, and therefore trust, peace and compassion, that is perhaps the greatest sickness we are facing today.

If this, then, is the context of 21st century Rosicrucianism and the role we might have in the modern world, *how do we actually go about doing it?* What practical steps can be taken and how do we know when they are working? This is a deeply personal question, with many different answers, but I'm going to briefly consider a simple overarching concept to try and give some structure that can then be tailored to each individual's place and means.

The most important thing to consider is that your identity as a Rosicrucian should be completely integrated into your life. This doesn't necessarily mean that you need to go shouting it from the rooftops (or putting it on your social media profiles). It does mean, however, that you shouldn't see the spiritual side of your life as a switch that can be turned off and on when most convenient to you. Often people completely isolate this part of their life and identity from their family and professional career. In reality, it isn't possible to separate our spiritual, physical and emotional selves and so we need to be cautious of times in which we seem to be attempting to do this. What we are doing when we compartmentalise our spiritual practice (or perception of ourselves as spiritual beings) into something that only occurs during specific rituals, ceremonies or special meetings is that we are accepting the illusion that our material selves take priority over the spiritual component of our being. That the routine of our daily life can only spare brief moments of spiritual nourishment. When it comes to those closest to us and our family, it can also have the effect of drawing us further away from some of the primary sources of Love and compassion in our lives. Rather than embracing these connections as pure and sacred expressions of the Divine, we might see them as burdensome or frustrating; even to the point of using our involvement with Rosicrucianism or other forms of religious and spiritual activity as a form of escapism that is deeply detrimental to both ourselves and those closest to us.

The ultimate goal of the Rosicrucian is not just to be reminded from time to time that we are eternal, metaphysical beings. It is to live and experience our role as divine agents as an all-encompassing vocation that informs and guides everything that we do. Rosicrucianism is not something that exists as separate from the rest of our identity and path through life. It *is* the path through life and must therefore act as a foundation for everything else, even though it might be one that acts subtly and quietly rather than overtly and evangelically. Genuine evangelism comes through the works conducted in God's name that transform and overcome, not through words that seek to convince or comfort. When one acts with the authenticity and dedication that true Rosicrucian vocation requires, others are impacted by this kindness and outpouring of Love; they feel the guidance of the divine hand and themselves turn towards the source of Light that we are embodying in that specific moment. Healing the world, free of charge and without fanfare, is our sacred mission. Through outward acts of compassion that actively aim to engage the world without any expected result or return, other than the purpose of healing itself, we act as unknown agents of Christ in conducting the transformative work of God.

In order to solidify this kind of vocation in one's life, I suggest a cycle of progress to reconcile our modern lifestyles with the Rosicrucian path. This cycle has different kinds of output and manifestation, but can be understood conceptually as the journey from *Personal Practice*; to *Social Engagement*; to *Spiritual Retreat* and then allowing this cycle to repeat throughout our lives.

Personal Practice is the conscious effort to embody the task of exploring the makeup of our being and how it relates to the world around us. By doing so, we find time to remove ourselves from the desires and motivations of daily life; conducting ourselves in a way that connects with God and reunites our physical agency with the eternal Christ Within. This takes many forms, but all share the purpose of opening ourselves to the Divine; of hearing the still voice within and heeding its call. It is also important for us to better understand those aspects of ourselves that require attention in order to be useful to a life in service to God. Self-discipline; humility; consistency; spiritual knowledge; concentration; all of these are enhanced by the methods of prayer, mystical and/or magical practice that we engage in. They should also be developed in harmony with the inner circle of our own lives; our family, close friends and other loved ones whom we rely on for support and who, in turn, we must uplift in becoming better versions of themselves. This doesn't mean we can't conduct ourselves privately, but we must always be aware of the impact our journey is having on those closest to us; because in the end, their path and ours are intertwined.

It is from this wellspring of personal practice that we emerge into the second part of the cycle: *Social Engagement.* Here we learn that our own relationship to God is but one of an infinite number of expressions and channels, each one unique and important even though it is but a speck of sand in eternity. Our inward-looking practice and prayer now has an outward purpose and the development we have undertaken helps to restore the fractures of a material world in need of repair. Importantly, it is also through social engagement that we learn to temper the arrogant excesses and delusions of religious life; which has a tendency to deceive as much as it does to lead people to the voice of Truth. By acting in service to humanity, we thus present ourselves with humility and seek to heal our own wounds alongside those we are working with. We place ourselves in a position to see things from the perspective of others, stripped of our own tightly controlled notion of identity. When our social engagement as Rosicrucians is conducted successfully, we learn that the prophetic voice and hand of Providence that emerges from us is not our own. Rather it is a small outlet of the eternal stream that has found expression throughout all of human history, inspired by the Light of the Most High and directed by the Spirit of Truth towards the regeneration and salvation of all.

If the social engagement that follows personal practice is an act of breathing out and sharing in God's Providence with others, then it is the act of *Spiritual Retreat* that provides the breath in and allows our inner spark to become inflamed with inspiration and visionary clarity. Social engagement has a deeply meaningful effect and is the true purpose of Rosicrucian endeavour; but just as it provides balance to the internal world of our own practice, it can also lead to becoming subsumed within the boundaries of society. Boundaries that can often serve to restrict progress and stifle momentum in favour of that which is familiar and comfortable. Spiritual retreat, which can take many forms from a single weekend through to months or even years, from silent monastic life to a simple hike through the woods, removes ourselves from the burdens and boundaries placed on us by modern life.

Personal practice exists by necessity alongside worldly obligations of family, work and community; but spiritual retreat strips all of this away and allows us to truly see what lies beneath the routine and patterns of day-to-day existence. It is here where the heights of religious and transcendental experience can be attained; whether experienced as soft light in a still valley, or as lightning strikes on Olympian mountains. It provides us with the radical shifts of perception and understanding that allow for the prophetic voice to emerge and with enough magnetism to have an impact on the world. All while reinvigorating the philosophical and religious practice as a serious component that nourishes and directs our lives.

The breathing in and breathing out that this cycle of Rosicrucian progress brings – from private internal, to engaged social, to intense focus on the Divine – is analogous to the cosmological formulation of the Tetragrammaton (*YHVH*). Our participation in the Breath of Life then echoes the incarnation of Jesus Christ and the formation of the Pentagrammaton (adding the *Shin* to create *YHShVH*) through its manifestation in the material agency of intellect, emotion and will. In this cycle of inward/outward, personal/social, passive/active, we mirror the nature of God as both infinite and finite, transcendent and individual. When repeated throughout one's life this cycle ensures that we can maintain balance between the esoteric and exoteric pillars of our lives and their personal and communal manifestations. It continuously reminds us to be humble while also requiring the discipline and confidence necessary for real progress. It integrates our physical, mental, emotional and spiritual aspects into one cohesive identity; focused on participating in the Will of God and allowing Providence to work through the agency of a well-trained and Truth-speaking ego. God's Love and Light finds its magnificent expression in, of and through us, following the redemption of humanity with its divine creator through the incarnation and resurrection of Christ Within.

21st century Rosicrucianism is not merely a personal pursuit that helps us overcome our own desires and insecurities, nor is it just a path of spiritual transformation for the individual to have an ecstatic experience of divine realms. Rosicrucianism has always been deeply connected with the spiritual destiny of Western society as a whole, particularly in those times where values of freedom, liberty, personal agency and social compassion are threatened. By taking these three categories (*personal practice*; *social engagement*; *spiritual retreat*) and ensuring that we fulfil them in our own lives, through whatever forms are available and resonate with us most, we are continuing this Rosicrucian legacy.

Success means that we recognise that it is not just an exercise in historical re-enactment that we are partaking in, but one of meaningful societal re-construction and prophetic re-creation that is required for humanity to continue on a path towards that which is eternally Good. In our modern lives, the context of mass global communications and an ever more enmeshed planetary destiny means that we have a duty to destroy the illusions of corruption that surround us and speak out against them through whatever means we have available. This should always be done with the respect that comes from recognising that all people are born into dignity and co-create the world with the Divine, while acknowledging that not all pursuits or motivations should be seen as acceptable to those that seek to uphold the tenets of Love, Light, Peace and Truth. In order to act as healers of the collective illnesses of humankind, we must conduct ourselves as guardians of these forces. We must truly understand our own selves and motivations, accepting our weaknesses with the discipline to overcome them rather than a guilt that burdens us to inaction, but we cannot become obsessed with self-exploration to the extent that we forget to engage with the world around us and have an impact on the form it will take in the future. We are living through a turning point in human evolution and development that requires all those attuned to the hidden mysteries of Nature, Science and the Divine to take responsibility for the collective destiny of humanity. Rosicrucianism in the 21st century, as it has done in centuries past, must play an active role in influencing the thought forms, practical applications and lived experiences that will create the boundaries of human existence for future generations.

By conducting ourselves with a seriousness that is open and compassionate, we accept the obligation of such an important and challenging task. We can then walk through the door to our collective future and confidently begin the next act of our cosmic destiny. Restoring that which was lost and emerging triumphant into a new phase of heavenly existence.

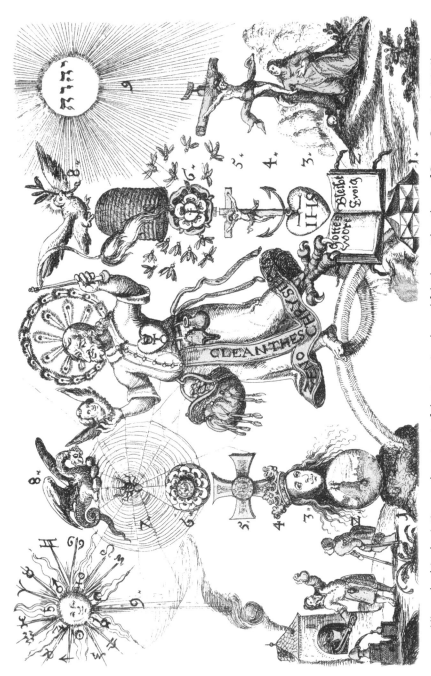

Hieroglyphic depiction and contrast of the true simple and falsely sent brothers of RosenCreutz (c.1649)

Image cropped from original (CC BY 4.0) Wellcome Collection

THE PRACTICAL PATHS OF ROSICRUCIANISM

Having posited that we should see our work as a cycle of three activities: *personal practice, social engagement* and *spiritual retreat.* We will now explore the first of these in more detail, considering the different forms of practical work that fall under the umbrella of Rosicrucianism. By doing so, we can embolden our personal practice and continue moving forward with the confidence that our work is inherently transformative while also being authentically Rosicrucian in nature. Understanding what the core ethos and egregore of Rosicrucianism consists of also allows us to create stronger bonds with one another as we walk our many paths of individual spirituality while being lifted along by the same currents of mystical air.

With this relatively brief overview, I hope to provide some guidance that maps out the general landscape of Rosicrucianism as a tradition while also giving an overall framework that might help us traverse it more readily. On the finer and more advanced details of what you might find along the way, I defer to the experience and wisdom of many others who are true Adepts; but by providing a contextualising framework of the practical paths of Rosicrucianism, the intention is to find a common ground in which we might meet and share our discoveries in a fruitful and productive way.

The Original Manifestos

Let's begin, then, by taking a look at the three original pamphlets released in the early 17th century. Without delving into speculation about who might have written them and why, we can ask a simple question: *what practical paths do the manifestos speak of directly?*

The *Fama Fraternitatis* gives us the lofty goal to *"renew and reduce all Arts...to perfection"*[1], and in practical terms tells us of the studies of Brother C.R.C. in *"Mathematica, Physick* [Medicine]*, and Magic"*, along with the 'Cabala' of Fez and the alchemical 'transmutation of metals'. There is mention of a *"magical language and writing, with a large dictionary, which we yet dayly use to God's praise and glory"*; references to 'our ROTA'[2]; as well as the *"discourse of secret and manifest philosophy"*; 'to cure the sick'; and the use of 'two Sacraments'. Importantly, there's also the clear statement that they *"[esteem] little the making of gold"*, along with the admonishment that there are many books and pictures 'under the name of Chymia' that are an insult to the glory of God. The *Fama* then closes with the assertion that all those of like mind and temperament should write or speak such truth openly and from the heart.

In the *Confessio Fraternitatis* there is a further call to action. The *Confessio* again calls people to write and speak out – to create and distribute the means for a wider awakening – but here the continual study of Sacred Scripture is put forward as the sole, only and assiduous practice required of the Aspirant. This is to occur not just in word but also deed, making:

> *"the Bible the rule of their life, the end of all their studies, and the compendium of the universal world, from whom we require not that it should be continually in their mouth, but that they should appropriately apply its true interpretation to all ages of the world."*

To achieve this, the *Confessio* calls us to read and understand the 'great book of nature' for which they *"made for ourselves a new language, in which the nature of things is expressed"* while again, in similar fashion to the *Fama*, admonishing the use of practical alchemy for profit in favour of a more

---

1. All quotations from the *Fama* and *Confessio Fraternitatis* have been taken from the Thomas Vaughan translation into English (under Eugenius Philalethes), published in 1652
2. Papus equates this to TORA / TARO in his book *The Tarot of the Bohemians*, 1896

compassionate and spiritual kind. It does offer a more nuanced view here than the *Fama*, though, in recognising that the search for the 'tincture of metals' is not inherently wrong, but that it tempts people away from walking the entirety of the path. Because in the end it is not enrichment, or status, or power that they seek, but human welfare; co-operation in the work of God; and the perfection of the arts through the steadfast observation of Nature (i.e. the macrocosmic Universe).

The Chemical Wedding of Christian Rosenkreutz

Which brings us to the third pamphlet released as part of the commonly acknowledged original manifestos, almost certainly by the self-professed hand of Johann Andreae, entitled *The Chemical Wedding of Christian Rosenkreutz*. It's worth noting that Andreae stated that this work was satirical in nature and you can certainly see a thread of ostentatiousness that runs throughout, with its long asides to tell riddles and parlour games played with dozens of virgins. However, to dismiss the piece as unimportant because of its satirical elements is to overlook the depth that it simultaneously displays. *The Chemical Wedding* is, by far, the most symbolically intricate of the three pamphlets, with allusions to black crows, white doves, Virgin guides, lions, unicorns, ceremonial rooms, ocean pearls, death, resurrection, Knights of the Golden Stone, holy nuptials and even door-keeping. The alchemical allegory is clearly present and, even without diving into the deeper symbolism involved, ultimately looks at the journey of one man towards the centre of his being and the heights of royal attainment to be found in the soul.

Prayer and meditation, that is 'humble and fervent', form the backbone of practical work referenced, with a focus on consuming oneself with the thought and glory of God, yet to 'reserve in silence' that which is entrusted and ensure that it is committed to the 'spreading of His name'[3]. There is the criticism of those who would either represent themselves and their attainments dishonestly, or think too highly of themselves and thus lead to their own destruction. Of particular interest to our focus here is the reference to the different paths that can be taken to the Royal Palace. There are offered to the Aspirant four paths: one that is short, but dangerous; one that is long, but easy (as long as you stay on course); the third which is the Royal way, filled with pleasure and joy (but offered only to one in a thousand); and the

---

3. English transation quotes as in Waite, A. E., 1887, *The Real History of the Rosicrucians*

fourth that cannot be completed except by 'incorruptible bodys'. Although this doesn't give us a direct steer on *what* the paths of Rosicrucianism are, it does provide some idea on the choices available and the manner in which they are walked.

Towards the end of the text, there is an obligation made that helps us understand a few more areas of practical work that should be avoided: namely to *"at no time ascribe your order either unto any Devil or Spirit, but only to God, your Creator, and His hand-maid Nature"*; and that we *"shall not be willing to live longer than God will have you."* Without getting too proscriptive, it seems that the search for longevity and immortality might be out of the question; even though it is regularly found in the work of physical alchemists and part of the Universal Medicine referred to in the earlier manifestos. The first of these obligations also shows us that, although we might consider both alchemy and various forms of magic to be part of the Rosicrucian tradition, it is only when directed by and for God and Nature (rather than devils or spirits) that we serve our duties true.

Contemporary Authors

Even though there might not be many direct instructions on practical paths in the original manifestos, it is clear that the founders of Rosicrucianism saw it as in line with Hermetic science and other strands of esotericism present at the time – particularly the resurgence of alchemy – but that it needed to be steadfastly aligned with a God-focused theurgic intent. This is proven effective by how strongly the publication of the pamphlets resonated and the flurry of activity that followed, with many commentaries and other manifestos circulated by numerous authors and often printed with one or more of the original documents themselves. We can also look to other key influences published immediately *before* the original manifestos were made public; that we can consider within the same milieu and part of the Rosicrucian ethos. When these things are combined with the content of the three primary texts, we begin to see a clearer picture of the practical paths of Rosicrucianism as envisaged at the time.

Before the publication of the original manifestos, Christian Alchemy was widely spread among the esoteric corridors of Europe. One of the first editions of the *Confessio* was published along with the *Secretioris Philosophiae Consideratio brevis* (*A Consideration of the More Secret Philosophy*), written under the pseudonym Philipp à Gabella, that was heavily influenced by and quotes substantial sections of John Dee's *Monas Hieroglyphica*; the symbol of which also appears in *The Chemical Wedding* and links the tradition directly to this powerhouse of alchemy, astrology and angelic magic. At the same time as Dee, Giordano Bruno was espousing an esoteric theology that linked the consciousness of Man to Nature and the Divine through mathematics – a key component of the learnings of the legendary C.R.C. in the *Fama* – and was also developing a highly sophisticated form of *Ars Memoriae*: the art of memory. Paracelsus is named directly in the *Fama* and his work on the *microcosm* and *macrocosm*; the *quinta essential* (soul of objects) and the role of Man as the 'fifth substance'; alongside extensive efforts in medicine and both natural and astrological magic, are clearly one of the primary influences on Rosicrucianism.

We can also thereby consider the important influence of Johannes Trithemius – who not only taught and mentored Paracelsus, but also Agrippa and was extensively involved in the development of angelic magic and the use of magical languages; indeed, it was one of his ciphers that was used in the infamous 'Cipher Manuscripts' that created the Hermetic Order of the Golden Dawn. Immediately following the publication of the pamphlets we then have things such as the ten publications released by Jakob Böhme between 1620 and his death in 1624, which solidified an evolved Christian Theosophy along with the notion of the 'union of opposites' that lies at the core of the Western esoteric tradition. Rosicrucianism was thereby born in a time of seismic shifts in the esoteric landscape of Europe; both heavily inspired by the many influences surrounding it, while also highly influential on what was to come.

Among all of this excitement and hidden depths of esoteric knowledge, it is still important to recognise, though, that the most important practice to those who considered themselves Rosicrucians was *Medicine*. Then an evolving science that straddled disciplines, medicine (or *Physick* as it was called then) sat between notions of the spiritual and physical components of mankind and spoke strongly to the concept of our shared duty towards the uplifting of humanity. There's a reason why the first and foremost duty of the Rosicrucian is to 'cure the sick, and that gratis' as it was absolutely front and centre in importance (and controversy) at the time. Michael Maier in his *Themis Aurea or Laws of the Fraternity of the Rosy Cross* published in 1618[4],

---

4. An english translation from 1656 is available on the Internet Archive, as part of the excellent Getty Research Institute collection a year after his landmark alchemical work *Atalanta Fugiens*, spends the first half of his book detailing the role of the Rosicrucians in the restoration of Medicine as an honourable practice that had fallen into disrepute. This notion of revitalising Medicine, similar to the work of Basil Valentine that was also popular at the time, admonishes the extravagances of the medical professions; which not only debased many of the things they were working with, but did so while overcharging and often outright deceiving their patients.

Overall, Maier shows us that the path of a Rosicrucian is an inherently practical one. Not just solely based on learning and reason, but on experiment and experience; on the transformative effect of practical work that can be witnessed and embodied rather than merely discussed or alluded to. While in today's world Medicine has a clearly defined professional path, there is still something powerful in the worldview of the original Rosicrucians that we can learn from in how we approach our practical work today. This is primarily because there wasn't as clear a distinction between material and spiritual alchemy – incorporating not only medicine, but astronomy, chemistry, geology and many other natural sciences that were developing at the time.

Indeed, unlike the post-Enlightenment world that divides material and spiritual pursuits, to the Rosicrucian they are forever intertwined. Even though to a modern viewpoint it might seem that Rosicrucianism was just defending 'real science' from the ravages of religious superstition (which, in many ways, it certainly was), it was also imparting the Hermetic notion that the spiritual subtleties involved have a very real impact on the success (or failure) of physical processes. This is partly because physical processes are an alchemical externalisation – a talismanic focal point – that enables the practitioner to be transformed through the cyclical nature of their material work; but also because the development of spiritual sensitivities allows for the occult qualities of material things to be perceived, so that they can be properly maintained and worked without unknowingly altering (or destroying) their essence.

This notion of the combined work of physical and spiritual spheres is strengthened by other contemporary texts. Robert Fludd in his *Apologia Compendiaria*, published in 1616 in defense of the Rosicrucian Brotherhood, states plainly that the *"spiritual and worldly secrets…may be accomplished… by the outpouring of the Holy Spirit in men…or by the revelation of the mysteries concealed in Nature, which also requires the assistance of the Spirit."*[5] This is a common theme among early Rosicrucianism. *The Speculum Sophicum Rhodo-Stauroticum* (*The Mirror of the Wisdom of the Rosicrucians*), published in 1618 and often referred to as the 'fourth manifesto', has the idea directly on its title page with the references to 'Ora' and 'Labora' (Prayer and Work); alongside the balancing titles of 'Physiologia' and 'Theologia'. The text itself tells us that faith, wisdom and study are the 'true philosophy' of the Rosicrucians and that we must *"therefore hasten slowly. Pray, work and hope"* along with the recognisable encouragement to 'know thyself' and 'amend our ways and life'. All of this is encapsulated within the practice of alchemy as the primary path for the aspirant, but it still remains of great importance to be properly prepared to walk it; for as the text suggests:

> *"whoever wishes to know the daughter of alchemical wisdom, resplendent in her brilliant white dress, should, before he sets out on this crystal sea, first train his eyes and prepare his strength for the struggles ahead"*[6]

This preparation involves other, lesser Arcana that build up the practitioner's concentration, willpower, intuition, visualisation and contemplative faculties to such an extent that the challenges found on the alchemical path can be overcome and the wisdom that it offers properly reconciled within the being of the practitioner themselves. Rather than forever remaining an external form of knowledge, the path becomes embodied and manifest through the transformation of the Adept as both craftsman *and* tool. Following the hand of Divine Providence, by understanding things greater than just our immediate situation in the material world, is the path that unlocks the *"lovely art and treasure house"* in full.

Practical Rosicrucianism therefore requires a combination of faith, intuition and wonderment at the miraculous nature of existence, while also needing the grounding principles of rationality, reason and observation to steer true. One or another of these will not suffice alone, but all need to be kept in balanced motion to achieve the alchemical and theurgic goals being sought.

What we find, then, is that at the core of Rosicrucianism is a Royal Art: the knowledge and understanding of the processes that develop the

---

5. Hoffman, W. (ed.), 2001, *Robert Fludd: Essential Readings,* North Atlantic Books, p52
6. The full text translation can be found on the Alchemy Website, levity.com

Universal Medicine[7] and the Philosopher's Stone. This is the Great Work and transformation of the Adept, but it is heavily veiled in allegory and requires material, astral and divine components to be properly aligned and purified through *'solve et coagula'*: the cyclical process of drawing down Divine Will into the physical realm, while sanctifying our own material form and intentions through contact with Divine Wisdom. Within this cycle of drawing down and rising up we can see that, when it comes to the day-to-day journey, there are many different steps to be taken, over many different types of terrain. Terrain that varies in distance and magnitude from individual to individual, depending on their particular lot and location in manifested existence.

There is some added context to this developed in another early Rosicrucian text, the *Ara Foederis Theraphici* (*Altar of the Theraphic Brotherhood*) published in 1618, that explicitly highlights the importance of sharing the knowledge gained while on travels around the world; something that was mentioned as a central duty for the original Rosicrucian fratres of the *Fama*. No one person can obtain omniscience of the near infinite experiences and practical paths that the human condition has enabled to flourish in its relationship with Nature and the Divine. Sharing our discoveries with like-minded companions – working together towards the common goal of redemption – therefore becomes a key component of practical Rosicrucianism and part of our duty and terms of achievement.

The *Ara Foederis* also builds upon the alchemical emphasis of other early Rosicrucian texts by giving an indication that the primary goals were contemplative and theurgic, as opposed to the involvement of more occult practices. This is echoed in a Rosicrucian prayer by John Hendon, published in 1662, that strengthens the notion that the ultimate goal of Rosicrucianism was to allow the aspirant to properly receive, understand and embody the, as he called it, 'Illuminating Spirit' through obedience to God's Will and a lifestyle properly aligned so as to *"wound not my Conscience with vice"*. This repeats the often found notion in the early texts, including all three of the original pamphlets, that it is only through pure intention and an adequately virtuous life that the aspirant can reach the destination they are seeking.

In this manner, one of the most powerful practical tools we have is *prayer*: an open adoration, communication and subservience to the presence of the Divine within our own beings and throughout all of Creation. Indeed,

---

7. Also referred to as *Azoth* per Basil Valentine's text published in 1613

the rituals of the modern SRIA state at the outset that our aims will be accomplished by *"prayer and perseverance in the paths of knowledge and virtue."*

In regards to magical workings, although not heavily present within the original manifestos it is widely considered a key component of the practical paths of Rosicrucianism. Returning to Maier's *Themis Aurea*, he is a huge proponent of 'magick' as *"the highest, most absolute and divinest knowledge of Natural Philosophy advanced in its wonderful works and operations"*[8]. Robert Fludd, in a letter of response printed in 1631 with the snarky sub-title *The Squeesing of Parson Fosters Sponge*, answers the assertion that all magic is evil (Diabolical) by asking:

> *"As if there were not a natural Magic, by which Solomon did know all the mysteries in Nature, and the operations therefore; yea, as if the three wise Kings of the East did discover that the true King of the Jews was born by Diabolical Magic…were these three wise men Cacomagical Magicians…?"*[9]

Gabella in the *Consideratio Brevis* of 1615 reminds the reader of the importance of 'geometry', 'mechanical magic' and 'cabbalistic expression' which, with a broader view, we know are all central components of angelic magic. While there might not be consensus on just how central a role assertive practices such as ceremonial magic should play, and there have certainly been many missteps in Rosicrucian history, there is a consistent recognition that, as long as the overall path is a restorative one, it can be considered a Rosicrucian one. This applies equally to any specific practice, on any of the four types of path outlined in the *Chemical Wedding* that the Rosicrucian might take. As Gabella also reminds us: *"By the Will of God he is that most famous Mercury, he is the Microcosm, he is Adam"*[10].

The final text that I want to consider today is perhaps the most famous outside of the original manifestos, almsot solely because of its beautiful and

---

8. Interestingly. this definition of 'magick' is also found in 17th century manuscrips of the *Lemegeton* grimoire and the definition is often attributed to it. Aleister Crowley quoted it as such in his *Magick in Theory & Practice* without mention of Maier, for example. Although parts of the *Lemegeton* do go back further, I can't track down an earlier source than Maier's Latin text for this particular definition, although it seems it could be a variation of that found in Agrippa's *Three Books* (Book One: Chapter II) published in 1533

9. Hoffman, W. (ed), 2001, p207

10. Full text English translation available on the Alchemy Website, alchemywebsite.com deeply meaningful emblems taken from a variety of esoteric sources, and that is the compendium known as the *Geheime Figuren der Rosenkreuzer* (*Secret Symbols of the Rosicrucians*) that were connected to the Orden des Gold- und Rosenkreutz (although not necessarily first collated by them) and published in multiple volumes between 1785-1788.

We can see right from its title page[11] that the compendium is for those *"Practicing daily in the School of the Holy Ghost"*. The numerous aphorisms inside its compiled pages all revolve around this notion; including *"If a philosopher you wish to be, let only patience dwell in thee"* and *"the outer and the inner Mind, without God's light you cannot find"* while we *"always watch the inner centre"* and *"look well for the golden magnet"* to pick out just a few of the dozens of inspiring lines found throughout the collection.

What this pivotal text presents throughout is the Christian Trinity of Father, Son and Holy Spirit; alongside the tri-une structure of God, Nature and Humanity; with the likewise ternary alchemical foundation of Sulphur, Mercury and Salt; the quaternary of the Tetragrammaton and Elements; Pentagram of the magi; the Hexagram of the cabalists; and Septenary of the astrologers. Suffice to say, there is no other volume that so readily gives us all the tools needed to understand the practical paths of Rosicrucianism as the *Geheime Figuren*.

This overarching and emergent structure forms the basis for almost all of the Rosicrucian orders that we know of, whether they be more focused on contemplative mysticism; proponents of precise ceremonial practices; or practical alchemical work. When combining this with the earlier texts of the 17th century we can see that there are, essentially, two grand paths of practical Rosicrucianism: *Alchemy* and *Theurgy*. Within each of these interrelated paths that dovetail like the snakes of the Caduceus, we have a number of different and more specific practices that could be considered.

Under Alchemy, we have both medicine and chemistry; but also herbalism, astrology, natural magic and practical paths such as talismanic work or the art of memory; as well as the symbolic guide of the Major Arcana of the Tarot (which helps to bridge both). Theurgy then consists of the more prayerful practices, whether contemplative or ecstatic, that are encapsulated by Kabbalah; angelic magic; meditation and prayer; guided by the Scriptures and Sacraments and fuelled by Faith, Hope and Charity. Underneath all of

---

11. High quality scans of multiple versions of this text are available online from the University of Wisconsin-Madison's History of Science and Technology collection. English translations can be found on the Internet Archive

these terms, and others not mentioned, is a kaleidoscope of different advice on specific programmes of action; but I would argue that they ultimately all return to those two grand paths: *Alchemy* and *Theurgy*.

These practices strengthen the physical, mental and astral components of the practitioner so that they can better understand and perform the operations referred to as the *Great Arcanum*. That secret doctrine of the Western Mystery Tradition which is inherently about the creative act itself. Focused on the formation of influence and construction that emerges from the source of all things, while also present in its highest forms within the personality and consciousness of humanity in our physical materiality.

It is our duty as Rosicrucians to align ourselves true in order to assist with the reintegration of material existence with the Divine; not just to escape the velocity of physicality or gain mastery over it for personal wealth, but to heal and restore the Universe to the former glory of the Heavenly Paradise present before the Fall.

To put it another way: Alchemy is working with the emergent substance of Material Form; Theurgy is our alignment to divinely inspired intelligence and intuition. Alchemy is the Act of Creation through Divine Will; Theurgy is the Sanctification found through Divine Wisdom; and in their Sacred Union lies the Redemption of Humanity and the Material Universe in Divine Love.

This is the practical path of Rosicrucianism, combining both *Alchemy* and *Theurgy* to ensure that the *Great Arcanum* is used for the Restoration of Creation to the Divine Glory of the Kingdom of Heaven.

The Role of Rosicrucian Orders

When considering what this looks like in action, it is clear that part of the practice of Rosicrucianism is to find like-minded individuals and align ourselves towards the collective goal of spreading Love, Light, Peace and Truth. Indeed, the original pamphlets outright call for us to, as the *Confessio* says: *"addict ourselves to the true philosophy, lead a worthy life, and dayly call, intreat, and invite many more unto our Fraternity."*

Working, meeting, praying and walking the path together is embedded within Rosicrucianism and should be seen as vital to the practical paths of the tradition as they might be envisaged today.

Consider that, though you are often doing this work *by yourself*, you are not doing this work *for yourself*. The goals are universal, sacramental, sanctifying and communal, bringing us (as Waite states in his *Way of Divine Union*) to that *"still, glorious and essential oneness, beyond the differentiation of persons, who are united in fruitful love, as in a calm and glorious unity…the crown and recompense of love made perfect in eternity"*[12].

This contrasts with the scene in *The Chemical Wedding* in which *"every one strove to reach the cord, and only hindered each other."* We can act in hindrance to one another and ourselves if we are all scrambling for achievement or possession of spiritual enlightenment without compassion or patience. Joining a Rosicrucian order can be a test of one's progress as it provides a landscape in which to see where instinctual reactions lead you and how adept you are at noticing when you are veering off course.

Practical Rosicrucianism in the World Today

The practical paths of Rosicrucianism are not only roadmaps towards illumination through the Divine, but also serve as training for the aspirant to help ensure strong spiritual, mental and physical foundations for the restorative task ahead. In today's busy and distracting world, a large number of initiates have trouble with implementing regular practice into their daily lives; but by doing so consistently and purposefully, great strides are made and new avenues of understanding open up almost immediately. Discipline, willpower, intuitive capacity, creative ability and intellectual fortitude are all enhanced by undertaking these practices. Serving the adept well in not only achieving the heights of the steep ascent up the Holy Mountain, but also developing the ability to assist others and improve the world with the knowledge and understanding that they find there. In many ways, the practical path you choose is less important than the resolution and resilience to continue with it *daily* for long periods of time. The goal here is to make it your normal state of being, so that the lessons learned and experiences gained are fully integrated into your life as a focal point that enables Divine Will, guided by Divine Wisdom, to manifest within the material plane.

Rosicrucianism is not just something that you *do*; but rather something that you *become*. It is an all-encompassing experience of realisation of the Presence of God within (Theurgy) and the Emergence of God without (Alchemy), so that your actions move beyond the motivations of seeking attainment for self-gain and become the nourishment of a life lived in the Spirit. In this way, such practices are the motivator and the outcome alike:

---

12. Waite, A. E. 1915, *The Way of Divine Union*, Kessinger Publishing Co. facsimile, p71

they sustain, inspire, enlighten, strengthen and embolden your existence as a praxis point for Divine Will; in sacred union with Divine Wisdom; so that the magical child might be born of Divine Love.

Rosicrucianism is not a tradition petrified in the stone of the past, to be studied and dissected, but is one in constant movement and effect in the world; filled with the living soul of our collective efforts and achievements today. God waits for us in the sanctuary of our inner selves that has always acted as a temple to the highest aspirations of humankind and meeting place for the most graceful servants of Providence. For those who feel like this might all be too difficult or time-consuming; understand that, though it is challenging and requires real commitment, the sanctuary is always open and ready for you. There is little resistance found once personal circumstances are aligned and the journey begins, or continues, except that which has built up in your own mind and surrounding dross of materiality. Another helpful image from A. E. Waite is worth holding here:

> "...the door which opens inward is not so much a closed door as one that is always ajar; it is not so much ajar as open; it is not so much a door as a curtain; and indeed it is scarcely a curtain, for it is an arch rather, with a free space beyond."[13]

The archway is always there for you to step through; between the pillars, underneath the keystone, and into a communicative experience of collaboration with the Divine. Taking the first few steps is the hardest part, but you are a Rosicrucian and listening to the still voice within has brought you here. Which means that you have already heard the eternal call and sooner or later – in the past, present, and future – walk the path you will.

The practical paths of Rosicrucianism relate to the creative act itself. Not just the final result but an understanding of the source of inspiration, how it emerges into consciousness, and the ability for it to cross the threshold into material being. This is the simple truth, yet it is an experiential one; universal and present in all things, animate and inanimate. The practice and embodiment of such a mystery is a complex matter, but the path is clear. As a recently translated prayer from the 18th century mystic Karl von Eckartshausen states: *Love in knowledge is the good, and love in practice is the true*[14].

---

13. Ibid. p234
14. Translation available on the Theomagica website by Frater Acher, theomagica.com

Humanity has arrived at a crossroads, in which our ability to harness the power of creation has reached a point in which our future form will be dictated by the visions that emerge from within ourselves. It is more important than ever that we walk the path of Rosicrucianism with confidence, knowing that we will need to direct the holy centre that we discover towards the restoration of humanity before humanity loses itself to its own corrupted thought forms and self-generated destruction.

Creation takes many forms, both evolutionary and involutionary; spiritual and material; intellectual and emotional. Its flame flickers in the creation of beings and in their final moments of return. Its seed can be planted in others and we in turn bear the fruits of those around us within our own hearts and minds. It can be the greatest force of progress and liberation, or give birth to the most horrific forms of oppression and destruction. Which is why the process of preparation is so important and the formation of the Elixir requires not only a deep understanding of the wellspring of inspiration and how it can be wrought into material existence, but also the golden chain that connects us to the source of Divine Providence and enables the embodiment of the Highest Good: together known as the Philosopher's Stone.

From the *macrocosm* to the *microcosm*, the Hand of God is present, but it is with the emergence of consciousness that it takes a more dynamic form. Within the sacred sanctuaries of our own being, guided by the source of Light, we can learn to experience the subtleties of the creative act – the *filius sapientiae* or 'child of wisdom' – and direct it towards specific inflections in space and time, even as they exist against the backdrop of eternity. There are many Arcana involved in this: but here you will find that Silence and Patience are your guide to Wisdom and Truth.

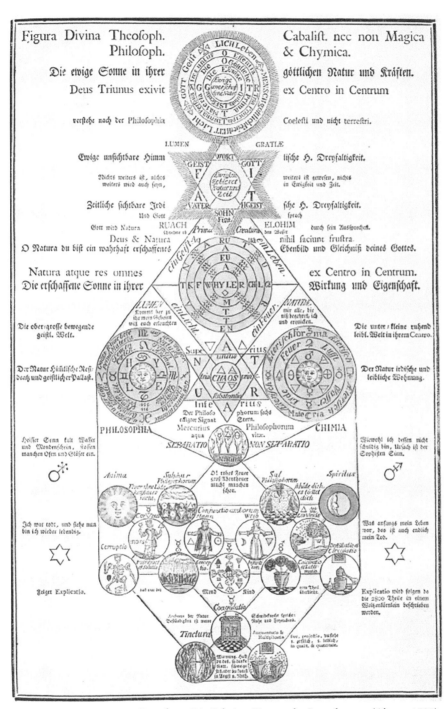

Page from *Die Geheime Figuren der Rosenkreuzer* (Altona, 1785)

Frontispiece of *Speculum sophicum Rhodo-Stauroticum* (1618)

PATHS TO UTOPIA:
ROSICRUCIAN ENGAGEMENT IN THE WORLD TODAY

In the previous two chapters we have considered how the Rosicrucian tradition is relevant to our lives in the 21ˢᵗ century, while also exploring the practical paths that are promoted throughout its history. Where we choose to take this practical work is highly personal, but each of us should ask the question: *what is the purpose of such work?*

The answer to this question is multifaceted and so we will now take a look at what it means to proactively engage with the world as Rosicrucians. If we are conducting this work for more than just our own relationship with God, what approach can we take to public engagement and how should that inform our actions throughout our lives?

In similar fashion to how we examined the practical paths of Rosicrucianism, it is beneficial to look at the original manifestos and surrounding materials to consider how they approach the idea of engagement in the public sphere. By doing so, we can see that our tradition speaks directly into ideas of social change and has a well-served thread of speaking truth to power; while also challenging many of the professional avenues we might undertake or other activities that could have a detrimental effect on the human condition. It is therefore important for us to view Rosicrucianism today as an assertive tradition. One that, from its very beginning, has sought to stand in opposition to many of the problematic areas of society in order to strive for a more harmonious and spiritually glorified way of being.

Rosicrucianism has had a long and illustrious past. From the initial outburst into public consciousness; to the numerous organisations that have left their mark and individuals of significant influence; through to educational, theological and scientific reforms. However, in the 21st century our tradition has been relatively detached from the public sphere. Although there have been plenty of publications produced, they tend to fall into areas of historical research or promote an individualised spirituality that removes the tradition from direct engagement with the social contexts of the modern world.

This stepping back into intellectual and/or personal pursuit has coincided with large shifts in global society, including the rise of social media; the power of tech companies; and media outlets that find it difficult to merely report accurately on the news, let alone properly scrutinise those in power. The cynicism found in many of our political and socioeconomic institutions today highlights how they have moved increasingly further away from a well-defined sense of common good. Instead, in many instances, they seem to be working towards the dissolution of truth in order to enhance profits and power; coupled with a turning away from compassion so as to become detached from accountability for the impact of their operations. This is the global context in which Rosicrucianism needs to play an active role in our collective destiny, as it has done so since its formation, and we must therefore reconsider our identity along such lines.

Social Purpose in the *Fama* and *Confessio*

Public engagement is a central component of the original manifestos and their purpose. This is found not only within the actions that define a Rosicrucian (such as 'curing the sick' and to 'follow the custom' of other cultures), but within the worldly context that the legend of Brother C. R. exists and the travels of the original Brethren to bring together different forms of knowledge *"so that finally man might thereby understand his own Nobleness and Worth, and why he is called Microcosmus"*[1]. Beyond even their content and primary instruction to *"cure the sick, and that gratis"*, the manner in which the manifestos were released and the way in which they

---

1. All quotations from the *Fama* and *Confessio Fraternitatis* have been taken from the Thomas Vaughan translation into English, published in 1652

were able to inspire discourse at the time shows how public engagement is held deep within the DNA of Rosicrucianism.

Within the *Fama Fraternitatis* we have direct examples not only of social engagement, but an international mindset that looks to harness the knowledge of different nations around the world. It is clear from the outset that Rosicrucianism is not merely an insular tradition existing along monastic lines, but rather one that builds up theoretical and experiential knowledge so that it can be shared with others of like-minded temperament and mission. Indeed, the *Fama* is an avowedly communal document and the members of the Fraternity travel far and wide without worry about national identity, concerned only with the corpus of human wisdom as a whole:

> *"they separated themselves into several Countries, because that not only their Axiomata might in secret be more profoundly examined by the learned, but that they themselves, if in some Country or other they observed anything, or perceived some Error, they might inform one another of it".*

This is further acknowledged in the 'five languages' that the *Fama* was originally distributed in (and the affirmation in the *Confessio* that it will *"be set forth in everyone's mother tongue"*) and is indeed self-evident in the assertive public declaration that the two initial pamphlets consist of. Because, after all, the goal presented in the *Fama* is none other than a *"general reformation, both of divine and humane things"*.

Supporting the reformative foundations in the *Fama*, large sections of the *Confessio Fraternitatis* are focused on how the mysteries and secrets of Rosicrucianism should transform the wider world around them. There is a clear acknowledgement that such knowledge *"be manifested and revealed to many"* which provides the notion that they should be used to seed new ways of being. There is no doubt in the *Confessio* of the public nature of the tradition, as its Trumpet:

> *"shall publiquely sound with a loud sound, and great noise, when namely the same (which at this present is shewed by few, and is secretly, as a thing to come, declared in Figures and Pictures) shall be free and publiquely proclaimed, and the whole World shall be filled withall."*

Thus, an outlook of public engagement is undeniably part of the core modality of Rosicrucianism (even though the adepts behind such announcements remain invisible) and with the expected results being that the Fraternity *"inrich the whole World... and endue them with Learning, and might release it from Innumerable Miseries"*. This is formulated, though, with the added recognition that these things would be overlooked or misunderstood by those who weren't ready to receive them (*"wherefore we neither can be seen or known by anybody, except he had the eyes of an Eagle"*). All combined with a call for people to request to join through public affidavits, while the Fraternity would be protected from any 'false hypocrites' by the fact that, unless their intentions are aligned with the Will of God, *"our Treasures shall remain untouched and unstirred, until the Lion doth come, who will ask them for his use, and imploy them for the confirmation and establishment of his Kingdom"*.

The degree to which public engagement is present within the original manifestos cannot therefore be overestimated, as it is essentially the entirety of the message. That which was previously hidden would now come forth and shine light on the future to come:

> *"what before times hath been seen, heard, and smelt, now finally shall be spoken and uttered forth, viz, when the World shall awake out of her heavy and drowsie sleep, and with an open heart, bare-head, and bare-foot, shall merrily and joyfully meet the new arising Sun."*

What we see, then, by looking back at the original manifestos is that they were clearly aimed at having a societal impact. Not only through the way in which they were disseminated and the recognition that they would *"dayly call, intreat and invite many more unto our Fraternity, unto whom the same Light of God likewise appeareth"*, but also through the primary purpose of curing the sick accompanied by the rallying cry for an all-encompassing reformation. As Michael Maier states directly in his *Themis Aurea* (1618) that applauded the release of the manifestos:

> *"The end for which these laws were made was the common good and benefit which partly belongs to the brethren themselves, and partly respects others, either in their minds or bodies to the furnishing of that with knowledge, and to the remedying of the diseases of the other, for they being ambitious to profit and advantage others, have taken a course suitable to their intentions."*[2]

---

2. Maier, M. 1618, *Themis Aurea*, English translated edition published in 1656, p23

This is echoed by the passionate words of Eugenius Philalethes (aka Thomas Vaughan) in his preface of the first widely available English translation of the *Fama* and *Confessio:*

> *"This will be the right kingly Ruby... that he doth shine and give light in darkness, and to be a perfect Medicine of all imperfect Bodies, and to change them into the best Gold, and to cure all Diseases of Men, easing them of all pains and miseries.*
>
> *Be therefore, gentle Reader, admonished, that with me you do earnestly pray to God, that it please him to open the heart and ears of all ill hearing people, and to grant unto them his blessing, that they may be able to know him in his Omnipotency, with admiring contemplation of Nature, to his honour and praise, and to the love, help, comfort and strengthening of our Neighbors, and the restoring of all the diseased."*

Looking at the material surrounding the original manifestos, we see that at the core of the Rosicrucian tradition is a form of healing-based spiritual activism that crosses boundaries of religion, politics and science. A call to put right many areas that had gone astray; restoring the relationship between Humanity, Nature and the Divine that should be found at the heart of all our endeavours. They were concerned with forms of control that would denigrate the role of the sacred in our lives, mostly due to the corrupting influence of the search for wealth and power. They were standing against the negative elements of institutional religion, overreach of political organisations, and even the shady practices of their equivalent to profit-driven 'Big Pharma' that we still find issues with today[3]. Even though our level of scientific and academic knowledge has progressed substantially, there remains a pressing need to stand against de-harmonising structures and mentalities in a world that can quickly become off-balance if left unchecked.

Visions of Utopia

There is a limitless field of activity in which such a proactive reformation could take place, but it's interesting to consider how the Rosicrucian manifestos

---

3. This was also being called out in *The Triumphant Chariot of Antimony*, attributed to Basil Valentine, and other alchemical works that saw wider publication in the late 16th/early 17th century and rallied against the excesses of exploitative medicinal practices.

existed within the sphere of the burgeoning *utopian* genre popularised by Thomas More's *Utopia* (1516). The search for ideal forms of human society, integrated closely with both divine and natural order, was hugely popular as a precursor to the worldviews that Rosicrucianism emerges alongside and, in many ways, helped evolve.

When exploring this aspect, there are two key texts that stand out: *Christianopolis* (1618) by Johann Valentinus Andreae and *New Atlantis* by Sir Francis Bacon (published posthumously c.1627). What is particularly intriguing about these texts is that their authors are both considered potential contributors to the genesis of the anonymous Rosicrucian movement. Indeed, in the case of Johann Andreae he was the self-stated author of the 'third manifesto' *Chymische Hochzeit Christiani Rosencreutz anno 1459 (the Chemical Wedding of Christian Rosenkreutz)* published in 1616. There are also many who presume that he was the author (or at least one of the authors) of the original *Fama* and *Confessio Fraternitatis*. Whether that is true or not, both Andreae and Bacon were central to the development of the Rosicrucian tradition in its first decade and these two texts are a key part of the 17th century movement that took on its own dynamic life as it swept across Europe. Looking at the themes that appear in both *Christianopolis* and *New Atlantis*, then, allows us to consider how they might apply to our idea of social engagement and the purpose of being a Rosicrucian in the 21st century.

Andreae's *Christianopolis* presents us with a highly structured community, used to convey ideas most important to a flourishing society. At the outset is the acknowledgement that this can also be seen as a device for exploring the human condition, applicable within each individual (*"if you should call my own insignificant body by this name, perhaps you would not be so far from the truth"*[4]) as much as they are to how a society could function as a collective whole to become a *"stronghold of honesty and excellence"*[5]. There's importance placed on education and learning, from mathematics and astronomy to music and art; collective work effort with creative freedom; as well as agriculture that is *"attentive to natural simplicity"*[6] with a food system that provides for all. Educating the young is seen as a primary task and undertaken in a flexible manner that promotes the strengths of each

---

4. Andreae, J. V. 1619, *Christianopolis*, Felix Emil, Editor and Translator, 1916, p140
5. Ibid. p144
6. Ibid. p151

individual. Combining an erudite approach with a strong moral compass, developed through religious devotion and ethical conduct, is paramount. This extends into the family unit, with state-provided housing and an acute sense of marriage as a sacred act.

The utopian vision presented by Andreae is one where *"religion, justice, and learning have their abode, and theirs is the control of the city"*[7]. He uses such foundations to create a communitarian outlook highly supportive of mutual respect; applauding the dignity of women (albeit with segregated responsibilities); and highlighting the importance of science and education over hollow superstition, in order to discover that:

> *"This is the summit of happiness, to be able with one and the same effort to preserve the safety of the republic and the adjustment of the future life, so that the children which we bear here, we may find to our satisfaction have been born for the heavens as much as for the earth."*[8]

In sum, we are presented with a forward-looking vision of society in which a great deal of faith and confidence can be placed in the notion that *"the champions of God, or the servants of a good cause...remained unafraid...[for] nothing is more intolerable to impostors, than truth and uprightness"*[9].

An inspiring view, even if in some areas it can fall into hand-waving in which negative traits such as gossip or jealousy simply disappear and *"no one enters into legal dispute with another"*[10]. There are also aspects that, particularly from a modern perspective, veer into the overbearingly righteous (*"the only ark which can contain those to be saved"*[11]). This is not exactly surprising, considering also the kind of 'general reformation' that the Rosicrucian manifestos were positing, but it's worth recognising that the search for purity can risk overwhelming the central components of love and compassion that are so desirable. A reminder that we must direct our transformative capacity to that which uplifts the human spirit and allows it to flourish in all its forms, knowing that: *"No power commands more effectively and none serves more readily than love."*[12]

---

7. Ibid. p173
8. Ibid. p206
9. Ibid. p136-37
10. Ibid. p246
11. Ibid. p233
12. Ibid. p182

Contemporary to Andreae's work, the drive to formulate a utopian ideal was also being undertaken by Sir Francis Bacon; whom had served as Lord Chancellor of England and whose *New Atlantis* provides an interesting companion to *Christianopolis*. Bacon is not as easily connected to the formation of Rosicrucianism on the European Continent, but it is clear that his works, such as *The Advancement of Learning* (1605), carry the same sentiments around a 'fraternity in learning and illumination' and provide an English counterpart (and potentially key influence) to the excitement that the Rosicrucian manifestos would themselves cause in Europe a decade later. In regards to *New Atlantis* specifically, Frances Yates states that *"it is abundantly clear that he knew the Rose Cross fiction and was adapting it to his own parable"*[13]. Regardless of whether or not Sir Francis Bacon was directly involved in the materials surrounding the Rosicrucian manifestos, he has come to be acknowledged as an important influence that the tradition calls upon and his work – even if in an apocryphal manner – provides further context with which to consider the purpose of Rosicrucianism as an agent of change in the world.

New Atlantis, through the meritocratic island of Bensalem under rule of King Salomona (after Solomon), presents another utopian vision built upon strong foundations of collectivism, familial bonds, universal education and scientific endeavour. Less focused on structural particularities and a much shorter text than *Christianopolis*, it assertively presents ideas on the importance of science and technology. While this text was unpublished (and left unfinished) during his lifetime, it exists within the wider body of Bacon's work that had a substantial impact on the intellectual direction of English society and institutions that began to form around it such as the Royal Society.

Bacon's use of Atlantis as a framing device not only builds upon the utopian provenance of Plato, but also places Bensalem within an internationalist mindset (albeit one that prefers to remain unseen). At the core of its purpose lies an institution (Salomon's House) dedicated to scientific observation, analysis and enquiry of all kinds with an all-encompassing mission as *"The end of our foundation is the knowledge of causes, and secret motions of things; and the enlarging of the bounds of human empire, to the effecting of all things possible."*[14]

---

13. Yates, F. 2007 (1972), *The Rosicrucian Enlightenment*, p166
14. Bacon, F. 1627, *New Atlantis*, 'Two Classic Utopias' Dover Thrift Edition, 2018 p31

This is strengthened further when the purpose of the community and its outreach is laid out in description of its productive focus:

"we maintain a trade, not for gold, silver, or jewels, nor for silks, nor for spices, nor any other commodity of matter; but only for God's first creature, which was light; to have light, I say, of the growth of all parts of the world."[15]

Facilitating this keen focus 'to have light' within the utopia envisaged in *New Atlantis,* is the idea of intellectual and scientific outreach. There are numerous categories of employment, including those designated as 'Merchants of Light', 'Mystery-Men' and 'Lamps' – terms that feel immediately relevant to our discussion on Rosicrucian engagement. Merchants of Light are learned travellers tasked with exploring the world to *"bring us the books and abstracts, and patterns of experiments of all other parts."*[16] Mystery-Men concern themselves with collecting *"the experiments of all mechanical arts… liberal sciences, and also of practices which are not brought into arts."*[17] While 'those we call lamps' are tasked with directing *"new experiments, of a higher light, more penetrating into Nature than the former."*[18]

There are numerous other categories besides, but these three together show both the wide variety of different forms of understanding gained through outreach with other cultures; alongside subtle underpinnings of a theurgic mindset that can also be found in brief descriptions, such as that: *"There was somewhat supernatural in this island, but yet rather as angelical than magical."*[19]

New Atlantis acknowledges that there is much to learn from proactively engaging with the world. Hospitality of strangers from afar and openness to the knowledge of other cultures (even if undertaken incognito) is key to the enlightened mindset put forward. There is an obvious parallel to the influential travels of Brother C. R. in the *Fama Fraternitatis* and the importance placed on multicultural learning (while 'wearing the habit' of others) as well as the receiving of wisdom from afar by the eight original Brethren. What we have, then, is not only an overtly Christian tradition, but one based upon a global outlook that seeks out and embraces the wisdom

---

15. Ibid. p21
16. Ibid. p38
17. Ibid. p38
18. Ibid. p39
19. Ibid. p15

A.   Magna moles & quafi rupes,in rotunda planicie,in eámq. adfcenditur viis
     quinque,quarum initia funt à portis quinque vrbis Veri.
B.   Gradus fcalarum quinq. in rupe incifi, quibus in fummum adfcenfus eft.
     Inter gradus autem ipfos,parte infima effigies , à læua SENSVS COM-
     MVNIS & VIS IMAGINATRICIS : à dextra MEMORIAE.
C.   Flama quæ in cælum adfcendit, fplendore fuo denotat MENTEM fiue
     INTELLIGENTIAM : calore VOLVNTATEM.
D.   Templum SCIENTIAE.
E.   Templum ARTIS.
F.   Templum PRVDENTIAE.
G.   Templum INTELLIGENTIAE.
H.   Templum SAPIENTIAE.
I.   ARISTOTELES.
K.   REGINA.

Illustration from *Civitas Veri sive Morum (The City of Truth or Ethics)* (1609) found in other cultures to form a more complete understanding of the material universe and our purpose within it.

An interesting side note is that there is no indication that Andreae and Bacon were personally acquainted by one another, even just through correspondence, although it is possible that they shared mutual acquaintances that could have acted as a bridge between English and Continental intellectual circles[20]. However, they are clearly both feeding into the same drive for a new form of enquiry that is simultaneously faith-based and scientifically-minded. They share many literary devices and narrative elements (found in another contemporary utopian work, *The City of the Sun* by Tomasso Campanella, published in Frankfurt in 1623[21]); along with the fundamental similarity of a perfected form of Christian society with a finely tuned devotional rhythm underpinning it. It is clear that *Christianopolis* is a more fully realised text than the posthumously published *New Atlantis*, that is best viewed in the broader context of Sir Francis Bacon's work and successful efforts to help bring about a new scientific era. Ultimately, they share the same general understanding of the collaboration between faith, culture, learning, science and the importance for each individual to have a deep relationship with both wider society and nature as a whole. We should thus consider them pre-eminent texts within the contemporary tradition of Rosicrucianism at its birth, that can directly inform us on the role of social engagement in our undertakings today.

Having examined these utopian ideals, it's important to recognise that there are elements in both texts that themselves need substantial reform. These include casual discriminations based on race or sex and there is often emphasis placed on puritanical ideals that have proven in practice to be just as detrimental, if not more so, as they might be beneficial. Rather than retaining any misguided notion that we have a fixed duty to uphold these texts in all their details, we should seek to understand their deeper purpose and continue on the path towards a more harmonious society that they were trying to envisage. Humanity moves ever onward and those in the future will correct our wrongs, as we must strive to correct the wrongs we ourselves inherited from the past.

Texts such as *Christianopolis* and *New Atlantis* show us that the ideals

---

20. For a detailed look, see Dr. Felix Held in his 1916 translation of *Christianopolis*
21. Also foreshadowed and likely influenced by other works of the time, such as *Civitas Veri sive Morum (The City of Truth or Ethics)* that was published in Paris in 1609

conveyed through Rosicrucianism are not merely for study or curiosity. In order to be of true value, they must be lived and embodied. Not just at an individual level, either, but if we are to be custodians of universal truths then they must be applicable to society as a whole. These foundational texts were followed by many others throughout the centuries, including the scientific cataloguing and mystical expressions of Robert Fludd; the formation of schools of hidden learning such as the Orden des Gold- und Rosenkreutz and all that emerges from them; the 'Way of the Heart' expressed by Louis Claude de Saint-Martin; the birth of new movements in art through the Salon de la Rose + Croix of Joséphin Péladan; the codifying of the occult tradition into accessible terms by Dion Fortune and Israel Regardie; through to new forms of education and wellbeing as implemented by Rudolf Steiner, to name just a few. All of these expressions exist, at least in part, under the banner of Rosicrucianism and build upon a loosely connected but undeniably inter-related body of work, one that illuminates the many paths to utopia found within Rosicrucian activism. Paths and means that can even be extended to the likes of the *Social Contract* from Jean-Jacques Rousseau or the era-defining life and career of Benjamin Franklin.

Rosicrucian engagement is imminently practical and focused on bringing people together so that they might form new ways of being and overcome the shortcomings of each era in which they exist. The formation of communities that harness Wisdom, Truth and Love as manifested through peaceful living, learning, scientific study and compassion is part of our intergenerational mission. That might sound like sentimental fancy, but there are numerous examples of attempts to realise such aims and envisage how they might actually come to fruition. Having an erudite and literary mind is not sufficient alone, but when combined with the radical message of illuminated enquiry that emerged from the mysterious Society of the Rosy Cross it can provide both the inspiration and praxis to shift the course of history and redeem some of the misfortunes that emerge from the human condition.

Rosicrucian Engagement in the World Today

All of this presents a lofty goal and we shouldn't expect every Rosicrucian to commit themselves to becoming lifelong activists for the common good, nor necessarily feel comfortable with the idea of acting as guardians of spiritual liberation. There are two things, though, that we should always keep in mind. First, that there are no boundaries to the aspirations for social change that Rosicrucianism should consider possible. That is to say, collectively, we should be aiming high (Most High) for the impact of our tradition on the world around us. Second, that Rosicrucianism is inherently a path that actively seeks to engage with the world at both the scale of the individual and that of society as a whole. In regards to each individual Rosicrucian, this means that we must see our work as being done for the purposes of the greater good and not just our own ends, peace of mind, or spiritual achievement. We are here to *'cure the sick, and that gratis'* and that is our primary goal and key trait that defines the Rosicrucian path apart from others that emerged out of the Hermetic, Neoplatonic and Christian theurgic landscape.

Holding this idea in mind brings up interesting points to consider. On a professional level (the point at which we 'labour at the furnace'), there are clearly livelihoods that should be considered incompatible with living a Rosicrucian life. Professions that prey on the vulnerable or seek to maximise material gain to the detriment of others (or with uncontrolled destructive impact on the environment) might be deemed acceptable under many political or socioeconomic understandings, but they should be considered at odds with the Rosicrucian goals of general reformation. It's difficult to talk about, as there will be some reading this who fall into professional categories that could be considered undesirable[22]. In this regard, nuance should always be considered and so it's important to remember that:

a)   Our lives are influenced by external circumstances and should be understood holistically, with our career being one avenue for social impact among many.

b)   We can all evolve as we come to a deeper understanding of our spiritual purpose and the sacredness of a life lived in service to the common good.

Changing one's profession to pursue something more meaningful, whether in terms of social impact, spiritual vocation or creative output, is perhaps the most difficult part of living a life fully realised in the Spirit. We must also acknowledge that those with wealth and privilege will find such a shift easier to instigate (perhaps harkening back to that Royal Path mentioned

---

22. I have not named any directly, even though our Rosicrucian forebears certainly did!

in the *Chemical Wedding*). This is not only a difficult thing to talk about while avoiding any conceited superiority that forgets we are all guilty of spiritual and moral transgressions, but it is an even more difficult thing to bring about such changes within our own lives. There are so many different factors working against such a pursuit that it can be detrimental to your own sense of peace and personal fulfilment to see this avenue as mandatory, so succeeding at such a task is truly a sign of deep spiritual and ethical maturity. Which also means that it deserves a great deal of respect and admiration when achieved, something that often seems to be lacking as we are conditioned to see success in primarily financial terms.

With these caveats in mind, to ignore one's professional output and compartmentalise it away from your spiritual practice will only prove detrimental in the long run. The concept of vocation is relevant here, because when we are able to discern what truly speaks to us we are able to find fulfilment while also having the greatest potential for positive impact in the world. This shouldn't just be seen as some unattainable goal of success, with many accolades and a lasting legacy. Indeed, such things can become a distraction to finding your vocation and allowing your life to grow within its labour.

For many people, vocation is found in reducing down one's sense of worldly ambition into a more localised and realised perspective of your role in the communities you find nourishment from. This applies equally to those in religious life as it does to teaching. It can be found in politics (if you have deep-seated integrity), but also in charitable work; present in medicine and science, as much as it is art and culture. There is even a great deal of need for it in the world of business and commerce, that desperately need to find new modes of operation outside of a sociopathic drive for endless profit.

In a real and meaningful sense we need to address the concerns of our modern age just as they were approached by the wise and learned of the past. Importantly, it is not good enough to presume that each of us can take a passive role in the formation of society. As Rosicrucians, we must proactively seek to better the world and fight against those forces which work to oppress the spark of the Divine within humanity. The texts of the past placed a great deal of importance on issues of education, restoration and devotion and so we must likewise continue to see our mission in these broad terms. The rapidly changing contexts of our digital age provide new avenues and modes through which to do so, but equally new challenges and distractions that draw us away from such a task. As we have more access to stimulus both information-based and sensory, we can quickly become overburdened and negatively influenced by the agendas of others who do not share our noble task.

Speaking truth into these new digital spaces and protecting the innocent through our ability to act with humility and compassion, in service of the common good, is as vital in today's world as it was for Rosicrucians of the past to enter the academies, councils and public squares of their own day. We must meet people where our presence is required most, embracing different means to act as beacons that hide not in the shadows but shine brightly from the centre of our souls – emboldened by the knowledge that *"whatever breathes the spirit, will have tremendous effect; [while] whatever smacks of artificiality will be powerless."*[23] The modern world is facing a crisis of authenticity in which the artificial has begun to rule in both ideology and form, slowly corrupting the experience of goodness to be found at the core of the human condition. The utopias we envisage must not, therefore, be seen as distant islands separate from humanity, but rather as global networks of like-minded seekers; present in every community and bolstering one another's efforts to prove that there are genuinely uplifting and alternative paths that can be walked alongside others.

The transformation of humanity toward Light and away from darkness is an ongoing struggle. Not only in the historical context that Rosicrucianism emerges into, but perpetually as part of the inherent nature of humankind and the internal dichotomy that we collectively represent. This is why our own daily practice, as discussed in the previous chapter, is a vital component. Social engagement quickly veers into hypocritical and corrupted, even violent forms if it does not emerge from a spiritually mature and self-reflective body of individuals. The relationship between *macrocosm* and *microcosm* applies to the societies we create, just as it does to the experience of humanity within the universe we inhabit. That which we create within ourselves emerges out as the constructive force of society just as, equally, society moulds the context within which our individual identity and perspective is born.

There is both inheritance and responsibility. We must transmute all that has been provided to us into a more enlightened form through our own influence and actions. Both of these things (*personal practice* and *social engagement*) aren't really optional, in the sense that they will occur automatically as we go through our lives. We must therefore decide how to

---

23. Andreae, J. V. 1619, p212

focus these functions of life in order to turn otherwise automatic processes into conscious acts of divine purpose and influence. As Rosicrucians embodying our path, we thus seek to move humanity toward the formation of a living Heaven and the expression of the Kingdom of God in the material realm. For all the intellectual, academic and even political terms we might consider our tradition in, it is these mystical truths that speak to generations of fellow seekers as we each hear the call and follow our duty to heal the corrupted ills of humankind.

The creative force of the cosmos can emerge from within ourselves and impact the material universe. Rosicrucian engagement does not merely hope for a better and more harmonious future, it works to *create* such a future through our own active being. To participate actively in the formation of society is a central component of 21st century Rosicrucianism and it is not afraid to challenge established ways of thinking, particularly when they are having a detrimental effect on the collective soul of humanity. This could mean the intellectual exercises conducted by Andreae and Bacon; or it can manifest as other cultural, scientific or artistic expressions. There are also those whom, in the true spirit of the original manifestos, focus on healing whether medical, psychological or spiritual. Rosicrucians are confident to stand up against power, but do so in a way that does not require recognition for it. Indeed, the fact that these manifestos had such a significant impact can arguably be placed down to the fact that they were released anonymously. There was a detachment from the shortcomings of individual personalities so that the higher ideals could properly resonate. Most forms of social engagement, of course, do require one to be identifiable as you are present and participating in an activity of some kind, but you can seek to do so with humility and as little projection of your own ego as possible. Healing for healing's sake alone. Love for the purpose of compassionate salvation. Truth that pierces through illusory structures.

To cure the sick, and that gratis.

Such a selfless approach is particularly poignant in our current age; in which not only is there a global multiculturalism to wholeheartedly embrace, but also a growing sense of distrust (often rightfully so) for ideological viewpoints that are too rigid and demand adherence. Within this context, the pointedly Christian nature of our work as Rosicrucians can sometimes lessen the impact of what we are trying to achieve. Which is why it is important that Rosicrucian engagement often happens under the guise of 'wearing another habit', assimilating with the communities around us so that our works might have the greatest impact without undue attention to ourselves or any requirement to acknowledge the source of our actions.

This is not to say, at all, that Rosicrucianism should move away from the Christian outlook that lies at its core (*Jesus Mihi Omnia…*), but that we should conduct ourselves in a manner that acknowledges the heights of spiritual nourishment provided through the Living Christ, while recognising the detrimental outcomes that can result from unnecessary proselytising and dogmatic worldviews. We cannot deny the mysteries of the eternal flame as they shine within different sanctuaries of the human soul. Wherever the Merchants of Light are to be found, we must recognise their wisdom and uplift their search for Truth and Peace; for we share the same goals even though we might be walking different paths to utopia.

So far, we've been looking at the idea of Rosicrucian social engagement in a conceptual manner that is essentially timeless. However, it's important to respond to the fact that we live in unprecedented times and that the digital world is far beyond even the more fantastical visions of the mystics and mages of the past. Modern communications technology would be mind-blowing to a 17th century magician working with scrying; consider also our ability to cure the sick from afar through virtual surgical procedures; or the tools we have for effective clairvoyance through AI and pattern recognition that would seem unimaginable even to adepts of the early 20th century.

It is still true that, from a metaphysical perspective, the advances of modern science and technology are but mimicry of the creative potential held within even a single cell of the infinite universe, but what they are mimicking is truly miraculous so they too should be understood as such. The tools we now have at our disposal need to be considered in light of our vocational duty as Rosicrucians. Immediately we think of the many different ways that they can do us harm: through addiction, obsession, manipulation and deceit. All of which must be carefully warded against. But just as the enemies of Love and Light are rushing to utilise these new all-encompassing channels, so must we too seek to harness the power they hold and ensure that an avenue always remains open for those called to find their way home.

In recent years, due in large part to the strange world that the pandemic has brought, we have seen an explosion of esoteric activity that has risen to meet a growing sense of hopelessness. We should be encouraged by this, as many have turned themselves with renewed vigour toward the search for Love, Light, Peace and Truth. Rosicrucianism today includes social media, video conferences and online workshops, as much as it does activism, charity work or community organising. All these things are now inseparable, ultimately enabling the Providence of God to find a leverage point within the crucible of our own souls so that we can *"observe the harmony and truth of the prophetic spirit"*[24].

Utopian literature emerges in times of social upheaval or crisis, when there is not only a need to re-envisage how society functions but also enough people that recognise a different path must be taken in order to survive. You already know the reasons why we are currently in such a period. We see it daily in the lack of empathy shown by structures that are meant to serve society, but are instead preventing us from repairing the injustices and imbalances of the world. We see it in our hollowed-out education and legal systems; in our housing and healthcare crises; in systemic inequality, racism, abuses of power and the pillaging of the environment with our insatiable need for more. It is manifest in the technology that has provided us with the capacity for infinite creativity and expression, but is often used to manipulate, invade, shame and dull the eternal spirit within every single one of us.

Humanity is at a cross-roads in which the thought forms that we create will become the future that we embody. We can be encouraged by the fact that in every period of crisis there has always been those guided by Light, agents of Truth emboldened to act as champions of Love and Peace. This is what lies at the heart of Rosicrucian engagement in the world today. We no longer have the luxury of delaying our actions and must stand alongside all those who act from a position of universal justice and compassion, with the humility to do so for the sake of others and not just themselves. That seek to *cure the sick, and that gratis.*

Part of our duty as Rosicrucians is to bring forth new visions of utopian society and work to enable them in a measured and holistic way. There is a need for a greater sense of integrity and authenticity that speaks into the trajectory of human destiny, rather than the selfish concerns of those seeking fame, wealth or power for their own devices. Some will be called to speaking Truth and championing the sanctuaries of Grace found both within and without in the world. Others will find their purpose in more practical terms, constructing the institutional avenues required to bring about social change. Some work to heal the physical, socioeconomic and spiritual maladies that face our fellows in humanity or beyond in the natural world. Others stand in opposition to those in power that are dampening the light of humanity under the shadows of narcissistic control. There are even those that see it

---

24. Ibid. p243

best to stand aside and amplify the Light found in others, so they can share new perspectives in spaces previously held away from them.

Through whatever avenue we find our calling, it is vital to administer ourselves to it with the passion and dignity deserving of those who would bear the title Servants of the Lord. For it is only by doing so that we conduct ourselves in a manner befitting the birth-right provided to all of humanity through our relationship with the Divine. Nobody will do it perfectly and none of us are entirely free from guilt or responsibility, but each of us, with each passing moment, chooses which path to take and we know the destination we should be aiming for.

There are no fixed set of proscriptions or rules that will bring you there. It is brought about by an individual journey into communion with the Word of God, along with the openness required to collectively manifest the results such experiences can bring.

For in the end there is but one Universal Medicine that will bring Love, Light, Peace and Truth to your soul. To experience and then *act upon* such instruction is to call yourself a Rosicrucian and be worthy of that sacred name.

A Winged Figure by Abbott Handerson Thayer (1904)

THE SACRED ART
OF SPIRITUAL RETREAT

The mystical experience is a source of guidance that hides in plain sight. Recognised for its paradigm-shifting importance yet ridiculed and persecuted throughout history, a large part of the strength (and perceived threat) of the mystical path is that it is attainable without anything but your own being. It is a path open to all and found within our own consciousness, requiring no books, institutions, items or anything else other than your own mind, body and soul. At the core of the human condition, stripped back of all its pretense, lies an experience of communication with the infinite majesty of God and Nature. One that reminds us of our role as co-creators of reality and provides us with the resilience to overcome any challenges, along with the visionary wisdom to form a brighter future no matter how corrupt our surroundings might have become.

How we come into contact with this source of guidance, however, can be an obscure and difficult process. The needs of our daily lives and distractions of the material world work to diminish our ability to hear its voice. So it is that we rely on those rare Adepts from many different traditions and cultures to help light the path so that we might find our way in the darkness. The ideas, practises and experiences to be found have been shared through the generations for as long as humanity has existed and will continue to do so for as long as we survive into the future. Much of this wisdom has been gathered into social institutions, or codified into spiritual practices that we can learn from and integrate into our own lives. We have already looked at the components of *personal practice* and *social engagement* that together form the central component of our religious expression. But there is a third component to this journey that can feel elusive and, at times, unattainable for many of us. This is the sacred art of *spiritual retreat*.

It is easy to be intimidated by the idea of spiritual retreat. The concept immediately brings up visions of monastic life and sparse surroundings without material temptations of any kind. If not a life lived in solitude, we are used to seeing the concept in religious retreats or other intensive practices (such as yoga) that can raise red flags of pressured group dynamics or duplicitous gurus. From an esoteric perspective, spiritual retreat usually comes with the idea of lengthy devotional activities and complicated ceremonial workings. All of these examples require a great deal of commitment. Many take place over weeks, months, or even years as one works toward the promise of brilliant, awe-inspiring communion with the Divine.

Spiritual retreat can be (and usually is) *all* of these things, of course, and for those who are able to find the time, resources and discipline to complete such undertakings we owe a great deal of respect and interest in hearing what they have to share about their experiences. Lives truly devoted to the mystical path are a rare and beautiful thing, which is why they capture our attention and imagination. It is also why they are often seen as threatening to those in power, that have the most to lose from people in touch with higher sources of authority and new ideas of how to organise our lives. It's equally important, though, that as we try to make our way through the many competing motivations of modern life we aren't paralysed by the idea that such exemplary models are the only path to success. If we consider what the purpose of spiritual retreat is, particularly in relation to the idea of the Rosicrucian cycle put forward in this book, then we can find a way to apply that understanding in a manner that fits our own circumstances and temperaments. One that works with the fast-paced and often distracting realities of life in the 21st century. We should also note from the outset that we will return to this part of the cycle numerous times over the course of our lives, which means that spiritual retreat will mean different things at different points along our journey. Sometimes it will mean simply going for a hike in the woods, or perhaps a more substantial experience that allows us to reconnect with the natural world in a way that many have lost touch with. For those who seek more community, it can be found in organised retreats whether full of prayer, meditation, working with the land or an intense exploration of creativity and craftwork. Sometimes it can be as simple as sitting in a dark, quiet room by ourselves for extended periods of time. For the most part we will want to seek spiritual retreat alone over a number of days, weeks or months, whether it be in the form of an intensely devotional theurgic working; as physically gruelly as a martial arts camp or yoga retreat; or more about embracing silence and solitude in order to listen for sources of inspiration both internal and external. There are times when it might be more meaningful to embark on a spiritual retreat with others: family, friends, people of similar faith or skill, brothers and sisters of any ilk. Then there are times when it is best done alone, because the work we have to do is intensely personal and the experiences that result emerge from our own particular situation at that point in time. Spiritual retreat takes many forms within an entire spectrum of intensity. You do not need to chastise yourself for not going far enough, as long as you retain a sense of what the purpose of such retreat is for and pursue it accordingly.

Throughout this chapter we will take a look at a number of different ways you can think about spiritual retreat in your life, each connected in some way to Rosicrucianism as it emerged and has been practiced over centuries. How you end up approaching this part of your own spiritual cycle is a deeply personal decision and dependent on many factors within the context of your own path. But by looking at a broad view of what this undertaking could mean, you can think about what it might look like in your particular circumstances; or perhaps more importantly, you can be honest with yourself about when it is not taking place, but should be, and try to find a way to overcome whatever is holding you back from doing so.

Spiritual Retreat in the Rosicrucian Manifestos

One of the key elements of the *Fama Fraternitatis*, that adds a particularly mythological tone to the text, is the idea that Brother C. R. was widely travelled and gained knowledge from many different people and cultures. This element was discussed in the previous chapter on social engagement, but it also factors into our considerations of the meaning and purpose of spiritual retreat. Travel is often seen as an important component of personal growth, allowing one to receive new experiences and inspiration through the many avenues that an open-minded sense of adventure can bring. It also helps break down our own narrow self-perception and realise that we are part of a much more varied and intriguing world than we often recognise. Through travel, we can better understand the universality of the human condition and our shared experience of consciousness that binds us all together, beyond culture or location. This duality between difference and unity is key to developing a strong sense of compassion and empathy, which in turn is vital for both our personal practice (so that the work we do is not merely aimed at gratifying our own desires) while also energising and directing our social engagement toward the common good.

To start our exploration of spiritual retreat with a basic form, then, travel is often viewed as a way to bring us out of our comfort zone and into an experience of our lives that is more exploratory than our daily routine. This gives us a useful starting point and indeed one from which transformative experiences can result when the right approach is taken. It is for good reason that depictions of spiritual retreat are almost always accompanied by the idea of travel. Whether heading off to an ashram in India, a monastery in Europe, or a commune in the Americas, we have a clear concept that spiritual retreat best takes place at a distance from our normal day-to-day lives. In the Rosicrucian manifestos, travel is discussed specifically as a way to engage with new forms of knowledge and cultural understandings of God and Nature. This remains a hugely beneficial pursuit today, if one has the means and time to do so, but months-long travel to the extent often seen in the texts of the past is a rare occurrence in our lives today (if it ever happens at all). Even so, extended travel can be a focal point on the horizon of our lives that our personal practice and social engagement actively builds toward. Travelling for the purpose of spiritual retreat also doesn't just have to be a grand adventure, but can be as simple as a cabin in the woods or retreat centre just a few hours away from home. These all have somewhat different purposes, connotations and efficacy, but we can see how the concept of travelling – of removing ourselves from the routine of our daily lives – brings opportunity for personal growth. How we go about creating such opportunities for ourselves is a vital part of understanding Rosicrucianism as a cyclical path of great benefit to life in the 21st century.

This idea comes together in the third provision of the *Fama* – that they should all assemble once per year or send notice of their absence – which can be seen as a form of collective spiritual retreat. Travelling from their daily lives and bringing all they have learned into communion with one another, in order to share the Light and Truth they had discovered through individual explorations of the hidden mysteries of Nature and Science. As we've also seen in the previous chapter, this theme of travelling throughout the world in order to bring back knowledge and wisdom is a central part of the utopian vision embedded within Rosicrucianism. It facilitates the connection of our internal worlds with wider society. Sharing and growing with one another towards something with the potential to be uplifting for all, even if it might so often fall short due to the corrupting influences of our material lives. Travel can be seen to go hand-in-hand with spiritual retreat, then, because it is not only central to our depictions of such endeavours, but also conducive to the processes involved. But to think of the experience in only this way can be to lean too heavily into the social and/or geographical elements and overlook the importance of the internal alchemy that is taking place. This is expressed straightforwardly in a small part of the *Fama*, in the period of time that occurs after extensive travel, when Brother C. R.:

> "*returned again into Germany... There, although he could have bragged with his Art, but specially of the transmutation of Metals, yet did he esteem more Heaven, and the Citizens thereof, Man, than all vain glory and pomp.*"[1]

Here we see that travel not only serves for the purpose of great learning and social engagement, but also plays an important role in the inward life. A period of 'five years' passes where the wisdom that has been gained from travel is integrated into a quiet life, before emerging again ready to spread a vision of worldwide Reformation and forming bonds with other like-minded people. The quiet life of a group of dedicated seekers aiming to bring as much Truth and Light into the world as they can muster; birthed from travel, encapsulated in learning and embracing the knowledge of other cultures. Available most readily to those who have lived life in the Spirit and are energised by coming into contact with their peers and seeing how they themselves have evolved, in a meeting of souls that share the experience of spiritual service to such an extent that one another's mere presence can be enlightening. It comes from the energy of social engagement and the diligence of personal practice, but can only really be fully expressed after the integration of retreating internally and becoming more attuned with the bare

---

1. English quotations as found in *The Fame and Confession of the Fraternity of R.C...*, 1652

reality of life and the radical honesty that we can develop between ourselves and God. From such periods of nurturing contemplation, a *collective* form of spiritual retreat (one that is quite rare) can be found and should be deeply treasured whenever we are able to experience it.

All of this a roundabout way of saying that travelling across the world can certainly be a powerful form of spiritual retreat, but travelling great distances alone isn't enough. The real meaning will still only truly be found by exploring your internal realms and the power of spiritual retreat comes from integrating all of the stimulating events, landscapes and cultures into the quiet contemplation found within a peaceful mind and life well-lived.

I have already mentioned in the previous chapters some of the relevant utopian depictions contemporary to the birth of Rosicrucianism (particularly *New Atlantis* and *Christianopolis*), that provide us with a look at the quest for 'General Reformation of the Whole Wide World'. Tomasso Campanella, in his book *The City of the Sun* published in 1623, adds some additional dialogue *"between a Grandmaster of the Knights Hospitallers and a Genoese Sea Captain"*. This provides an evocative view in which the travel out of our comfort zones and into new surroundings, into new ideological frameworks, provides the key from which a vision of utopian society can emerge and be obtained. It also gives us a steer through its allegory as to the conditions required for spiritual retreat to stand in contrast to the trappings of our normal lifestyle:

> *"They are rich because they want nothing; poor because they possess nothing; and consequently they are not slaves to circumstances, but circumstances serve them."*[2]

Jumping right into the means and desired outcome of spiritual retreat, another example in the early Rosicrucian texts comes from a treatise called *The Pegasus of the Firmament*. Credited to the pseudonymous Josepho Stellato, but attributed to Daniel Mögling whom is also linked to the *Speculum Sophicum Rhodostauroticum* (*Mirror of the Wisdom of the Rosy Cross*), this text was published in 1618 alongside the three manifestos and openly explores how one might go about *"arriving at the font of true wisdom, that is, the middle path"*[3]. There are three primary methods given: *"serious*

---

2. Campanella, 1623, *The City of the Sun*, 'Two Classic Utopias' Dover Edition, 2018, p.62
3. Translation by Dr Shawn Daniels and Christine Eike, published on Pansophers.com

and diligent prayer to God, faithful establishment of principles, and the most dedicated reading and contemplation of the Chief Books." Although these might seem quite standard in our understanding of spiritual practice, as indeed they are, it is in the extortion that they are 'serious and diligent'; 'faithful'; and 'most dedicated' that we can see that the kind of devotion that will bring us to the heights of spiritual experience goes beyond the usual effort we might put toward such things. The 'Chief Books' in question are those of Holy Scripture and the Book of Nature; a gamut of material that ranges from intensive study of Biblical texts (through direct contemplation rather than the interpretation of others), through to the likes of Hermes Trismegistus, Paracelsus and Basil Valentine that are all named in *The Pegasus* as 'authentic interpreters' of the Book of Nature. There is also an account of the 'seven pillars of wisdom' that will allow a virtuous alignment to *"this true practice of Ethics, since all praise of virtue lies in Action alone"*. All of this presented in a vibrant and almost ecstatic tone (at times quite biting and evangelical) that not only gives the means, but also outlines some of the outcomes that we might expect. Put simply, there are three 'Gifts of Grace' that result from such intensive spiritual devotion: *divine inspiration*, *prophetic dreams* and *prophetic visions*. The true Rosicrucians are thus in possession of such wisdom, the author states, and it is this visionary output that will be their legacy:

> *"If the Outcomes of the famed and exceedingly wise Men in the worshipful Society of the Rosy Cross match their predictions even a whit, they will have drawn the Secrets of nature out of the abyss into bright light; the blessed Righteousness of life, the true love of one's neighbour, the glory of justice long-sought, will scatter the brightest rays throughout the whole of Europe, as is now obvious. Absolutely no Lettered person of sound mind will rightly hold such a noble Society in hatred; rather, it will be kept in a singular love and with everlasting honour. Lastly, it must be known that it comes from this Light of Grace, insofar as it results in a real, true Kabbala, as it is known in Hebrew; in Greek, it is called prophecy or Prophetic Illumination."*

So we can see that the ultimate purpose of the Rosicrucian tradition, as outlined in the *Pegasus* text, is to enter into states of 'Prophetic Illumination' that can put forth new visions of how society should function in accordance to the Will of God and in harmony with Nature. Aligning our lives in a manner conducive to achieve such states is part of the journey that we must therefore undertake. There will always be reasons not to do so, to avoid dedicating ourselves to such tasks or find excuses for why they must occur in some undefined future. But we must recognise such excuses for what they are, knowing that ultimately we do have the ability to construct our lives in a manner conducive to achieving such a goal and that spiritual retreat is a key part of doing so. It does not need to be in the form of complete monastic commitment – that path is only suitable for very few – but if we find ourselves without time for spiritual retreat, then that is a consequence of our own actions. If we can't manage to prioritise our lives to the processes of mystical attainment, at least for certain periods of time, then how can we hope to achieve the kind of visionary states sought after and be worthy to be held in 'singular love' and 'everlasting honour' through the reception of a 'true Kabbala'? Our actions must at least attempt to match our words, even if the true heights of mystical experience are rarely attained, and so it's important to identify the ways in which we can genuinely seek to do so while recognising the full scope of the task at hand.

This chapter opened with the concept of travel not only because it is so central to the original manifestos and their surrounding material (and the focus they have on *global* reformation), but also because it is something that almost all of us can relate to. Particularly in the hyper-connected world of the 21st century where, compared to the time period discussed in the *Fama*, or the world of the manifestos over a century later, we have far greater access to this basic mechanism of spiritual retreat. When considering the three elements of 21st Century Rosicrucianism outlined in this book (*personal practice*, *social engagement* and *spiritual retreat*) the final element can seem the most obscure and is seeking a visionary goal that can feel unobtainable. But by exploring what it meant for those most dedicated to such practises, we can begin to understand some of the tools involved. We can see how it is constructed and therefore begin to find ways for it to become expressed within the context of our own lives and circumstances. The greatest examples of spiritual retreat that we hold in our minds are important to aspire to, necessary even if you want to attain the truest heights of the journey undertaken, but they are ideal forms. There are many steps leading up to those all-encompassing moments of pure commitment and worshipful devotion. It is therefore important that we understand the process of spiritual retreat as a gradual one, that we will keep returning to and receive greater and greater gifts in return. By doing so, we can begin to identify avenues that enable us to steadily climb the Holy Mountain rather than being intimidated by staring up at its peak from the valley of our daily lives.

The idea of being worldly and well-travelled is thus central to the Rosicrucian mythology and the manifestos that formed our tradition. Spiritual retreat in a classic sense often takes place a long distance away from home, often involving a pilgrimage that requires a long and challenging journey. Although there's less need in the 21st century to seek out spiritual masters in new lands, often relying instead on virtual spaces, the knowledge that was sought from such an undertaking was only a part of the overall purpose of why such a journey would take place. The commitment, drive and openness that is required to successfully embody seemingly simple terms such as 'diligent prayer' and 'faithful principles' is the key element here that was part of the drive behind such travels that led people to doing amazing things. Something that modern tools such as the internet can't fully replicate, even though they can serve to motivate and provide knowledge for the seeker. In some ways, the elements of traditional spiritual retreat or pilgrimage can now be separated out into component parts. Some can be fulfilled online at home, while others still require the physical journey (and all the fortitude such requires) to take place in order to be fully realised. One of the things that the pandemic showed many practitioners is that there is real community to be found online, that can lead to real practical work even of a group nature. But virtual engagement can only take one so far and shouldn't be seen as something that can completely replace the need for spiritual retreat to be physically embodied in one form or another.

Gathering Together as Rosicrucians

Let's look at another example many of us will have experienced today. Because of the manner in which our tradition emerged, Rosicrucianism is often expressed in the form of initiatory organisations that meet in person to learn from and practice with one another. Such gathering together, taking time to meet and focus on what it means to be a Rosicrucian, can be seen as part of our undertaking of spiritual retreat (albeit one that crosses over with both personal practice and social engagement) – even if a relatively basic one. This is particularly so if it happens with a significant period of time between each occasion, thereby creating more of a distinction between daily practice and the environment of the meetings. As mentioned above, this kind of collective spiritual retreat is even built into the obligation of the original fratres of the Society to meet each year, travelling to the Domus Sancti Spiritus so that they might be:

"assembled together with joy, and [make] a full resolution of that which they had done. There must certainly have been great pleasure, to hear truly and without invention related and rehearsed all the Wonders which God had poured out here and there through the world."

When we do this, we open ourselves up to new information and perspectives. We move beyond the internal experiences of our own daily practice and seek to reconcile them with the experiences of others on a similar path. This enables us to not only learn from others, but also to gauge our own experiences and get a better sense of where they might be situated in the wider scheme of things. When done outside of the normal context of our personal and professional lives (more akin to the social engagement discussed previously), it becomes a form of spiritual retreat that allows new inspiration to take hold within us. This kind of collective retreat can also prove important as a sounding board that helps make sure we aren't veering into areas that might be illusory, self-defeating or even perhaps dangerous to our wellbeing.

Both of these opening examples, travel and collective meetings, are easy starting points to explore the idea of spiritual retreat. We can immediately engage with them (indeed have almost certainly done so already) and they should be seen as worthwhile pursuits. But we must also acknowledge that they will only take us so far. They are an important part of the Rosicrucian journey, but they will not take us into the depths of spiritual experience that we are ultimately seeking. However, it is useful to think of spiritual retreat as something that can start small but grow in importance as you mature and evolve throughout the course of your life. It is also something that can be found throughout all cultures (some more ritualistically expressed than others) in the idea of *rites of passage*, which our initiatory orders today are a form of. These rites of passage involve the individual stepping outside of their normal mode of being, entering into a liminal state outside of social categories (usually accompanied by an ordeal, whether real or allegorised) in which they are consumed by archetypal forms and enwrapped in cultural meaning that is bigger than individual identity. They then emerge with a new status as an evolved member of society, capable of taking on new roles and responsibilities that were previously closed to them. Such rites are expressed in the initiation ceremonies of modern Rosicrucian organisations and other similar institutions, although they are usually in a softer form than these ceremonial demarcations were done in the past and, indeed, are still done with intensity in many cultures around the world today.

We can see through all of this the overlap of *social engagement* with *spiritual retreat*, bolstered by our own *personal practice* and the depth of understanding it brings to such activities. There are no hard lines here, all aspects of our journey bleed into and influence one another, but we can see how particular aspects can be brought to the forefront during different phases of our journey. Spiritual retreat is perhaps the most difficult part of the Rosicrucian cycle, particularly today with busy lives and a growing number of distractions, but it is also an irreplaceable one. Just as personal practice and social engagement are pivotal elements that can't be overlooked, so too is the transformative impact of the discipline and devotion required to truly enter into spiritual retreat. This isn't something that most of us can do every week, month or even year (although if you can incorporate it consistently into the rhythm of your life, all the better), but it is necessary in order to ensure that you continue to make progress. By committing to periods of time in which spiritual retreat is your primary focus, your ability to embody the True and the Good becomes more reliable and effective. You learn how to distinguish between your own internal voice and that of higher inspiration and can incorporate the latter into a meaningful form when it arrives, taking this wisdom back into both your personal practice and social engagement in order to enhance their impact and visionary foundation. Strengthening these processes is one of the main benefits of spiritual retreat and thinking of this part of the cycle in such a way will help you identify how it can most readily manifest within your own circumstances (and also how it might change over time as you grow into a more holistic form of Rosicrucian spirituality).

When thinking about how our spiritual development matures into a more authentic and devoted form over time, another insightful text is the theological-utopian treatise from John Amos Comenius entitled *The Labyrinth of the World and the Paradise of the Heart*. Published in 1623 and even putting forward views on the Rosicrucians in one chapter (XIII), the book follows the trend of utopian texts as a tour of an ideal city. However, in Comenius' case he spends the first half of the book (the Labyrinth) pointing out the hypocrisies of the world and how our endeavours are usually clothed in virtue and progress but underneath are hollow, corrupt and/or absurd when looked upon objectively. There are pointed remarks that speak directly to the disingenuous way we often present ourselves, such as noting our ability to hide our true nature in public and:

"how artfully some handled [their] masks, quickly removing them and then again putting them on, so that they were able to give themselves a different mien, whenever they saw that this was to their advantage."[4]

Comenius also identifies one of the key issues that humanity faces, which is our ability to drag one another down and attack anything new or novel:

"Among them all there was none who spoke, or did something, or erected an edifice, without the others laughing at it, misrepresenting it, destroying it. One fashioned a thing with vast labour and expense, finding in it great pleasure, then another, approaching him, overturned, destroyed, and injured it, so that I saw that never in the world a man made a thing without another injuring it."[5]

Observations we could learn a lot from today as our world seems to be increasingly divided along tribal and ideological lines and the masks we wear become ever-more prevalent. Funnily enough, Comenius proceeds to spend the 'Labyrinth' half of the book doing exactly that – tearing down the edifices of human endeavour in its many forms from labour to law, religion to learning. His views on astrology and alchemy are generally unfavourable, seeing them as complicated trivialities with little tangible results and plenty of excuses made by practitioners. But it is his brief chapter on Rosicrucianism that provides an interesting perspective with which to consider what it means to be a practicing Rosicrucian today. As an opening point, he recognises that the message of universal reformation found in the manifestos implores that many of the activities of humanity are in need of redemption and should be refocused towards Godly ends. However, as with many things in this labyrinth, Comenius ultimately feels that there is a futility behind the spectacle. That the promise of the manifestos failed to materialise for the many seekers who reached out to praise and devote themselves to the purpose behind this illustrious and elusive organisation:

"Those whom I had at first most seen running and rushing about, these I afterwards beheld sitting in corners with locked mouths, as it appeared; either they had been admitted to the mysteries (as some believed of them),

---

4. Comenius, J.A. 1623 (1905), *The Labyrinth of the World and the Paradise of the Heart*, published by J.M. Dent, London, p.28
5. Ibid. p29

and were obliged to carry out their oath of silence, or (as it seemed to be, looking without any spectacles), they were ashamed of their hopes and of their uselessly expended labour. Then all this dispersed and became quiet, as after a storm the clouds disperse without rain.[6]

Those of us seeking to live as Rosicrucians do need to sit for a while with the idea that what we are doing could be inconsequential or a waste of our time and energy. On a surface reading, perhaps we are to understand that the mysteries of Rosicrucianism – particularly in its modern institutionalised forms – are but hollow promises, acting more as a spiritual mirage rather than anything attainable by the labours and personal sacrifices made in their name. Yet it is here – after 'the clouds disperse without rain' – that the process of spiritual retreat begins to provide results. For those who are able to look beyond the notion of spectacular treasures, glittering like gold, and instead peer through the veil to the subtle threads of creation, there is something miraculous to discover. Spiritual retreat strips us of our pretense and allows us to be with who we truly are, both from a psychological and emotional perspective but also in terms of our divine being and its praxis. It's important at the opening stages of this journey to be skeptical and question both our own motivations and the efficacy of any organised systems that we are part of, but there reaches a point when all of this is stripped away, including our misguided vanities, and we stand silent before the Most High ready to accept that which has been offered and willing to *"Be still, and know that I am God."*[7]

By stripping back the expectations and vanities of the world we are confronted with our true self and must sit with it honestly and without hypocrisy. It takes time to let the pretensions and denial fade away, so that we can open up a space of transformation to overcome the darker sides of our identity that may have been allowed to develop and negatively influence our lives. This is why the concept of spiritual retreat is so often coupled with extended periods of solitude and isolation, because the longer we are able to live without the masks of our social pretences the more they fade away until eventually we are able to see what lies beneath. The intense periods of devotional activity are then designed to strip away the final mask that we present even to ourselves, filling it instead with the image of God

---

6. Ibid., p95
7. Psalm 46:10

and receiving a clear view of the potential of what we could be. So that we can return from our isolation with a greater vision for what the ideal manifestation of humanity has to offer and begin to enact it.

The Highest Forms of Rosicrucian Devotion

Rosicrucianism is a symbolic and experiential mechanism, through which personal interaction with the Divine can become manifest and evolve humanity toward Heaven. There are many different ways in which it can do this: through prayer and practice; activism and revolution (large and small); through healing and love; wisdom and truth; vision and guidance. All of these avenues are dynamic and adjust according to the context of each individual, their surroundings and ability to act in a transformative manner. There is no *fixed* path in Rosicrucianism because, from its very outset, it was designed to be a universal form of Christianity, with a mission even broader than that. One that sought to overcome many of the structural shortcomings that institutionalised forms of religion and politics inherently have. Having said this, there is a *progressive* path at the core of the Rosicrucian tradition. A path is a journey that requires movement, after-all, and attainment is (at least in great part) dictated by effort and commitment. Progress is not just something that you will be bestowed with; nor is it something that everyone is equally graced with, although it is available to all. Results emerge in correlation to the extent in which individuals are willing to do the Work. This is why so many Rosicrucian groups over the centuries are based upon a series of successive grades of initiation, because at the core of the tradition is the understanding that true knowledge of the Divine requires dedication; both in time spent and the depth to which one is willing to sacrifice of themselves in its pursuit.

Spiritual retreat becomes one of those areas that sorts the wheat from the chaff, as it is a necessary part of the cycle for anyone seeking to walk the prophetic path to its full extent. If *you* want to truly understand and experience what Rosicrucianism has to offer in the 21st century, then it must be embodied at an increasingly all-encompassing level. At any point along the way one can decide they have experienced enough. Have changed enough to have a positive impact on their lives and those around them. Have understood enough about how the different levels of material, psychological and spiritual reality interact and can be content with where one has arrived. Indeed, if you're anything like myself, sometimes spiritual retreat can even mean pulling *away* from all such pursuits in order to take stock of your life and where everything is at so that you don't get lost down some esoteric alleyway or too exhausted by what the process is asking of you. All of these things are legitimate stops along the way, or even end points, but it's also to acknowledge that you can't expect further progress without continued effort. You can't expect to enter into states of 'Prophetic Illumination' (or maintain them) simply through a desire for such or knowledge that they exist. Dedication and continuous action is required to experience attainment of the hidden wisdom. Which isn't necessarily only found through 'action' in the sense that we might think, as we know that sometimes sitting still and doing *no-thing* is the best way to actually walk the path! However, when one's mind and emotional attention are directed elsewhere then the foundation of our spiritual identity starts to shift accordingly. It will bring with it everything learned and developed, hopefully enough to eventually steer back on course, but it is a diversion from the path all the same. Part of our spiritual evolution as Rosicrucians is therefore to be able to identify when this has occurred (because it *will* occur) and have enough sense of direction to be able to steer ourselves true once more. Thankfully, there is always that shining Light to guide us back when we are ready.

If we look back again to the original manifestos, there are a number of examples within the *Chemical Wedding* allegory that speak directly of this conflict between choosing to live life in the Spirit or focusing more on our Material existence. Indeed, the whole narrative goes through many different pitfalls that we can fall into that draw us away from spiritual attainment (as has been discussed in previous chapters of this book). Even the opening moment of self-examination outlines clearly the conflicts that we've been discussing here:

> *"For whereas I before imagined, that to be a welcome and acceptable guest, I needed only to be ready to appear at the wedding, I was now directed to Divine Providence, of which until this time I was never certain.*
>
> *I also found by myself, the more I examined my self, that in my head there was nothing but gross misunderstanding, and blindness in mysterious things, so that I was not able to comprehend even those things which lay under my feet, and which I daily conversed with, much less that I should be born to the searching out and understanding of the secrets of Nature, since in my opinion Nature might everywhere*

find a more virtuous disciple, to whom to entrust her precious, though temporary and changeable, treasures.

I found also that my bodily behaviour, and outward good conversation, and brotherly love towards my neighbour, was not duly purged and cleansed. Moreover the tickling of the flesh manifested itself, whose affection was bent only to pomp and bravery, and worldly pride, and not to the good of mankind: and I was always contriving how by this art I might in a short time abundantly increase my profit and advantage, rear up stately palaces, make myself an everlasting name in the world, and other similar carnal designs. But the obscure words concerning the three temples particularly afflicted me, which I was not able to make out by any after-speculation, and perhaps should not have done so yet, had they not been wonderfully revealed to me.

Thus stuck between hope and fear, examining myself again and again, and finding only my own frailty and impotence, not being in any way able to succour myself, and exceedingly amazed at the forementioned threatening, at length I betook myself to my usual and most secure course – after I had finished my earnest and most fervent prayer, I laid myself down in my bed, so that perchance my good angel by the Divine permission might appear, and (as it had sometimes formerly happened) instruct me in this doubtful affair. Which to the praise of God, my own good, and my neighbours' faithful and hearty warning and amendment, did now likewise come about.[8]

So we can see a relatively clear picture of what we are trying to obtain – alongside the broad strokes of how to get there – and we've discussed some of the reasons why we would want to do so. Let's take a look now, then, at some specific examples that can help codify what is often meant by intense devotion within the Rosicrucian context as we seek to bring about this 'good angel'. There are numerous examples within the grimoire tradition that build towards this experience, which we won't go into detail on here but thankfully are readily available today and tend toward the extended efforts of prayer and devotion outlined already, combined with more direct engagement with the spiritual and celestial realms. There are also visionary states described as found through the use of the Urim and Thummim – harkening back to the gem-stoned breastplate used as a source of divine oracle by the ancient

---

8. Taken from the Foxtrot English translation of 1690, as modernised by Adam McLean and Dierdre Green on alchemywebsite.com

Hebrews – as mentioned in the esoteric writings of Heinrich Kunrath and found as a central component of the high-order scrying rituals of Der Orden der Gold- und Rosenkreuzer[9]. Another interesting example, that combines a lot of these influences, can be found in an 18th century text with connections to this Order that outlines a magical process in which the aspirant must:

> *"Purify thy heart, convene thy soul, choose loneliness and pray to God and make thyself worthy to receive the highest grade of holy magic… Separate thyself for several days from all men and their worldly affairs and contemplate the importance of solitude and silence".*

With the end goal being to:

> *"Purify my soul and unite me through the bond of innocence with Thy holy angels…All is vanity except to love and serve God alone…May from now on my heart be God's temple and my love my altar."*[10]

Along similar lines when it comes to attainment of the prophetic vision within Western esotericism, there is perhaps no text more renowned than *The Book of Abramelin*. Indeed, particularly in regards to Rosicrucianism in the late-19th and 20th centuries it was the primary model of spiritual retreat that many relied upon (although few ever went through with). Dating itself as a text from the mid-15th century (note the similarity to the Rosicrucian biography of Brother C. R.), the earliest manuscripts available come from the early 17th century in Germany. Running alongside the Rosicrucian manifestos, the text is certainly part of the mix of Kabbalah, Hermetic wisdom and the grimoire tradition that so strongly influenced that period. Presented as a book handing down knowledge received by a wise man named Abra-melin residing in Araki, Egypt, it presents a similar weight to the notion of intensive periods of prayer, contemplation and purification as our previous examples. Starting again within a framework that applauds learning from other cultures and bringing back wisdom from periods of travel, it outlines how this knowledge can be harnessed through lengthy periods of devoted isolation away from society; emerging out the other

---

9. For a detailed overview of texts referring to the use of the Urim and Thummim see Tilton, H. 2016, *The Urim and Thummim and the Origins of the Gold- und Rosenkreuz*
10. *The Highest Symbolic Grade of the True Magic*, from the earliest known English translation as found in the SRIA London December MMXXI pamphlet, srialondon.org

Illustration from *Quinta Essentia...* by Leonhard Thur Thurneisser zum Thurn (1574)

side in communion with our divine counterpart and in possession of the prophetic voice, ready to overcome the malevolent forces that surround us.

The translation from a French manuscript by S. L. MacGregor Mathers became of central importance to Rosicrucian magical orders such as the Hermetic Order of the Golden Dawn, laying down the path for many to whisper in esoteric corridors about the 'Knowledge and Conversation of the Holy Guardian Angel'. Recent translations[11] have highlighted how this manuscript was flawed and missed many nuances of the original, indeed whole sections, but even so, the work that Mathers did in conveying its meaning and purpose allowed many adepts to cross into new areas of spiritual discovery. The fact that we now have a more accurate version, based upon the earliest existing German texts, allows this primary example of spiritual retreat within the Western esoteric tradition to be discovered afresh by new generations seeking greater communion with their 'good angel'.

However, while access to the material is certainly easier than it has ever been, in some ways it is perhaps more difficult to fully commit to such a pursuit due to the many competing pressures and motivations of our modern age. Not least of which because, as now understood, the *Abramelin* working is an endeavour of spiritual retreat requiring not just six months of increasingly intensive work, as the Mathers' translation required, but rather *eighteen* months in order for its intended results to see fruition. Throughout the generations, numerous people have attested that this is certainly possible within the shorter framework of the Mathers translation, but this shift in the scope of such a highly revered working highlights the levels of dedication needed when considering the notion of spiritual retreat taken to the highest levels. Given that we now have a more accurate translation, the newer edition is certainly the recommended one for those keen to learn more about this working, although there are useful insights from Mathers as to the nature of the working and its intended effect:

> "[Man] is the middle nature between the Angels and Demons, and that therefore to each man is attached naturally both a Guardian Angel and a Malevolent Demon, and also certain Spirits that may become Familiars, so that with him it rests to give the victory unto the which he will."[12]

11. Dehn, G. 2015, *The Book of Abramelin: A New Translation* (2nd Edition), Ibis Press
12. MacGregor Mathers, S. L. 1897 (1976), *The Book of the Sacred Magic of Abra-Melin the Mage*, The Aquarian Press, U.K., p. xxvi

Here then, Mathers outlines a vital aspect of spiritual retreat and its ultimate purpose. Which is to allow the Adept the time, space and dedication required to overcome any malevolence attached to them and to build relationships with those celestial and divine forces that might assist them; doing so through a reintegration with the Divine that establishes an ongoing communion and the aforementioned 'Prophetic Illumination'.

The Book of Abramelin provides us with an approach to spiritual retreat that we can directly utilise, focused on intensive periods of prayer and exaltation, that combines theurgy and ceremonial magic in a form that has resonated throughout the centuries. Indeed, it has become for many the epitome of advanced esoteric workings given the amount of time and devotion involved. It's certainly not the only possible approach that one can take (and it does have its detractors), but it can teach us a lot about the processes involved so that we can begin to formulate our own approach to spiritual retreat. We can also start to plan out how to build from smaller efforts into long-term workings such as this that require total commitment.

In a related, but more realised, sense there are also examples of Rosicrucian-influenced sects that lived a monastic life and took this concept as far as would seem possible. The 'Zionitic Brotherhood' was a small mystical society that resided at one of America's earliest religious communes known as the Ephrata Cloister. Outlined by Julius Sachse, a prominent Masonic scholar, in two books published in the 1890s[13], the Ephrata Cloister was established near Philadelphia in 1732 with an interesting blend of German Baptist, Theosophical and Rosicrucian strands manifest within the context of a monastic life lived in rural Pennsylvania (home to other well-known sects such as the Quakers, Amish and Mennonites). Their story starts with what is referred to by Sasche as 'the virtual successors to the Mystics on the Wissahickon', in reference to an apocalyptic group of 'true Rosicrucians' that landed in Philadelphia in 1694 led by the German mystic Johannes Kelpius (who himself would often retire to a nearby cave for extended periods of prayer and contemplation). The mystics that followed the leadership of Kelpius expressed their monasticism through a holistic form of devotional living that not only centred upon prayer, celibacy and contemplative solitude but also regularly used occult talismans; had a keen interest in astrology and astronomical phenomena (searching for portent signs); and cultivated

---

13. Sachse, J. *The German Pietists of Provincial Pennsylvania* (1895) covers in great detail the community surrounding Kelpius and *The German Sectarians of Pennsylvania* (1899) covering the later period that includes the history of the Ephrata Cloister

a large garden in what *"was probably the first systematic effort made to raise European medicinal plants for curative purposes in America."*[14] Their efforts are described by Sachse in familiar terms for a rural monastic community, but with particularly relevant underpinnings that provide an outline for spiritual retreat that can be adapted to our own circumstances today:

> *"Here in the solitude, far away from the bustle and gossip of the village, these Theosophical students when not employed on errands of mercy were free to devote their spare time to their esoteric studies, undisturbed by the temptations of the world or official interference – seeking Theosophical light, as set forth in their secret and zealously guarded symbolical manuscripts."*[15]

The notion of unifying the different strands of Christian identity found in Pennsylvania at the time was at the forefront of Kelpius' ethos, similar to the universal reformation sought by Rosicrucianism. This openness was also combined, though, with a desire for solitude in the wilderness and a devoted mysticism that kept them at arms-length from many of the other communities flourishing at the time; even though they were often the source of spiritual guidance and nourishment for many who found their way to them. As an aside, and important to our notion of Rosicrucian engagement, the community also wanted to ensure that *"all services of a spiritual, educational, and medicinal nature were given free, without price or hope of fee or reward."*[16]

The community led by Kelpius, that came to be known by outsiders as 'The Society of the Woman in the Wilderness' (a reference to a symbolic figure in Revelation[17]) and referred to by themselves as 'The Contented of the God-loving Soul', has a rich and varied story well worth closer examination. For the topic we are exploring now, we can see how this became an active form of Rosicrucian-inspired monasticism with a notion of spiritual retreat that continued to have great influence in the area. Without covering the story in detail, which I highly recommend for further study, there are then connections to the founding of the Ephrata Cloister three decades later (the

---

14. Sachse, 1895, p75
15. Ibid., p77
16. Ibid., p83
17. *"and the woman fled into the wilderness, where she has a place prepared by God, so that there she can be nourished for one thousand two hundred sixty days."* Revelation 12:6 (NRSV)

death of Kelpius in 1708 led to the dissolution of the community surrounding him) that also took up the mission of reformation and maintained central teachings of spiritual seclusion and mystical devotion. Known to its members by the name *Ein Orden der Einsamen* (the Community of the Solitary) and founded by Conrad Beissel (under the name Friedsam Gottrecht) the community that formed was built upon similar tenets to that of 'the Mystics of the Wissahickon' that came before them:

> "[Their] chief aim was to attain spiritual and physical regeneration and perfection. Here for over half a century the secret mysteries of his occult philosophy were explained and the sacred rites practised without fear of molestation or official interference, while the votaries lived undisturbed in their voluntary seclusion. Here for years the most profound occult sciences, combined with the simple Sabbatarian tenets, were taught and promulgated, and possibly in no other community in this country was there so complete a renunciation of the world and as much simple Christian faith manifested as there was among the recluse Sabbatarians of Ephrata."[18]

Like the community surrounding Kelpius, the Ephrata Cloister has a fascinating history that feeds into the promulgation of esoteric ideas out of Europe and into the American colonies. However, it is within a smaller initiatic subset of their members known as the aforementioned 'Zionitic Brotherhood' that we can find a particularly interesting example of spiritual retreat that is both deeply mystical and intensely practiced. As the wider congregation at Ephrata grew, a smaller mystical order was formed by some members that sought a more devoted monastic lifestyle. They even established their own building within which to do so and it is stated by Sachse in his history of the community that:

> "these brethren in the Berghaus passed their time in speculations as foreign to the pure and simple Sabbatarian teachings as they were to the Rosicrucian tenets; the rites which they practised were similar to what are now known as the 'strict observance,' or the Egyptian cult of mystic Freemasonry…The professed object and aim of the members of the Zionitic Brotherhood was to obtain physical and moral regeneration."[19]

---

18. Sachse, 1899, p30
19. Ibid., p354

This sect-within-a-sect included a range of ceremonial and monastic practises, including periods of 40-day seclusion and complex ceremonial work in closed chambers done in similar fashion to the high-degree Freemasonry that they took inspiration from. This included a circular chamber within which 13 cots would be situated, surrounding a central lamp that burned for the duration of their lengthy periods of mystical seclusion. The third floor of the lodgings also contained a chamber with similarities to the ideal room described in *Abramelin* (which makes sense given the German links to both), being a plain square room with:

> *"a small oval window in each side, opening to the four cardinal points of the compass…[and] it was in here that the ceremonies of the rite was performed by the thirteen brethren who were striving for their moral regeneration and seeking communication with the spirit world."*[20]

The forty-day collective ritual, which followed a period of intense physical preparation that also consisted of forty days of individual isolation spent fasting and praying in the forest, is described by Sachse as follows:

> *"At the conclusion of certain religious services, among which was the saying of the 48th Psalm, a procession was formed, and the thirteen elect were escorted up the hill to the portals of the building, which, as soon as the adepts had entered, were securely locked to prevent any intrusion or interruption during the forty days of their retirement from the outside world. These days were spent as follows: six hours of each day in silent reflection; three hours in public or common prayer, in which each votary offered his body and soul as a living sacrifice, or offering to the glory and honor of God; nine hours were devoted to the study and practice of the esoteric problems of the ritual; lastly, six hours were spent in communion among themselves looking toward the regaining of the lost of ineffable world.*
>
> *The ritual further states that at the end of the thirty-third day of seclusion a visible intercourse commenced between the brethren and the seven archangels, viz.: Anael, Michael, Raphael, Gabriel, Uriel, Zobiachiel and Anachiel; this visible communion lasted until the end of the fortieth day, when they labor was finished, and each of the adepts received from the senior archangel a parchment or scroll, on which was*

---

20. Ibid., p358

the seal, or the sacred pentagon, containing the ineffable name. The attainment of this great treasure completed the 'moral regeneration,' or, as it was known among the Bruderschaft, the 'state of primitive innocence' (unschuld). The fortunate adept who had thus successfully completed the ordeal, with physical body as clean and pure as that of a new-born child, his spirit filled with divine light, with vision without limit, and with mental powers unbounded, would henceforth have no other ambition than to enjoy the complete rest while waiting for immortality, when he should finally be able to say to himself – I AM, THAT I AM."[21]

Thus we have an example of how the intensive practices of spiritual retreat, as practised within the grimoire tradition of Europe, were placed in central importance to an 18th century community. Not only as esoteric rites hidden away in rare books, but collectively practiced in a rural township in Pennsylvania.[22]

There are some reasons to doubt the accuracy of the account from Sachse, though, not least of which because of the rather fantastical way that psychoactive substances, alleged to grant superhuman regenerative powers, are said to be utilised in the first period of solitary isolation that brings about 'physical regeneration'. There are also those who question the names of the seven archangels that don't seem to appear in that specific configuration until Cagliostro nearly 50 years later (which doesn't disclose that the brotherhood at Ephrata could have been working from earlier unknown sources, or perhaps even been a source themselves)[23]. Regardless, we can be confident from the primary sources and materials used by Sachse that the account is, at least in large part, a relatively faithful portrayal of the broad practises undertaken by this mystical order. We can also readily say that they are not something that we must try to mimic to the letter in how we go about Rosicrucianism in the 21st century (similar to how many grimoire and alchemical texts cannot realistically be strictly adhered to, either). Rather we can use such accounts to understand the intensity in which spiritual retreat was understood and practised within Rosicrucian-inspired communities of the past. An intensity that goes well beyond what many of us practicing

---

21. Ibid., p358-59
22. It has even been postulated that Joseph Smith, the founder of Mormonism and a known occultist, could have potentially been influenced by these very communities
23. Levenda, P. 2009, *The Secret Temple: Masons, Mysteries, and the Founding of America*

today are likely willing or even able to undertake ourselves.

Such examples harken back to a long and varied tradition of theurgic monasticism, not just in Christianity but through to examples in the ancient world such as the Pythagoreans that were influential on Western esotericism in general and the utopian ideals of Rosicrucianism in particular. We can see through these examples how the notion of spiritual retreat is taken to its most intense and encompassing form, with strict rules on diet and lifestyle; long periods of silence; and highly structured forms of learning and worship. There are other contemporary 17th century efforts at religious living that we see championed, such as John Pordage and his 'family' of religious seekers; and Jane Lead and the Philadelphian Society that adhered to many of the pansophic theories of Jacob Böhme and for whom *"Revelation came through the via negativa, the shedding of all acquired knowledge."*[24]

These movements, in all their diversity, disseminated the theosophical strands held within the Rosicrucian tapestry into a more widespread and utilised form. I've chosen a few interesting examples to briefly show how the notion of spiritual retreat, when brought to the forefront, is able to nourish and embolden the source of visionary thinking within us. This can then manifest in ways that not only change the course of our own lives, but of society more broadly and how we relate to the Divine across centuries of thinking and practice. But even without such epoch-defining outcomes, which are not only rare but often the result of circumstances beyond individual control, the process itself is life-changing and one that we should incorporate into our own path to whatever extent we can.

For most of us today, the monastic lifestyle is not feasible (although it can be available for shorter periods such as a week, month or even a year). However, it is interesting to consider the elements that can be tailored to our own context and ability to pursue such things. It's important to know that this isn't an 'all or nothing' equation. The monastic lifestyles mentioned above are intimidating and unattainable for many, but there is great spiritual nourishment to be found from short methods of a few days, or even in some cases a matter of hours, that take us out of the distractions and obligations of our busy lives so that we might be able to better listen to the still voice within. We can be encouraged by this and continue in our own capacity, as long as we acknowledge that those who put in the most effort and commitment to the process will be (for the most part) the ones that receive the greatest fruits.

---

24. Hessayon, A. 2013, *Jacob Boehme's Writings During the English Revolution and Afterwards*, p93

We also need to acknowledge that, at least in most parts of the world, there is more access to information and an ability to live a more openly mystical life today, which in previous centuries would often be seen as heretical or seditious. People were burned at the stake in England up until 1612, while censorship, book burnings and criminal charges of blasphemy continued for far longer. Thankfully we can now tailor our own programme of spiritual retreat from a wide variety of sources, doing so in a manner that is more open and able to reach out for advice from others pursuing similar goals. It seems like a simple thing to say, but the freedom in which most of us can operate today should not be taken for granted as it enables us to pursue spiritual retreat to whatever extent we feel called to. We can take inspiration from the monastic lifestyles of deeply religious communities, whether they be on the fringes of society or the more well-trodden forms of Christian monasticism found in religious orders. There are tools that we can use such as the contemplative approach of St. Thomas Aquinas; the pilgrimage and spiritual exercises put forward by St. Ignatius; or options more directly related to Rosicrucianism such as the previously explored *Geheime Figuren der Rosenkreuzer* or the symbolic emblems of Daniel Cramer published in 1617. The latter of these, made up of 40 illustrations depicting a process of heart-focused esoteric Christianity, have become known as the 'Rosicrucian Emblems' and provide us with a clear example of how extended contemplative efforts can enable a deeper understanding of the processes of the soul. Throughout all of this and by whichever approach we might end up taking, we can be assured that the mysteries we seek are able to be found through prayer and contemplation alone. That through committed acts of devotion and principled living, our periods of spiritual retreat will lead us into new areas of esoteric experience. The more we are able to give ourselves over to this process, even if only for finite periods of time, the deeper we will enter into modes of spiritual understanding. As Pico della Mirandola states in *Oration on the Dignity of Man*:

> "If you see a person living in deep contemplation, unaware of his body and dwelling in the inmost reaches of his mind, he is neither from heaven nor earth, he is divinity clothed in flesh...Let a holy ambition enter into our souls; let us not be content with mediocrity, but rather strive after the highest and expend all our strength in achieving it."[25]

---

25. Translated by Richard Hooker on the website of Prof. Paul Brians, Washington State University, 2016

Emblem VI and Emblem XV from Daniel Cramer's *Emblemata sacra...* (1624)

When looking at how Rosicrucianism is practiced today this kind of self-discovery and the application of different sources of inspiration is a central component that embraces the modern world and all its freedoms of information, travel and communication. While doing this, we also understand that there is personal accountability and a need to follow through with our spiritual ambitions in order to achieve the heights of experience sought.

As an aside, through the graces received in spiritual retreat we learn that there is one Universal Master and all spiritual teachers, gurus, shamans and priests et al. are but advocates for the celestial and divine realms. There is no strict requirement to prostrate at the feet of others, because you have within yourself the capacity to communicate directly with the source of Truth and Light that emanates throughout all of created existence. The advice in *Abramelin* states this plainly when it says that one should:

> *"Remember, even if you do not have a teacher to show you the secret of the Wisdom and its preparation, after eighteen months your Angel… will reveal to you everything that is necessary."*[26]

Each of us can forge a connection to the higher source of inspiration that will guide you where you need to go and, ultimately, only you will be able to know how successful you are in getting there. This is not a call to arrogantly proclaim your achievements, but rather to enter into a calm state of compassion that allows you to assist the presence of God in the world and bring about the goodness born from genuine wisdom that does not seek power, fame or money. Once you have entered into such communion through the processes of spiritual retreat, the path forward will become clear and you will know what needs to be done. Through distancing oneself from distractions, external responsibilities and material desires, the contemplative silence that quiets the mind can allow the messages of the soul to be heard. Through the faithful devotion that brings you into contact with the wellspring within, you will receive the aforementioned Gifts of Grace and be guided through the many trials and challenges that life brings.

The process of spiritual retreat, conducted wholeheartedly, removes any sense of doubt about the path chosen; replacing it with an insight that provides strength and wisdom to all our undertakings. Not blind obedience

---

26. Dehn, 2015, p38

to dogmatic forms, but inner alignment to divine purpose fortified by the assurance of direct experiential knowledge. An alignment that leads one toward the devotional heights required to become consumed by the Holy Spirit and able to view the esoteric mysteries that otherwise exist beyond reach. The true secrets of Rosicrucianism cannot be written down because they are lived and experienced. The subtle trails of our ascending path only become apparent through spiritual development, attained via ever-greater levels of devotion. Those able to surmount the difficulties of this journey and the many aspects that can lead one astray become enveloped in the illumination we seek, returning from the Holy Mountain with the transformative presence of the prophetic voice.

Sensual Spirituality and Senseless Technology

"Beloved, we are God's children now; what we will be has not yet been revealed. What we do know is this: when he is revealed, we will be like him, for we will see him as he is. And all who have this hope in him purify themselves, just as he is pure." 1 John 3:2 (NRSV)

Spiritual retreat not only allows communion with that which is higher, but reflection on that which we currently are. An honest assessment of our own life, mimicking the final moments of our Earthly existence before we pass and allowing us to recognise the joys of a life well lived while also being inescapably forthright in where we have done wrong. A reflection of that moment before we are subsumed into eternity so that we may return again in another form, for another fleeting moment in time. However we individually choose to pursue spiritual retreat – and there are many forms it can take – it is a process that at its heart requires radical truth in order to receive an experience of the Divine Rose unfolding within our own material incarnation of consciousness.

From an alchemical perspective, we can see that there is both an active and passive component to our spiritual workings that slowly merges into one unified whole. The active components of our consciousness and material self must be directed towards matters of the Divine; which requires time, energy and personal sacrifice. Without such actions we cannot offer ourselves in full completeness and so will forever remain separated (at least consciously so) from our birthright as co-creators of living reality. But with them and the purification that results, we construct a vessel capable of manifesting the eternal spark and bring ourselves to the point in which we can receive the Gifts of Grace and allow them to encompass our thoughts and being. Active and Passive; Masculine and Feminine; King and Queen; both are required and combined in the Great Work to bring about the Stone of the Wise.

Sanctification of the material world and materialisation of the sacred.

The modern Rosicrucian has this in common not only with our forebears, but with the esoteric traditions going back to the dawn of human endeavour. Not through an unbroken chain of teachings, however romantic such an idea might be, but due to the fact that we all share the same conditions as part of manifested humanity. This is why the ancient rituals and monastic traditions still have such a meaningful impact on people today. Even though we might have changed our worldview and understanding of the components of these practices, the core of the experience remains the same. It goes beyond ideology or belief and ties us together through the shared medium of consciousness and its ability to connect with something beyond our usual modes of being. Although we might be surrounded by modern conveniences that can help engage (or distract) us on this path, it is one that we share with all those who have walked before us. Indeed, it's important at this point to recognise that our modern lives, filled with relative comfort and privilege, have in many ways made it *more* difficult for us to attain the heights of religious experience. While much of how we need to see our work as modern Rosicrucians revolves around responding to the realities of a tech-centred world, our lives are now so enmeshed with the digital that our concepts of *spiritual retreat* should be seen in contrast to this new day-to-day reality. The retreats that we must find, whatever the length of time they might represent, will almost certainly require a detachment from the hyper-connectivity that technology has provided and, in significant ways, has imprisoned us in. This is required not just to regain control over our impulses and attentive desires, but also to find enough distance from the ideological influences that we have become saturated by and are even weaponised against us in very real and concerning ways.

Our spiritual retreat must find respite from this cacophony of sources demanding our attention and allegiance. Without such respite, it is all but impossible to find the stillness required to discover the hidden sanctuaries of our inner world. While recognising that there are many different forms of spiritual retreat, it thus seems important to consider all of them as necessarily removed from the distractions of our digital lives. Even so, we do have an obligation (particularly as Rosicrucians seeking reformation) to help transform our digital landscapes into spaces of meaningful advancement and collaboration for the betterment of humankind. The need to remove ourselves from the distractions of life is not a new challenge, but it is one that has become more pressing as our technology draws us deeper into the illusions of the material world in a manner that feels far more substantial than they really are. This is not to say that we must abandon such things entirely, but rather that our concept of spiritual retreat and purification should consciously seek to reduce such influences so that we can strengthen our ability to hear the call from within.

While this is a particularly modern challenge, we can also be reassured by the fact that all seekers of esoteric truth in the past have faced such a trial in their own way. Robert Wentworth Little, one of the founders of the *Societas Rosicruciana in Anglia* and its first Supreme Magus, states this plainly in an address given in 1868:

> "To the fitting contemplation of our mysteries we must bring minds divested of the cares and griefs of life–unfettered by the chains of custom–and free from the storms of passion and prejudice which darken and desolate the souls of men...Let no misgivings haunt thy soul, but press onward; bear with thee, like the memorable phylactery of the ancients, an unshaken trust in that great and glorious Name, which is associated with the mystery of our regeneration; bear with thee to the shrine of truth the tribute of an humble heart and a purified perception. From the dross of sensual life eliminate the gold of intellectual existence; and from the countless systems of human learning extract the atoms of true and heavenly wisdom."[27]

Which brings us back to a more practical application to overcome the 'chains of custom' and 'storms of passion' that lead us astray. Our lives have become so enmeshed with technology and the ever-present desire to be validated by others that we are surrounded by distractions and lost in our own damaging thought-forms to the extent that it is difficult to 'find the time' for more contemplative pursuits. Many of the forms of spiritual retreat discussed can feel elusive, requiring a great deal of commitment to follow through with. We know that this level of dedication is needed to truly experience the heights that our mystical traditions have to offer (and it is no coincidence

---

27. *The Rosicrucian: A Quarterly Record*, July 1868, available at srialondon.org

the allegories surrounding our spiritual treasures are often wrapped in epic quests), however, these examples of spiritual achievement are not the only forms accessible to us. This is even more true when taking into account the context that we now live in. We are all intimidated by mythological quests and feel inadequate to undertake them, but every journey starts with a single step and the will to begin. One first step that we can all take, although not as easy as it sounds, is to simply detach ourselves from the distractions we have filled our lives with. To alter a phrase from George Orwell: *In a time of universal technology, logging off becomes a revolutionary act.*

It feels worrying to say, but just leaving the house without your smartphone can be seen as a basic form of spiritual retreat that will start to strip away the external influences holding back an experiential relationship with the Most High. Doing so for extended periods feels similar to overcoming addiction (and indeed, for many of us, that's because it very much is). It is not only a challenging task, but an equally rejuvenating one that allows you to reconfigure parts of your life and how you prioritise things in deeply meaningful ways. This isn't a reactionary response to technology, but rather a purposeful view of how it is altering our perception of ourselves; our relationship with others; and even our concept of reality itself. If you can only take part in a single form of spiritual retreat, even if just for short periods of time, then consider this one act: *switch off your phone and internet.*

At the very least, by doing so you will discover that you have all the time you need for the more complicated and demanding tasks at hand. That the search to 'find more time' that was used as an excuse for inaction is overcome by the realisation that much of our modern lives is spent wasting time – or filling it with trivial things – and there is an incentive for many external forces to keep us distracted. They get paid for our attention, not for whether our attention is productive. Certainly not for whether our attention is beneficial to ourselves or others in any real sense of the term. Breaking this manipulative cycle is a vital component of how we must approach the concept of spiritual retreat in the 21st century and it is one we can all begin with to enhance any other practises that might follow.

The Cycles of a Rosicrucian Life

"the place where they had the Holy Vessel in keeping…is situated in a valley; it has a tower, and is approached by a bridge."[28] A. E. Waite

---

28. Waite, A.E. 1909, *The Hidden Church of the Holy Graal*, Rebman Limited, London, p129

What spiritual retreat looks like in practice will be different for each of us, yet all paths speak to the same essence. From a Rosicrucian perspective, this will most often come from a Christian framework in broad terms along with its esoteric roots. For many practitioners, there is also a great deal of folk magic or more pagan practices involved; and increasingly other traditions, such as Islam, Buddhism and Hinduism (among others) have become a strong influence on both the philosophical and practical manner in which progressive illumination might be attained. Rosicrucianism is an inherently syncretic tradition that is not afraid – indeed at its foundation celebrates – diversity of belief and the ability to learn from different cultures. What it does require, though, is an encapsulating self-sacrifice which speaks to the core of our desire to reconnect with the Divine and to do so with humility and trust for what incarnation brings. Not in a dogmatic sense which seeks to directly explain the infinite majesty of creation, but rather in our ability to fully commit to the path that we are taking and do so not merely for our own prosperity or power but so that we might participate in an act of communal, global healing. We give of ourselves (sacrificing our ego) in order that our actions can have a restorative effect on the small aspect of the world around us that we serve. We act as individuals, but it is our collective efforts that truly change things for the better and sanctify a greater and greater portion of the human experience and consciousness. Spiritual retreat allows us to better hear the voice of the Divine in its various expressions; our daily practices bring this voice as a beating rhythm into our lives; allowing it to burst forth and emerge through our words and deeds as we interact with others. Each interaction a moment of creation; each step reverberating infinitely even though it may seem insignificant at the time.

The cycle of *personal practice*, *social engagement* and *spiritual retreat* is one that occurs at different levels throughout our lives and with a lot of overlap between each stage. They are not discrete segments, but rather modes of spiritual being. There are cycles that occur within a single day, when we find time to commit to daily practice and also inevitably engage in some form of social contact (even if increasingly online). There are weekly cycles, where we find short moments for spiritual retreat that take us outside of our day-to-day activities and provide the environment for new perspectives to emerge. Then we can think in terms of months, working towards larger acts of regeneration whether personal, social or spiritual; and even over the course of years where some of the more truly impacting and defining examples of our spiritual life are to be found. Seeing things in this manner, as different cycles and timeframes of personal practice, social engagement and spiritual retreat, allows us to be freed from the paralysis of inaction and self-doubt and get on with living life as a Rosicrucian. We often think about these things in grand terms – a pilgrimage over hundreds of miles, a life of monasticism, or intensive ceremonies such as *Abramelin* – and that can hold us back from enacting them in our lives on an ongoing basis. Do not expect perfection from the beginning and do not hold yourself back through feelings of insignificance. By taking things one day at a time, while understanding that there is a bigger journey being undertaken, we can build toward the grand and spectacular moments on the path of mystical attainment. Because, in the end, even those spectacular moments aren't the final goal. Rather, they allow us to sanctify our being and bring back fleeting glimmers of the Divine that we have been graced with – like morning dew that reflects on the road ahead. Each step we take on this path is sacred, the spectacular moments are there to help align our actions accordingly.

Spiritual retreat provides us with the experiential knowledge that the universe itself is sacramental. Once we can understand and *see* this truth then we energise our practice with the spark of creation and become agents of Divine Immanence. This energy is built up through our personal (and group) practice, but becomes manifest through our social engagement. Our encounters with God and the Choirs of Angels are predicated not merely on lip-service or even good intent, but on the sacrifices of devotion and righteous action that emerge from an alignment of our inner sphere with the source of creative purpose and Love in the world. Once connected, our own microcosm is renewed at a higher plane of understanding and efficacy; enhancing its role in the destiny of the universe and thus the cycle continues anew. We act not merely as singular agents seeking our own goals, but as components of the collective sum of humanity in its sacred form. Ready to act within that space of Prophetic Illumination and able to discern the difference between our visionary and egotistical forms.

To close this section, we can for a moment step back and consider the previously discussed idea of *social engagement* as the act of living our spiritual path in an outward manner. Seeing our efforts as spiritual beings in this way connects us to the local reality of others that we share material existence with. How we dedicate ourselves to *personal practice* is not fundamentally important here, although it does provide us with the strength and fortitude to forge ahead, because what ultimately matters is the impact we are having and the extent to which we are helping bring about universal Love and Regeneration. Such practices need to be informed by something, though, and that can either be through obedience to traditional forms (and the teachers that represent them); or through direct experience and a close, personal relationship with the Divine. It is this relationship that we have been predominantly looking at now, one that only truly emerges when significant amounts of time and devotional energy are committed to the sacred art of *spiritual retreat.*

Spiritual retreat can take different forms and won't always fit the romantic ideals of lengthy ceremonies or monastic lifestyles. Although there are clear examples to be inspired by, they aren't always readily accessible to everyone and certainly aren't available to everyone *all the time.* For the vast majority of us, the best we can hope for are a few significant periods in our lifetime; combined with some kind of rhythm spent in periods of isolated contemplation. Following through with such aspirations will develop a strong devotional relationship to our spiritual path, but we should also find other, smaller avenues for spiritual retreat that are more accessible in our daily lives. By doing so we can be assured that the heights of spiritual experience won't forever remain a mirage in the distance, that we keep telling ourselves we'll get to one day…but never do.

There are many ways to proceed and you will know (and be guided to) what is needed for your own journey, even if you might not feel ready yet to undertake it. In a more general sense, what we are referring to is the process of removing the dross accumulated throughout the course of our lives in order to emerge a more integrated and purposeful being. Less swayed by primal instinct, negative influences and nefarious intent from a wide variety of external and internal sources. Importantly, such outcomes are not an end point but rather the beginning of a new cycle that draws us to ever more meaningful and impacting expressions of our relationship with God and the divine messengers found throughout all of creation – from the smallest quantum particle through to the largest galactic configuration and everything in between.

This process can look like many things and is something built toward throughout our life, but it comes to define everything else that succeeds it and will make sense of the journey that brought you there. It requires the will to align your material circumstances with spiritual pursuit and the wisdom to know when is the most beneficial time to do so. There are some individuals who are even so drawn to spiritual retreat that they make it the primary focus of their lives, which can provide great sustenance not only to themselves but as inspiration for all of us and even the course of humanity as a whole. Consider how many guiding lights emerge out of the monastic traditions of the world. Within the act of spiritual retreat there are truly real and miraculous experiences to be found, that can provide the creative vision for entirely new ways of being to emerge into the world. In our modern age, however, with all its responsibilities and distractions, these kinds of pursuits can feel unattainable or difficult to envisage. How do we find the space and time? Does it require disappearing for a year to benefit? What about family, friends and professional obligations? The answers to these questions will be as varied as those attempting the journey.

Personal practice is something that should be done as often as possible, ideally daily, as it will build the subtle changes in consciousness that bring you closer to an ideal form of human expression in the world. These practices create a rhythm that becomes a sacred heartbeat, driving everything else around it and providing the confidence to work through things that are difficult and overwhelming. From within that heartbeat emerge the guiding voices and visionary images that draw you further into a relationship with God and the majesty of Creation in ways that will both challenge and inspire you. Most of us will never experience the heights of this path, at least not within the confines of our material existence, but that doesn't mean that we aren't able to appreciate it for the source of Light that it truly is. Even a short glimpse is worth a lifetime of dedication. Thankfully we know, from the countless seekers that have walked before us, that such a reward is received for our journey into the source of all that is and can be. We should not be surprised that it is difficult and requires something extraordinary from us. But to even experience only part of the journey during our lifetime brings nourishment enough. It is not an all or nothing search for Truth, but one that unfolds over time into greater alignment with the sources of Peace and Love in the world.

Spiritual retreat strips everything back so that we can encounter the core at the heart of our existence. Rather than acting just as another foundation of belief to support our daily motions, it brings us into contact with the bedrock of existence itself. It provides a glimpse of the eternal stillness behind time and a point around which our spiritual lives can circle and ascend to new heights. By removing ourselves from egotistical concerns, we allow the natural language of the universe to be heard and understood more directly. This is not a place that we exist within permanently, for all of us are material beings and few can escape that fact, but it is one that, if we are able to find the motivation, will forever change the trajectory of our lives. All of human history, in all cultures, languages and times, speaks of the riches to be found within this space and gives us guidance in both allegorical and literal forms on how to get there. There are many paths to Truth, but all speak of its existence and transformative power.

As with the previous chapters, my intention here is not to tell you *what* to do but rather to provide a framework to consider *why* you might do it. There are many examples that you will find your own inspiration from. In a modern and more practical context we can think about the purpose of such experiences and, as discussed, there are different ways in which one can consider the undertaking of spiritual retreat. Conceptually, it is placing ourselves within an environment in which the structural responsibilities and influences of society (vital though they sometimes are) are consciously removed so that a direct relationship with reality, internal and external, and a one-to-one communicative experience with God can be achieved. An experience that allows us to become attuned to a state of visionary exaltation that has been identified by our Rosicrucian forebearers as 'Prophetic Illumination'. In the specifically Christian context of Rosicrucianism, our dedications through prayer, ritual and continual affirmation towards the Christ Within construct a mystical archway in the depths of our consciousness. An archway waiting for us to step through with enough humility to experience the sacred realities on the other side and wholeheartedly accept salvation. The path of internal pilgrimage is not an easy one, by any means, but it is universally accessible for those who choose to take it. Only our own shortcomings, through often influenced by circumstances outside our control, are holding us back:

> *Ever since the creation of the world his eternal power and divine nature, invisible though they are, have been understood and seen through the things he has made. So they are without excuse; for though they knew God, they did not honor him as God or give thanks to him, but they became futile in their thinking, and their senseless minds were darkened.* Romans 1:19-21 (NRSV)

If we take a moment to think 'what now' in terms of 21st century Rosicrucianism, then we can see how the central role of personal practice forms the basis for any external action to follow. Without the measured confidence of one aligned with higher purpose and disciplined against the misguided influence of the ego and the *in*voluntary forces found in the material world, it is difficult to successfully bring to fruition avenues of social engagement that will have a lasting positive impact. Once this has been achieved (a difficult task), it is then also important to find moments of spiritual retreat. Not just in a literal sense of pulling back from the engagement and practice that you have been conducting, but more importantly in finding the space (wherever and however that may be) to be embraced by silence and return to the centre of your existence.

21st century Rosicrucianism can thus be seen as a cyclical process, the phases of which have specific purposes and goals in mind. *Personal practice* brings the aspirant to a state of devotional selflessness; *social engagement* integrates us with the karmic riverbeds of our collective being; while *spiritual retreat* is a process of sanctification that embodies the greater forces of the universe and allows the micro/macrocosmic balance to be restored. In an age when the true scope of humanity's ability to create is becoming realised – in which we not only seek to leave the planet that gave birth to us, but also give motion to new forms of being ourselves – we must not lose sight of the vital responsibility that this balance represents. We are on the cusp of entirely novel forms of human-guided evolution that demand a high degree of intellectual, emotional and spiritual maturity. Just as we are created, we create. Just as we might feel gratitude at being offered life, so must we provide a proper degree of reverence to the sparks of creation that emerge from within ourselves.

Through spiritual retreat we learn that the subtle is just as important as the spectacular. We come to the realisation that our efforts do not have to attain the pinnacles of human achievement in order to be meaningful and contribute to the sanctification of Creation in all its forms. Our experience of the localised moments around us, down to the smallest perceivable level, is an expression of the ineffable. Though we might indeed achieve great things, it is with our self-sacrifice and embracing of the subtlety of the universe that we give honour to the miracles of existence itself. In these moments it doesn't matter what you have achieved externally, because you are stripped back of all those things and stand in direct communion with the cosmos as a unified whole. All things at all times, through the source of everything that rests within the heart of humanity. *I Am, That I Am.*

World without end.

Amen.

PART II:

LIVING
TRADITION

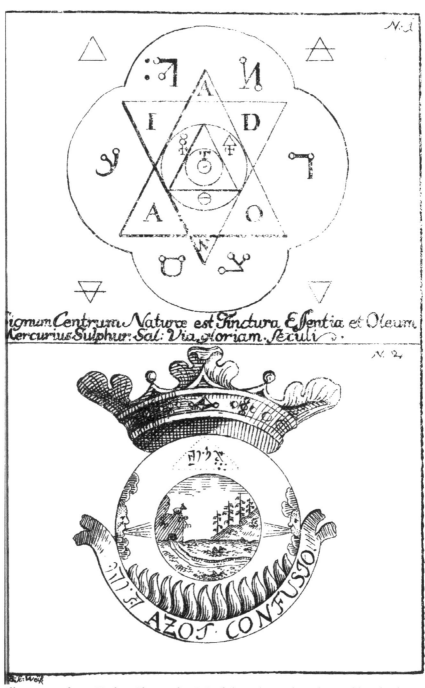

Illustration from *Uraltes Chymisches Werck* (1735), attributed to Rabbi Abrahami
Eleazaris and based on the work of 14th century alchemist, Nicolas Flamel

AN ALCHEMICAL INTERPRETATION OF THE ANNUNCIATION

Welcome everybody and thank you for being here to listen to this presentation. I want to begin briefly by saying that the topic of this talk is one that has proven central to my own personal journey and has provided me with inspiration at many different points over the last few years. So what I want to do today is share some of my findings and realisations, as well as allow time for discussion. Hopefully this will enable all of us to leave this session with something of value and I strongly encourage you to see the Annunciation as an image of true transformative power, depicting as it does a stage of initiatory and alchemical progress within the Great Work.

What I will be examining, then, are the common elements present in many depictions of the Annunciation, the moment at which Mary is told by the Archangel Gabriel that she is to be the Theotokos or God-bearer. This exploration will begin with the biblical text, before moving onto artistic interpretations, and shall examine the general symbolic import of the common elements that we see in the Annunciation throughout history. I will then move into more detail from an alchemical perspective and provide you with what I have found to be a powerful and spiritually transformative way of viewing this event. I shall be asking a number of questions: What are the common symbols and elements and how might we understand them in regards to the process of alchemical work? In doing so, can we see the Annunciation as an allegory for spiritual progression? And what can we, as Rosicrucians and Seekers of Light, gain from a more esoteric understanding of this core aspect of the Christian tradition?

So then, with the context and disclaimers out of the way, let us begin; and in order to begin it is important to briefly define just what it is that I am discussing when I use the phrase 'Alchemical Interpretation'.

Alchemy and Hermeticism

Alchemy, as used in this context, is to be understood as the practical application of the Hermetic tradition that plays such a central role throughout the history of esoteric thought. Let us presume that when I mention alchemy I am speaking of that form which predominately emerged out of the writings of Hermes Trismegistus, whoever or whatever that name may signify. These teachings form part of the foundation of the perennial tradition and its concepts can be found spread through the teachings of the Qabalists, Gnostics, Sufis, Neo-Platonists, Alchemists, Rosicrucians; and all the way through to the allegorical system of Freemasonry and beyond.

The core of the alchemical teachings of Hermes Trismegistus are distilled in an item known as the Emerald Tablet, and I want to read out a translation of its text before we begin in order to appropriately set the scene:

In truth, without deceit, certain and most veritable.

That which is Below corresponds to that which is Above, and that which is Above corresponds to that which is Below, to accomplish the miracles of the One Thing. And just as all things have come from this One Thing, through the meditation of One Mind, so do all created things originate from this One Thing, through Transformation.

Its father is the Sun; its mother the Moon. The Wind carries it in its belly; its nurse is the Earth.

It is the origin of All, the consecration of the Universe; its inherent Strength is perfected, if it is turned into Earth.

Separate the Earth from Fire, the Subtle from the Gross, gently and with great Ingenuity. It rises from Earth to heaven and descends again to Earth, thereby combining within Itself the powers of both the Above and the Below.

Thus will you obtain the Glory of the Whole Universe. All Obscurity will be clear to you. This is the greatest Force of all powers, because it overcomes every Subtle thing and penetrates every Solid thing.

In this way was the Universe created. From this comes many wondrous Applications, because this is the Pattern.

Therefore am I called Thrice Great Hermes, having all three parts of the wisdom of the Whole Universe. Herein have I completely explained the Operation of the Sun.[1]

Whatever the origin of this text, and however we might each understand the esoteric teaching that hides behind its words, it is one that heavily influenced the practical path of the alchemists. I don't want to delve into a detailed analysis of the Hermetic tradition, but suffice to say that I shall be exploring many of its themes in our examination of the story of Mary and the virgin birth of Jesus Christ.

Depictions of the Annunciation

Let me begin this exploration with the main biblical text that discusses this event: from the New King James Bible, Luke Chapter 1: 26-35

> [26] *Now in the sixth month the angel Gabriel was sent by God to a city of Galilee named Nazareth,*
> [27] *to a virgin betrothed to a man whose name was Joseph, of the house of David. The virgin's name was Mary.*
> [28] *And having come in, the angel said to her, "Rejoice, highly favored one, the Lord is with you; blessed are you among women!"*
> [29] *But when she saw him, she was troubled at his saying, and considered what manner of greeting this was.*

---

1. Hauck, D.W., 1999, *The Emerald Tablet: Alchemy for Personal Transformation*, Arkana, Penguin Group, p45

30 Then the angel said to her, "Do not be afraid, Mary, for you have found favor with God.

31 And behold, you will conceive in your womb and bring forth a Son, and shall call His name JESUS.

32 He will be great, and will be called the Son of the Highest; and the Lord God will give Him the throne of His father David.

33 And He will reign over the house of Jacob forever, and of His kingdom there will be no end."

34 Then Mary said to the angel, "How can this be, since I do not know a man?"

35 And the angel answered and said to her, "The Holy Spirit will come upon you, and the power of the Highest will overshadow you; therefore, also, that Holy One who is to be born will be called the Son of God.

Even though this is by far the most central and influential text, we must bear in mind that it isn't the only one. There are numerous apocryphal texts which discuss the Annunciation and many of them are influential when it comes to artistic depictions – particularly early Byzantine iconography. The Armenian Gospel, for example, describes two Annunciations – the first from an invisible angel that Mary dismisses as the Devil's work; which then leads to her seeking guidance through prayer and the more visceral experience of Gabriel's appearance, emerging through a closed door, and the Word of God entering Mary's ear.

From these textual descriptions of the Annunciation we get many artistic depictions, understandably so as such a central image within the Christian tradition. The elements that are taken from these source texts are straightforward and readily recognised. They are the inclusion of Gabriel as messenger to Mary, who is seen as a woman of purity, and the announcement that through a miraculous virgin birth she will bring forth the Holy One, the Messiah, who is to be called the Son of God. The first such depiction that we know of is a circa 4th century fresco in the catacomb of Priscilla in Rome (this has been disputed, but the similarity is there).

From this we get a very long tradition of artistic depictions of the event and it is from the evolution of artistic interpretations that some of the more powerful and alchemically relevant symbolism emerges. Without such artistic evolution, there is still a strong case to be made purely about the text; but it truly is from the art that the hypothesis and perspective is made much stronger and more impacting. Interestingly, it is not until the 15th and 16th

Byzantine Annunciation, 14th century

Earliest known depiction of the Annunciation, Catacomb of Priscilla, 4th century AD

An Alchemical Interpretation of the Annunciation 111

centuries that these artistic depictions really begin to take on attributes of the alchemical tradition widely practiced at that time. Tracking the progression and evolution of the symbolism involved is a daunting prospect, but there are a few observations that can be made succinctly.

The first of these is that the very early images show Mary and Gabriel, and little else. The inclusion of the dove as symbol of the Holy Spirit first appears in an early mosaic from the 5th century in the Basilica di Santa Maria Maggiore, Rome. This is likely due to the decision made at the Council of Nicea that the dove was a valid symbol that could be used to depict the Holy Spirit. Early depictions of the Annunciation tend to revolve around concepts of epiphany in general – Mary being amongst the first to have such visions and revelations of Christ – and we can often see curtains and other such veils presented to represent this.

One of the most important evolutions of the symbolism that incorporates elements outside of the direct text itself comes from the inclusion of the Lilies – a long standing symbol of the virgin Mary – however this element does not become universally used until about the 13th century, at which point it is more difficult to find depictions without the use of lilies than examples of those with them. The 15th century really sees a boom in many varied and more subtle symbolism than previously seen and the examples I have provided show this attention to detail that is prevalent throughout much of the images of that era. The depictions become, in many regards, crowded with objects and figures; sometimes referencing particular aspects of local celebration or just instilling the work with the personal touch of the individual creating it.

In the end, the Annunciation has become one of the most widely painted scenes in the history of religious art and it brings such a sense of sacred purity that it is always an incredibly powerful image to lay eyes upon. As with all powerful things, the true depth of its message cannot be understood immediately and even within a purely mainstream Christian context there is more than meets the eye; but when looking at it from the perspective of Hermeticism and its manifestation in the alchemical tradition we can catch a glimpse of something truly life-altering.

When we examine depictions of the Annunciation we begin to see common elements that run as threads throughout the many variations and stylistic decisions. So I am going to focus on a number of these common elements in order to provide an interpretation of the Annunciation through the lens of the Hermetic alchemists.

I have provided a number of artistic interpretations of this scene, taken throughout a cross-section of history, that display these common elements. Whilst I am discussing this interpretation I would encourage you to look through these images to help with visualisation, and also see if you agree with what I am saying – or more importantly, perhaps, if you come to any realisations as to where I may be off the mark. I have by no means completed my esoteric study of this work, and would thus greatly appreciate any comments, corrections or further insight you might be able to provide.

Alchemical Interpretation

Alchemy is a tradition of symbolism, both through necessity and nature, so there is no better place to begin with this interpretation than to examine the symbols present throughout the tradition of the Annunciation.

Of course, one of the difficulties that we have is that not only is the symbolic language of the alchemists designed specifically to obfuscate and lead astray, but different alchemists used terms and symbols differently. As an example: some merely refer to Sulphur and Mercury. Others, most famously Paracelsus, add in Salt to create a *tria prima*. We also hear of Gold, Silver and Quicksilver; or Sol, Luna and Mercurius. Each of these elements in turn has many many different contexts and qualifying statements and adjectives – there are many different types of Sulphur and Mercury. It can all get complicated very quickly if we merely presume just one reference for translation, so we must always remember that different contexts and individuals refer to these concepts in slightly different ways. Indeed, I will end up doing so as well. Although it must be said that, in my case, misinterpretations are likely the result of personal ignorance rather than a conscious attempt to conceal!

The result of this obfuscation and abstraction is that you find yourself grasping at phantasms, intuitively understanding certain aspects as feelings rather than well-formed thoughts that can be easily articulated. It makes it difficult to communicate these ideas, but that is the nature of the Work and is both its greatest frustration and most sublime beauty. So, I can but try and provide as lucid an understanding as I can humbly give – keeping in mind that I am still very much involved in the process.

Let us first, then, take each common element in turn and see how it could be related to the esoteric understanding of the alchemists, before bringing them together into one coherent picture so that the purpose of this conjoined symbol can be more fully understood.

5th century mosaic with Annunciation (top tier), Basilica di Santa Maria Maggiore, Rome

Annunciation with lilies from unknown German artist in Cologne (c.1330)

Middle panel of *Mérode Altarpiece* triptych, attributed to Robert Campin (c.1425)

15th century Annunciation by Netherlandish artist Rogier van der Weyden (c.1434)

Annunciation commissioned for the Palazzo Medici in Florence, by Filippo Lippi (c.1450)

The Annunciation by Nicolas Poussin (1657)

The Annunciation with Saint Emidius
Depiction with peacock's tail by Carlo Crivelli, 1486 (CC, The National Gallery, London)

The Annunciation by Federico Barocci (c.1596)

19th century depiction by Dante Gabriel Rossetti (1850)

The Annunciation as depicted in the Isenheim Altarpiece
by Matthias Grünewald (c.1515)

Bed Chamber

In almost all depictions, the Annunciation takes place inside and often within the confines of a private space such as a bed chamber or study. It is clear that Mary has been sitting alone in quiet contemplation, in most instances there is an open book before her – the Bible – and this ecstatic event has occurred from a state of contemplation or prayer.

In alchemy, the concept of a vessel is an important one as the Great Work requires a demarcation of the inner sphere from unwanted outward physical influences. When discussing this vessel, or *retort* as it is often referred to, we might immediately feel that Mary's womb represents this vessel – however in my opinion this vessel can also be represented by the inner chamber in which almost all depictions of the Annunciation occur. Such a chamber represents on a very literal level the space that an individual has demarcated as their own, different from the world outside of it and having a close relationship to their internal being.

Such a room can be translated succinctly into the language of spiritual transformation – the inner chamber as a backdrop for the Annunciation shows us that this is an internal process, and one that requires us to isolate our soul from external corrupting influences throughout the period of purification and exaltation. Consider here the words of Plotinus:

> "To purify the soul is to isolate her...preventing her from attaching herself to other things and raise her from the things here below to intelligible entities; also to wean her from the body, for in that case she is no longer sufficiently attached to it to be enslaved to it, resembling a light which is not absorbed in the whirlwind of matter".[2]

Virgin Mary

The next element, and clearly the most vital one, is that of Mary herself. Now, with Mary being at the centre of all depictions of the Annunciation by definition, I will be touching upon her significance throughout the different common elements being discussed – but let me begin by saying that we are to understand Mary as Mercury, Luna, the purified feminine principle.

---

2. Plotinus, *The Six Enneads of Plotinus*, translated by S. MacKenna and B.S. Page, Forgotten Books, 2007, Ennead III, 6: 5

Mary can be seen as the *argent-vive*; the receptive feminine Mercury that is to be united with the creative masculine Sulphur of God the Father in order to create the Philosopher's Stone. In her state of Immaculate Conception, free from the ravages of Original Sin and ego, Mary stands even before the Annunciation as Luna, the Moon: the Queen and bride of King Sol; the receptive principle; the purity that results from the cleansing of the subconscious and automatic processes of the mind and body; the One Thing.

Psychological speaking, she has been cleansed of primal emotions and ego-based desires and constructions, slowly replacing them instead with a more pure form of divine inspiration and perspective. The point of Annunciation is the moment at which the cycles of purification that Luna must go through have been completed and refined to perfection. The One Thing has reached its most pure expression and its previous forms have been dissolved in the Waters and cleansed of impurity.

Depictions of the Annunciation always display Mary as a passive form, in a state of receptivity and reverence for the Secret Fire to come unto her. Quite often she is to be seen in a seated position, signifying this passivity and respect for the divine presence – indeed in the depiction by Nicolas Poussin we see her in a state of meditative stillness. This feminine aspect is not to be understood merely as a matter of gender, of womanhood, it is a universal passive element within the One Thing that allows the creative force of the One Mind to forge it into different forms that coagulate and manifest into material existence.

Mary is thus the perfected feminine principle, her role in the Annunciation is as the purified and cleansed physical form Below through which the newly unified soul and spirit from Above can be born into material existence.

Emerging from this place as Luna, the womb of Mary is the perfected *prima materia* – the pure malleability of the One Thing from which all forms can be derived through the creative power of the One Mind. The virgin birth that results from the Annunciation is symbolic of the philosophical child that is the offspring of the Chemical Wedding of Sol and Luna. I will of course discuss this in more detail shortly.

Archangel Gabriel

When looking toward the archangel Gabriel we must recognise his place as the only other element of the Annunciation that is present throughout all depictions. In one regard, Gabriel seems immediately to be indicative of the

Mercurius substance that acts as catalyst for the Divine Marriage. Indeed, it is easy to make a comparison between the rod or stem of lilies that he often carries and the caduceus – the wand of Mercury that highlights the need for balance between earth and heaven; Sulfur, Mercury and Salt – and thus we could quickly define Gabriel as the catalysing substance that allows the union of opposites to occur. In another regard, it would be equally straight forward to classify Gabriel as the masculine Sulphur or Sol; and I was initially (and in some ways still am) tempted to do this. However, neither of these explanations do complete justice to the role of Gabriel, particularly because it is not Gabriel that is the source of Christ's conception, so I want to look a bit further than constructions of Gabriel as either the Mercurius substance or Sulphur while at the same time recognising that we certainly could settle for either (or both).

Nicholas Flamel writes in *His Exposition* that *"the natures then are here transmuted into Angels, that is to say, are made spiritual and most subtle, so are they now the true tinctures"*[3]. Gabriel, as an angel, can therefore be seen as the sublimated spirit, that substance of which the practical alchemists would describe as rising as vapour and that must be contained and coagulated once more within the body that remained at the bottom of the vessel. Zoroaster's Cave says of this process: *"Our Great business is to make the Body a Spirit, and the Spirit a body"*[4] It is the *solve et coagula*, one of the central axioms of the alchemical process, and thus we should not see Gabriel merely as an agent external to the Immaculate Mary, but rather we should also understand that the eternal spirit has emerged because of the purification process and Gabriel, as archangel and messenger, is the perfect culmination of this cycle. Gabriel acts as the divine aspect of the physical Mary, separated momentarily because of the state of purity but which will be combined once again following the process of *solve et coagula*: separation and coagulation that must occur multiple times, each time with more purity of the One Thing and more creative infusion of the One Mind until the *rubedo* state is achieved.

The appearance of Gabriel unto Mary thus harkens the period of separation that directly proceeds the *coniunctio*, the point at which the perfected spirit re-enters into the purified matter. Artephius, when discussing this cycle of dissolution and congelation in alchemy, even goes so far as to state that: *"their*

---

3. Abraham, L. 1998, *Dictionary of Alchemical Imagery*, Cambridge Press, p8
4. Ibid., p187

solution is also their congelation for they have one and the same operation, for the one is not dissolved, but that the other is congealed."[5] The process of the sublimated spirit (Gabriel) rising from the purified substance (Mary) allows then for the coagulation of the more enlightened spirit back into the material form. With each cycle of *solve et coagula* the material substance becomes more sanctified and instilled with that outer source of divinity – the Secret Fire. In the event of the Annunciation this process has reached its perfection and culminating stage, separation and coagulation has occurred multiple times; each return to unity bringing more strength and Light than the last until it is to culminate in perfect conjunction. Bernardi Penotus, a 16th century alchemist, described the final refinement of this process in his work *De Physici Lapidus Materia (Natural Philosophy of the Stone)*:

> *"As to how the Son of Man is generated by the philosopher and the Fruit of the Virgin is produced, it is necessary that he be exalted from the earth and cleansed of all earthiness; then he rises as a whole into the air and is changed into spirit. Thus the word of the philosophers is fulfilled: He ascends from earth to heaven and puts on the power of the Above and the Below, and lays aside his earthly and unclean nature"*[6]

With each cycle of this exaltation we must learn how to reintegrate what has been learned Above into our physical existence Below, until finally reaching a point where the two are able to become one and the same. When going back to the very source of the Annunciation we see that the figures at play are Gabriel and Mary – and the trick is to paradoxically see them both as aspects of the same being, whilst also simultaneously as individual agents. Mary is the purified emotional state of a perfected body and soul, the cleansed and washed ego which allows the spirit (Gabriel) to rise up from the Below and return, perfectly sanctified, as messenger from the Above. This process needs to occur multiple times throughout the course of the Great Work, but the appearance of Gabriel foreshadows the final distillation that occurs before the great union – before *'the power of the Highest will overshadow you [and] that Holy One who is to be born will be called the Son of God'*.

---

5. Ibid., p187
6. Hauck, D.W. 1999, p121

Lilies

The lily is an incredibly potent symbol and really a lot of our work is done for us even if we were to just examine this one element. To put it simply, it is a symbol of purity. Before the inclusion of the Lily in depictions of the Annunciation, Mary's purity was often displayed as a strand of yarn or basket of wool; alluding to her upbringing in the temple of Jerusalem where she would spin robes for priests.

In alchemical writings the Lily is directly and almost universally used as a symbol of the stage of *albedo*, the stage that occurs once the blackened matter of *nigredo* has been purified. It is interesting to note that in some alchemical texts there is a stage following the *nigredo* which is often referred to as the 'peacock's tail' – so called because of its rainbow nature – before the many colours are unified into a state of pure white. In one depiction of the Annunciation by Carlo Crivelli, which I have provided for you, we see prominently displayed the figure of a peacock hanging its tail down over the entrance to the inner chamber that Mary resides in.

The *albedo* is indicative of a state of being whereby all impurity has been absolved and there is no longer a threat of decay from corrupting forces. In psychological terms, this stage represents the dissolution of the ego. Mary's Immaculate Conception, the general understanding of her as absolute feminine purity – free from Original Sin – plays into this understanding of the Annunciation as representative of the *albedo* stage. It is the emergence of true consciousness and, in many ways, we might say that the Annunciation actually represents the culmination of the *albedo* stage. The symbols surrounding the event indications that all of this has occurred within the state of *albedo* and we are at the point of moving to the next stage of *rubedo* in which the Christ-consciousness finds physical manifestation.

God & Rays of Light

In most depictions we are to find the image of God – more often as Rays of Light that come from Above, but also quite regularly as an embodied masculine figure residing in the heavens – which in this context, reaching out from the formless infinite existence of the One Mind, represents the hot, dry, creative masculine principle of refined Sulphur or Sol: the circle with a dot in its centre; the energy and spiritual essence behind all things. It is that which emerges from the One Mind to grant form to the receptive principle present within the One Thing.

Sol is the Father of the Stone, the source of *"perfect incarnation which follows the illumination of the soul (Luna) by the divine spirit or solar ray"*[7]. Through attracting once more the agency of the Most High, the purified state of *albedo* is able to find exaltation as the embodiment of the eternal spirit in the material sphere and the renewal of the ultimate wholeness. Through gradual cycles, Sol imprints its golden image upon the seeker; the Work cannot be completed without this divine inspiration that comes directly from the One Mind. Heraclitus spoke of this creative principle inherent within Sol: *"Everything becomes Fire, and from Fire everything is born"*[8].

In the vast majority of depictions, the Most High is dressed in red garments – and the sulphuric or Sol principle is regularly referred to as the Red King or lion. It is the source of the solar gold that emerges during the *rubedo* stage of the Great Work. When united with the receptive Luna the Chemical Wedding may occur and at its most refined level the Philosopher's Stone – or Christ-Lapis – may be conceived. The perfectly distilled Spirit has been enabled to arise out of the purified physical matter and commune with the Godhead before returning as its messenger, finally culminating in the triumphant union of Sulphur and Mercury, Sol and Luna, masculine and feminine. This process is facilitated by a third party, the Mercurius that is present within all stages of the Great Work.

Dove

The dove is a symbol used regularly by alchemists to represent the *albedo* stage of the Great Work, but it is also often utilised as the symbolic manifestation of the Mercurius substance that acts during this stage (and all others) that is capable of uniting Sol and Luna in the Divine Marriage. It is that substance which acts at all levels and upon all things, existing eternally across all states of expression.

Of course, in the Christian tradition the dove represents the harbinger of the Holy Spirit – which in itself can be seen as the universal and eternal force that facilitates integration between the receptive and creative principles; the channel that can exist between the Divine and our material world. The Holy Spirit is the Divine Fire that is attracted to and illuminates matter when it is appropriately purified, and the dove is a representation of its process.

---

7. Abraham, L. 1998, p186
8. Hauck, D.W. 1999, p75

In the alchemical tradition, fire plays a pivotal role in the transmutation process. This fire is sometimes referred to as four-fold (Elementary, Secret, Central and Celestial), but when related to the individual there are two fires that flame: the Central and the Secret. The Central fire burns deep within matter and sits embedded, animating and providing the lifeforce and material from which form can be expressed. But it is the Secret fire that could be said to play the penultimate role in the Great Work, coming as it does directly from the Divine when we are ready to receive it and carrying with it the will of the One Mind unfettered. The consecration and perfection of the Central fire attracts the Secret fire to its receptive state in a cyclical relationship that was previously discussed in the idea of Gabriel and Mary as *Solve et Coagula*.

It is for this reason that the great cathedrals were created with such perfect geometry in mind, because geometry is an expression of the understanding and purification of the Central fire – and when perfected and situated in pure balance it attracts and brings rushing forth the magnificent Secret fire. The ancients always understood the power of pure geometry and the role that it could play in attracting this Secret fire unto the physical plane of existence.

Colours

Moving on, the colours that are utilised throughout many different artistic examples of the Annunciation allow us to bring together all of the different symbolism that I've just been speaking about. From the 15th century onward the colours of the robes of Mary (and quite often, but less universally Gabriel) are predominately red and blue – Fire and Water – Light and Darkness – Sun and Moon – Male and Female. In fact, it is quite astounding when you look through the history of Annunciation imagery just how consistent the colouring of red and blue is. Mary's inner layer is red and her outer garment is blue, and often – as in the depiction provided by Barocci – the Godhead is vested in the alternate manner: blue underneath, red on the outside.

In some other depictions these colours are red and white – Rose and Lily – Lion and Eagle – Sun and Moon – Male and Female. Even if not in the form of garments, we regularly see the colours red and white utilised in many other aspects. The depiction by Filippo Lippi contains a vase by Mary's feet that is filled with red and white roses; and in the image by Dante Rossetti the colouring is predominately pure white except for the hanging cloth which shines a bright red. The Annunciation image created by Matthias

Grunewald is a particularly interesting one in this regard, as we can see that not only is Mary clothed in black (the *nigredo*, or the act of dissolving the impure; killing it so that it might be reborn); but Gabriel is clothed in white and red. Furthermore, we see that the interior space has been separated into three sections by two coloured curtains: one black, the other red. Mary sits right on the cusp of this newly opened red curtain, and we then see in the final part of the triptych the resurrected Christ dropping the white garment to the ground as he is uplifted purely in red. I'll leave this image with you to ponder over (and recommend viewing the full colour version), but suffice to say there seems to be a strong correlation in this triptych with the three stages of the alchemical process; *nigredo*, *albedo* and *rubedo*.

It is worth noting that we must always keep in mind that reducing symbols to masculine and feminine is to merely replace one symbol with another, for male and female are themselves symbols in this context. Feminine principles represent a receptiveness to a new becoming and the fluid nature of the One Thing. Working upon them brings about a purification of the body and sanctuary from the corrupting influence of the physical sphere – in psychological terms, the dissolution of the ego. Masculine principles represent the creative possibility and generative power of the One Mind, as well as highlight the ability for all material things to participate in Divine Providence to a greater of lesser extent depending upon the depth of purity and receptiveness that the feminine principle enables. The perfection of the Great Work comes from combining both principles in absolute unity. All pure creative actions come from a place of receptivity to the Divine and are thus perfect participation in Providence triumphing over the ravages of individual desire and ego-inspired action. The united soul and spirit are able to reintegrate once more with the purified body in order to bring about the philosophical child. This dual working acts in favour of both the Above and Below, and is referred to in many different ways but most commonly surrounding the idea of sacred copulation.

Virgin Birth as Chemical Wedding

The crux of the interpretation that I am providing is that the Annunciation represents one of the stages of what is known, in Rosicrucian terms, as the Chemical Wedding. It is the marrying of two elements, one feminine the other masculine, that is facilitated by a third universal force in order to bring forth a metaphorical child of great spiritual purity and power. We shouldn't be surprised that some alchemists saw this third part as depicted by the Holy Spirit, and as such we see from the very earliest stages of our understanding of the Annunciation that Gabriel (the sublimated and perfected spirit), Mary (the purified soul) and the Holy Spirit (the Mercurius agent) were present at the moment when the conception of the Son of God could occur.

In order to produce the Philosopher's Stone the creative masculine principle of Sulphur must be united with the receptive feminine principle of Mercury. This concept is most often displayed as an intimate sexual relationship between two lovers which is to occur many times over (*solve et coagula*) until it reaches such a point of refinement that they emerge as one unified hermaphroditic form. This Son of the Sun and the Moon can be understood as the Christ-Lapis, or Christ-Stone; a figure which is neither solely Above nor Below, but exists at both points simultaneously: *combining within Itself the powers of both the Above and Below; it overcomes every Subtle thing and penetrates every Solid thing.* It is the reclamation of The Fall, the point at which the soul unites with the perennial spirit and realises its true nature to return and manifest within the newly purified body.

The moment being depicted in the Annunciation is the point at which the One Mind comes flooding into the prepared and purified material individual. With the purity of the vessel formed we attract the Secret Fire, the tongues of flame that can only be truly experienced when we have dissolved the ego and thereby expect nothing in return – a state of pure passivity. We become aware of the presence of the Divine within all things, of the role that the One Mind has to play in the formation of the One Thing in all its aspects. We are not seeking this experience to uplift ourselves or to allow us to have power or status over others – to lord over them with lofty titles or obscure ceremonies – we seek this because it is the path of spiritual evolution for the One Thing, the meaning of our being, and the true potential of our exalted existence as privileged creations of the One Mind.

This is the power of the culminating *albedo* stage, transforming triumphantly into the *rubedo* in which the passive purity can find true and perfect union with the active creative force. Once our consciousness has experienced the cleansing and uplifting power of the Secret fire it is not the end point, but rather a new beginning. A time in which we must nurture that flame towards a complete merger of our soul and body with the pure spirit of the One Mind, so that we might hand over our agency to the child that is born from this spiritual consummation – the Son of the Sun and the Moon; the Christ-Lapis. It is at this moment that we truly understand the correspondence between the Above and Below; between the Below and Above. For our journey was not done just to reintegrate our own spirit, to ascend up Above. The Great Work also allows the Above to descend Below. For what is perceived by us an act of reintegration, is from the perspective of the Most High a process of incarnation.

We have within us the potential to be an active co-creator in the formation of the One Thing and its development through the catalysing lens of the One Mind. We have a role to play that relies not just on us being receivers of Providence, but active participants in the reintegration of the physical sphere into the Divine so that it may achieve incarnation. This concept lies at the core of the Western Mystery Tradition and almost everything else is practical or cosmological commentary on this relationship.

As Rosicrucians we must dedicate ourselves to this alchemical process. There are many names by which it is called and many systems of symbolism by which it is explained, but they all have one and the same goal in mind: active participation in creation. We should not view the Great Work as a process merely of individual achievement or illumination, for to do so is to only see half of the Hermetic equation. We must seek redemption not merely for ourselves, but for the perfection of all substance. We are not just the one to be redeemed, but we can also be the agent of redemption – providing a means through which the Logos can be liberated from the labyrinth of the material world and find expression within it. I hope that you will now be able to look upon depictions of the Annunciation and be reminded that just as Below corresponds to Above, so does Above correspond to Below – and both for a solitary purpose: *to accomplish the miracles of the One Thing and achieve the consecration of the Universe.*

Further Reading & Bibliography

Bonardel, F., <u>Alchemical Esotericism and the Hermeneutics of Culture</u>, in

Faivre, A. & Needleman, J. (eds.), *Modern Esoteric Spirituality*, p71-100, The Crossroad Publishing Company, 1992.

Franz, M., *Alchemy: An Introduction to the Symbolism and the Psychology*, Inner City Books, 1980.

Hall, M.P., *The Secret Teachings of All Ages*, Penguin, 2003.

Hastings, J., *Annunciation*, Phaidon Press Inc., 2000.

Jung, C.G., *Psychology and Alchemy*, Princeton University Press, 1968.

Le Bouter, E., *The Two Marriages in Alchemy*, Rose Croix Journal 4., 2007.

McLean, A., *The Alchemical Vessel as Symbol of the Soul*, alchemywebsite.com

Obrist, B., <u>Visualisation in Medieval Alchemy</u>, *HYLE – International Journal for Philosophy of Chemistry, Vol. 9: 2*, pp. 131 – 170, 2003.

Roth, R.F., *The Archetype of the Holy Wedding in Alchemy and in the Unconscious of Modern Man*, Zurich, 2005.

Roob, A., *The Hermetic Museum: Alchemy & Mysticism*, Taschen, 2006.

Smith, R.F., *Iconography of the Annunciation*, theglobaldispatches.com

Thompson, C.J.S., *The Lure and Romance of Alchemy*, Bell Publishing Company, 1990.

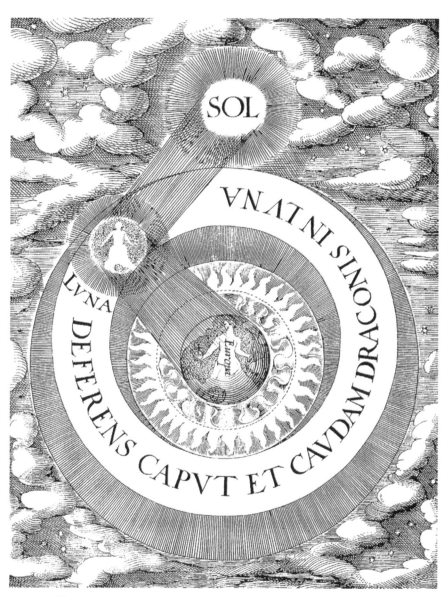

Illustration from Michael Maier's, *Septimana philosophica* (1620)
"Deferens caput et caudam draconis in Luna"
Bringing the head and tail of the dragon in the Moon

ON THE ESOTERIC VARIETIES OF LOVE

In almost all esoteric traditions you will find a term consistently used that transcends the practical applications of these traditions and at the same time provides their foundation. This term is Love. It is a mysterious term, and one that is widely used but quite often not fully grappled with or understood. If we try and delve a bit deeper beyond a surface level understanding of the term, we immediately begin to see that it is a truly remarkable one that covers many different experiences, emotions, and practices. There are exoteric and esoteric forms of Love, those related solely to the individual experience of existence (such as desire or sexuality) and those related to a higher form of being (such as compassion and Divine Grace). However, to create this distinction is to do violence to the beautiful variety that the term encompasses; presuming that some elements of it are lesser than others. Rather what lies behind the term 'Love' is a tapestry of deeper truth and intuitive connection to a higher form. A longing and yearning for something of which we often do not see clearly and yet know implicitly that it is good, just and worth striving for. It could even be argued that Love represents the esoteric tradition in its totality, that nothing that is to be found within the mysteries exists outside of this term.

With this talk I will explore some of the many facets of this term 'love' and how we see them manifest within the human condition. This will allow us to see a pattern of commonality emerge that hopefully sheds some light on the role of Love and why we have come to define many aspects of being human under this one phrase that is both evocative and full of mystery. This talk is intended to be an encouragement to see that what we are all seeking is to be found in the most obvious of places – it is there right in front of us and yet we often continue to search the ends of the Earth to find it elsewhere. By the end of this short paper, we will see that Love is the key to so many of the doors that we seek to unlock. That which we seek in the Divine is to be found through Love in its many varied forms, so in the end all esoteric study can be seen as the study of Love; more importantly, all esoteric practice can be seen as the implementation of Love, the mechanism of the Divine in the material plane of existence.

Beginning a topic such as this is incredibly daunting, and I have struggled for a while in deciding upon just how to do it. I did not want the paper to turn into a lesson on etymology, history or comparative religion. All of these things are important, certainly, but in the end they do not bring us any closer to the question at hand. Which is how does this term 'Love' and all that it encompasses bring us closer to the esoteric truths of humanity and our role in existence? To this end, I have sought to break down the term Love into three different contexts in order to explore its many nuances more clearly. For the purposes of this paper, these three categories are Love of the Individual; Love of the World; and Love of the Divine. In many ways this is an artificial distinction, a rhetorical device that hopefully can lead to further discussion at the end about its uses and limitations. I cannot possibly hope to cover the true depth and beauty that the topic entails, so I welcome any and all suggestions for improvement and hope that following the paper we can all engage in a discussion that brings together our many different areas of knowledge and experience. Let us begin then, with a discussion of Love of the Individual.

Love of the Individual

Love, when related to the locally manifested level of the individual experience, is the place where most of us make our first steps along the path. It is also where many things that pretend to be Love, or that we misinterpret as belonging to various aspects of it, are to be found; requiring either a purity of heart, or a watchful contemplative eye to overcome. These negative aspects of the colloquial umbrella of 'love' can be recognised by other names such as 'narcissism', 'infatuation', 'envy' or 'jealousy'. These things do not truly belong to Love but they can be found living in the same vestiges of the human condition, hoping to attach themselves to the eternal and universal desire for true Love that is to be found in all of us. Anything emerging from genuine Love cannot manifest itself negatively, only those things pretending to be are capable of corruption and the path of Love is in many ways a path of learning to distinguish these imposters from the true source. Any effort to move towards Love is simultaneously one that brings us further from ego, and can eventually flower into the most radiant of expressions when one finds Love of the World or, ultimately, Love of the Divine. But like all things worth having, the beginning stages are often the hardest to overcome and it is almost a certainty that when beginning to walk the path of Love – be it manifest in love for another individual, for love of knowledge of the book of life, or for the love of Wisdom and the book of the Spirit – we first encounter simulacrums pretending to be what we truly seek and we must remain vigilant against them.

Recently I was asked the question: *what spiritual practices do you do?* This kind of threw me a little bit, because although I used to do more 'practical' things (mostly related to ceremonial traditions) I have veered away towards a more contemplative approach and one that is sometimes hard to delineate and decide upon just what is a spiritual practice and what isn't. When asked the question, my mind immediately went to things I don't do regularly anymore: such as yoga; working with chakras; ceremonial work – many different things that immediately bring up images of activity and action and which we often classify as the 'correct' answer to this question about spiritual practice. Our daily, material lives are filled with concepts of success that revolve around distinct and measurable activity and we project this onto our spirituality as well. How much time did you spend meditating this morning? How many yoga poses can you do, and how long can you hold them? How many retreats have you gone on, and how many chakra exercises have you learnt on them? My mind drew a blank for a moment because it was focusing on those things, which for the most part are not an aspect of my path at this point in time.

I then went to the notion of trying to live in the presence of the Divine at all times, but for some reason dismissed this internal thought as possibly too trite an answer. So I ended up saying that I try and live my life for the benefit of others rather than myself and, although an honest answer, there was something about it that rang hollow and was missing the true spiritual practice that I do.

Upon having some time to consider further, I came to the realisation that it was because I overlooked a number of aspects of my spiritual life: which are the development towards Conjugial Love, involvement in Fraternal Love, and the embracing of the Love of Wisdom. All of these things are aspects of what I am referring to with the term 'Love of the Individual', and we shall now have a look at these different forms in turn.

Conjugial Love is a term coined by Emanuel Swedenborg in his 1768 text of the same name that explores the manifestation of Love in the bond between two individuals (to Swedenborg expressed as a man and a woman in faithful marriage). This bond develops from the recognition of personal completion in another being and can result in an eternal and true marriage of souls and the regeneration of both individuals within one another. This form of esoteric Love manifests between two people when they are in both a spiritual and physical relationship, involving a deep appreciation for the role of sexuality in spiritual progression and an understanding that at its most pure expression there is an example of how the spiritual path need not be one that must be completed alone.

When discussing the esoteric varieties of Love of the Individual, Conjugial Love can be seen as the pinnacle of development for the kind of Love that encompasses our intimate relationships. It is the twinned and tethered development of two souls, which become as one intellectually, emotionally and spiritually. The path towards such a state of being is by no means easy to travel, but rather is an endeavour that requires constant vigilance and purity of aspiration. Without this, the stages of this path can quickly succumb to illusory aspects that begin to manifest as negative behaviours that are usually extensions of the corruption mentioned previously. However, if embarked upon successfully, what ends up occurring is that the spiritual development of one member of the bond impacts directly and immediately upon the other. A reciprocal relationship spiralling upwards as each individual ego lets go of its need for personal achievement and the tethered souls begin to more and more closely imitate the masculine/feminine relationship that occurs within each individual (and, indeed, in all things). Even though it is incredibly rare for Conjugial Love to develop to such heights, the lessons learned about Love when we find its mirror in our personal relationships are among the most powerful tools we have to come to a true understanding of what spiritual practice really is.

Conjugial Love is not the only form of esoteric love to be found between individuals, of course, and the non-physical forms of Love between individuals can be equally impacting and important when trying to decipher the message of Love within our lives. The Love between family, or the Love of close friends, has no physical component but in many instances can be a stronger bond than those that do. In our own societies we can find great expression of the depths of Fraternal Love that is available. I don't think much more needs to be said about the bonds of fraternity and how Love between individuals provides the true backbone for such endeavours if they are to be fruitful. In esoteric societies, the egregore that is created begins to rapidly develop in a way similar to Conjugial Love (albeit without certain – sometimes very powerful – elements, such as the sacred sexuality that physical unions can embody); and the collective spiritual force and momentum of the souls involved becomes greater than the sum of the group's individuals. This concept lies at the very heart (pun intended) of all successful spiritual organisations; and disorder reigns in those groups – both sacred and profane – where this purity of motivation is not present.

Finally, we come to an aspect of Love of the Individual that truly provides the drive and motivation for many genuine seekers along the path towards light. This is the Love of Wisdom – the *philo sophia*. The Love of Wisdom is a deeply personal and individual form of esoteric Love. It is an intimate and secret relationship that cannot fully be expressed and shared unless with those who have also felt its effect. The Love of Wisdom is quite often the first glimpse of genuine esoteric Love that we come across as individuals. Before feeling this sense of aspiration towards higher Truth, we might instead long for results for personal gain; and what we approach as Love might more often than not be various forms of lust, whether for power, status or sensuality. But when we emerge into a relationship with Wisdom, this is the moment when our progression as spiritual beings flourishes; and we can often quickly find ourselves drawn along the path through no conscious direction of our own other than to trust implicitly in this flowering intuitive pull towards ultimate Truth. We know that it is a pure form of aspiration, because the Love of Wisdom is something that increases in inverse proportion to our personal desire to take advantage of it in a material sense. Rudolf Steiner expresses this concept well when he says that:

> *"Love of wisdom is not egoistic, for this love increases as we approach death. As our expectation of gaining something through our wisdom decreases, wisdom increases - our love for this content of soul steadily increases."*[1]

---

1. Steiner, R. 1998, *Love and Its Meaning in the World*, Anthroposophic Press, p179

The Love of Wisdom is a pure expression of Love within the individual, because like Conjugial and Fraternal Love, it draws us away from the allure of the ego and towards a clearer vision of our divine potentiality. The thirst for knowledge and wisdom, not for any particular result but purely for its own sake, is the most commonly experienced and universally accessible of spiritual paths and yet we have removed our understanding of this impulse so far from its original roots that it is often expressed in purely secular and non-sacred terms. I am often bemused by those within the New Atheist movement who scoff at all forms of religion as if they have nothing to offer but children's fairytales, yet find deep personal meaning via the triumph of Spirit to be found in the search for Truth. This feeling, even within the most hardline of atheists and humanists, is the Love of Wisdom and it is Divine.

Regardless of how modern society wishes to perceive it, this will always be one of the primary and most impacting forms of esoteric Love and it will always draw us towards its natural intended outcome, which is a greater appreciation of the multitude of perceived universes that exist outside of our own. This eventually culminates in the recombination of an infinite landscape into not only ourselves but the universal whole. Jürgen Moltmann, a highly esteemed Christian theologian, explores this contemplative process and the importance of its basis in esoteric Love when he states that:

> "Through this tarrying contemplation, the perceiving person participates in the object perceived, enters into it and corresponds to it. Pure perception transforms the perceiving person into what is perceived – not, conversely, the thing perceived into the perceiving person, as in the modern concept of reason...we perceive in order to participate. Consequently we perceive only insofar as we are prepared to let the object be as it is...said Augustine rightly: 'We only know in so far as we love.' The person who cannot love understands nothing."[2]

Love, here, is the infinitely faceted aspect of Creation that allows us to step beyond the constraints of individual identity and emerge into a more lucid view of the cosmic totality. Love, when expressed within the individual, is therefore a series of processes that enable us to receive the outside world and allow it to become a part of our own identity; releasing aspects of ourselves

---

2. Moltmann, J. 2010, *Sun of Righteousness Arise! God's Future for Humanity and the Earth*, SCM Press, p173

outward so that the rest of the cosmos might integrate with it once more. In this way, Love's true import comes from the fact that it is universally accessible and felt, in one form or another, by all of us. In many ways it covers the old adage of the deepest secrets being hidden right before our eyes. Indeed, the majority of people who experience Love within themselves are never fully aware of the miracle that is taking place with each moment in its presence. It is, in this sense, genuinely esoteric and hidden; for even when one experiences the 'lower' manifestations of it, is drawn to it, directed by it, fulfilled within it, this does not necessarily mean at all that one needs be fully aware of the process that is occurring. However, for those who are able to become aware of this sublime secret and consciously choose to embrace it, the Rose blossoms upon the centre of the Cross and they become in the truest sense of the term 'Rosicrucian'. Combining the material world material with the Divine and allowing the universe to find its full and eternal expression, even within the seemingly narrow confines of our individual identity. From this starting point, Love springs forth and develops outward; while the individual embracing that Love within becomes a co-operative in the continually unfolding Providence that lies at the heart of existence.

Love of the World

The development of Love of the Individual brings about a change in focus that eventuates in a more empathic and truly altruistic view of the wider world and our role in it. This is an important stage in the transition between stages of esoteric Love and, in many ways, is the most difficult. For the forms of Love that are discovered within the locus of our own identities – whether they be personal or co-operative – can feel incredibly powerful and transformative, often to the point that many people who discover them are content to not move deeper into the fold of Love. Having said this, it is the natural progression of esoteric Love to develop the focal point outward. To move from the Individual, to the World, to the Divine. Thus we come to the second major esoteric category: Love of the World.

When we discuss such a phrase, the behaviour patterns that immediately come to mind are those commonly labelled as 'altruistic'. There are many people who have argued that altruism is merely a self-centred behaviour brought about through conditioning of cultural, biological and evolutionary reward systems. However, while such a view is certainly applicable to many manifestations of altruistic behaviour (which it must be said doesn't, in most instances, make them any less beneficial), the expression that we are discussing develops into a far more pure form.

For those who experience the kinds of Love of the Individual we have already been discussing, the path will open up further through the selfless acts that such understanding begins to bring about. To Love a mate is an incredibly powerful experience. Love of the search for Wisdom is a liberating one. To Love a friend, a humbling one. This esoteric seed, once planted through such actions of individual Love, begins to grow and develop. A new perspective begins to form and blossom that brings with it a wider and more encompassing expression of esoteric Love. The forms that we are going to examine now are two that develop once we are able to hear and listen to the intuitive nature deep inside all of us: *compassion* and *stewardship*.

Compassion is an aspect of Love of the World that is seemingly universal throughout all forms of religion and spirituality. It is an incredibly important facet that brings us out of searching merely for personal fulfilment and allows us to understand the importance of uplifting all. The act of Compassionate Love is one that seeks to overcome suffering, both physical and spiritual, not only in the individual or those closely connected, but for all beings. A perfect example of this is the concept of *bodhicitta* in the Buddha Dharma tradition; seen as the purest form of compassion that emerges by recognising that spiritual attainment must be embraced to remove suffering for all beings, not merely for oneself. This requires an ability to become aware of the nature of suffering in its many different forms, including those of which we might not have any personal experience of. This recognition then evolves into a conscious decision not just to contemplate the suffering of all beings, but to do something about it.

Thus develops the Love of the World and the deeper embracing of the burden that the true Initiate must eventually carry if they wish to continue with the Great Work. At its pinnacle, this form of esoteric Love leads to the individual making the decision to forgo the highest levels of personal attainment, in order that they might best help others achieve them . A beautiful and awe-inspiring form of spiritual sacrifice that comes directly from this Love that brings us outside of our own identities and envelopes us in the experience of all beings simultaneously.

Stewardship is a form of esoteric Love that is most often heard of in a Christian context and typically understood as the recognition of our responsibility to look after Creation at the behest of our Creator. In the context of what we are discussing here, the Love of Stewardship often manifests as an even more all-encompassing form of spiritual experience than that of compassion. Compassion is inherently focused on the removal of suffering for sentient beings; while stewardship includes not only all beings, but all that exists. We can come toward an understanding of this process in an esoteric sense through a quick visualisation, indeed many of us may have actually experienced it already without fully knowing what it might indicate.

If we consider something that we have experienced within the Love of the Individual: whether that be through the Love of Wisdom; of another; of a friend; or something else entirely, what we experience internally when contemplating such things can be felt as tangible. It is present at the forefront of being yet it cannot be fully grasped nor located. We might have visual memories of moments in time, perhaps, but mostly it will be a strong sense of something simultaneously tangible and intangible; a sacred space of local identity enveloped in this individualised form of Love and forever holding its echo.

Almost all of us can then think of compassionate moments, where that same feeling was experienced for those who have not entered our close circle – homeless individuals we walk by on the street; animals suffering poor treatment; or people around the world suffering in war, famine or disaster. We can sometimes genuinely feel that intense longing to remove their suffering and many of us have turned that longing into action through various forms of charitable work or other personal efforts. For the vast majority of us, this feeling is just a fleeting glimpse into the true depths that Compassionate Love makes available to us and is not an aspect we can continuously hold onto as our daily lives begin to overshadow it. Sometimes, we might be able to hold onto this externalised identity for longer periods of time; but almost exclusively it will regress back to the ego-centred praxis that comes most naturally to us as human beings.

However, if we for this moment hold onto that feeling of Compassionate Love, we can take this compassionate feeling further than just other humans. It can grow into a true sense of longing for the perfection of all of nature; the perfection of all that is physical; recognition that all that has been Created basks in the Light of the Creator. Imagine the warm glow you feel when holding a loved one close. Stewardship is this feeling extrapolated onto all of Creation. Not merely of the animal kingdom, but everything physical from the birds that sing in the forest; to the grass that makes up a field; to the rocks that form a mountain. When you can wrap your arms around a boulder of cold stone and feel the universe breathing, this is when you have experienced the Love of the World that is stewardship.

Through this process, that cognitively connects different forms of Love we can experience immediately and somewhat easily with those more fleeting and egoless forms, we can start to see the spiritual journey that Love enables within us. Beginning from simple and universal feelings of closeness and attraction to other people; widening to embrace even those people we know nothing of other than that they share the cosmos as we do; and externalising even further until identification occurs not only with similar beings, but with other sentient beings and eventually all of existence. Here the Love of the World brings us not only out of ourselves, but out of our relative timeframe. For to embrace all of existence is to embrace all of its temporal flux, to feel Love for the flow of the universe as it traverses through the infinite number of relationships within it that we conceive of as time. We can relate to this Love of the World, in the famous opening words of William Blake's Auguries of Innocence:

> *"To see the world in a grain of sand,*
> *and to see heaven in a wild flower,*
> *hold infinity in the palm of your hands,*
> *and eternity in an hour."*

We have now been taken from the narrow focus of the ego-based consciousness, to one that embraces all of Creation from the largest and most awe-inspiring, to the smallest and most subtle. Encompassing all that has been and is to be, past, present and future. Through personal spiritual growth, powered by the esoteric nature of Love, we are able to perceive the inherent beauty and radiance that lies behind material existence. It is a natural process and a pure form of spiritual practice. Indeed, it could be said to be the only form of spirituality, because all other activities, practices, exercises, rituals and other trappings that we often label as such are mechanisms designed to better enable us to participate in the co-creation of Divine Providence that is Love.

Love of the Divine

Which brings us now to the final and most difficult part of this exploration of esoteric Love, those hidden depths that relate directly and perfectly with the pure essence from which Creation continuously and eternally emerges.

It is here, after walking the path from ego to world, that Love shines brightest and we begin to catch a glimpse of the vast depths of its beauty. This glimpse, if focused upon with a purity of motivation, can continue to grow for as long as we are able to submit to it, until eventually one comes to the realisation that the Love which was previously being felt coming from ourselves was actually gifted to us through the Grace of the Limitless Light. It is here, in these culminating forms, that we see Love for what it really is: the Key to all Creation.

Little can, or should, be said about the ultimate nature of God. But one thing we can observe comes from the aspect of Love that has often come to be labelled as Grace. This concept has been discussed in different forms throughout many of the world's religions, but ultimately amounts to an act of Love (or Light) extending from the Divine and providing insight and transformation for those who might receive it. Light in Extension (LVX). Grace is the basis of esoteric Love, for it is by understanding Grace that we see the true source of our spiritual progress. Despite what many lay claim to, there is only one Universal Teacher, provided to us through Grace. All spiritual acts emerge out of our relationship with that aspect of the Divine revealed to us through this process. We must always remain humbled to the fact that it is not through our own good deeds alone that we can walk steadfast towards supreme revelation. Our actions and efforts are certainly required for the relationship to manifest most clearly, but nothing would be possible were it not for the gift of Love originally provided to all of us at the core of our being. When we reach, we find that there was already present a reaching back. Our efforts are exemplified within the Divine Grace that stirred them in the first place, now discovered anew in order to carry us even further.

From a personal perspective, our journey through Love takes us from individually focused expressions to universally focused ones. The ego begins to embrace its role in the vast tapestry of Creation rather than fighting for independence. From this embodying of universal aspiration comes an appreciation of what lies behind merely a physical expression. The physical expression is that which has been actualised in material reality, but the deepest forms of Love show us glimpses of infinite potentiality. It is here that we see one of the strongest emotional reactions to the force of Love in our lives, which is the esoteric nature of *lamentation*.

Lamentation is a variety of esoteric Love that results when we begin to truly realise the radiance that has been forsaken by our physical, ego-based form. It is a pure form of sorrow, because it is sorrow directed entirely at the loss of our conscious relationship with the Divine. When we lament, in a spiritual sense, our emotions are overwhelmed by the injustice that has been committed against the source of all things. We feel both a mental and physical pain of regret which develops upon remembering the Fall. It develops into what the Sufis often refer to as *longing*, a drive that calls us back to the heights of Love of the Divine that have been discarded along the way toward physical incarnation. This kind of longing is one of the most pure forms of Love, directly related to the previous states discussed because it is this longing to be reborn into the light of pure Love that drives our soul to find meaning. First within itself, then within the world, until finally leading us towards complete reintegration with the all-encompassing essence of Creation that has immeasurable Love for us.

It is this longing for something which can only be satisfied by the Most High that evolves into a multitude of practices, rituals and states of being encompassed by the terms 'devotion' or 'reverence'. Both of these are the conscious act to commit oneself to higher aspirations that lie outside of the desires and drives of the individual ego. An act purely motivated by this unquenchable longing for the true source of the spark within. It often finds its practice in the truest forms of charity, compassion and stewardship that we have previously discussed. Indeed, it is present in all of these things when they manifest genuinely – although it is not always recognised as such. The beauty of these aspects of Love that relate directly to the Divine is that they unify the many processes and facets that we have been discussing into one eternally connected whole. Essentially, we emerge from an understanding of Love being projected out of our ourselves; to one in which Love in all its forms has been gifted to us, an experience that brings with it a sense of cosmic humility that paves the way for greater development along the spiritual path.

One of the esoteric varieties of Love of the Divine is the practice of theurgy, a form of ceremonial devotion that is most easily understood as a more nuanced type of prayer. The term 'theurgy' was originally related to the means and practices needed to communicate with the ancient gods and animistic spirits; in this sense, not always a selfless devotional act. It seems that the evolution of theurgy begins with its praxis in relation to an ultimately monotheistic worldview: primarily the latter Egyptians, Hinduism, Judaism, Christianity and Islam. With an understanding of a supreme being or reality that underlies all things, theurgy becomes less about contacting particular gods and spirits in order to ask them for favours or advice and more about striving upward and surrendering our will to the mechanisms both internal and external, hidden and exposed, of Divine Providence in its greatest mystery. Perhaps the easiest way to display this change in focus that Love of the Divine brings over other forms discussed earlier is to quote a theurgic prayer from one of its great modern proponents, Mouni Sadhu (an esoteric alias for the polish mystic M.D. Sudowski):

> "O Father Who art in Heaven, may the blessed time soon come when Thy Will, which is the wholeness of perfection, will be understood and accepted by human beings and will serve them as law. Purify and sanctify our souls which unite themselves in the ardent desire to hasten those happy days. Enlighten our understanding, absorb our wills, inspire with Thy Holy Spirit all our thoughts, actions and our sufferings, which we bind together to make a bouquet of thorny roses, in order to offer their perfume to Thee. Make us worth to be admitted to the ranks of those, who, in both the visible and invisible world, sacrifice themselves to achieve realization of Thy will on this earthly plane."[3]

This prayer continues with similar extension of the well known Lord's Prayer, until finally ending with the powerful invocation: *"I am not afraid of anything, for nothing can harm me since God is my only love and his will is my whole law"*[4].

Love of the Divine fully emerges when we no longer require a particular material focus for its expression, but rather begin to embody it and experience it in the most pure of forms. The previous forms of Love become understood as creative manifestations of the ultimate Love that is the Godhead. Thus the esoteric process of Love has one intended outcome, which is the recognition and recollection of the Divine source at the very core of existence. This Love includes all types that preceded. It includes everything in Creation, for it is creation itself. The successful Lover in this context forgoes any desire for personal spiritual advancements or attainment, any need for social recognition or mystical result, because of this devotional act that is Love of

---

3. Sadhu, M. 1965, *Theurgy: The Art of Effective Worship*, George Allen & Unwin, p68
4. Ibid., p69

the Divine. Here we find the circle completed, for where once the impulse of Love was thought to be for the gain of the individual it now becomes the individual whose existence is given over to the extension of Love.

Conclusion

With the final unification of that which is Above to that which is Below, and vice versa, the Great Work of Love achieves completion in the individual Spirit. Through this completion and refraction through multiple lenses, Divine Grace finds greater and more powerful expression on the material plane. This form of co-operative Providence is found through the mechanisms of Love, and the experience of it grows intuitively within the soul of each individual that hears its initial calling. Love is an intuitive aspect of human existence; and from the first inklings of it, that we find in our attraction to others outside of ourselves, it grows and is strengthened like a muscle requiring exercise.

That which is often tied closely to personal pleasure or result grows into one that recognises itself in others, even those who do not directly affect us at all. This empathy then develops into a Love that seeks to relieve the suffering of others in all its many forms; and further still to an identification with all that exists, whether it be sentient or non. As our intuitive understanding of Love grows in this way, we come to see that it has not grown out of us, but rather through us. It was not created by us, but found its expression through our being. This realisation that Love is a Gift of Grace and not merely a construct of 'I' brings us eventually to a devotion and uplifting of Self towards the ultimate reconnection with the Divine Source.

Out of this devotion to the Divine, this combination of Love of the Divine with pure intention, emerges one of the great esoteric truths: the co-operative Providence that emerges from the unification (or reintegration) of Creator and Created; of Lover and Beloved. We are not merely made in the image of God, but rather our spiritual selves are the image of God expressed through material bodies. The Light that shines in the darkness, yet we comprehend it not. The role of Love in all its many and varied forms is to reunite that which has become dislocated by the temptations of physical existence to its more pure and perfect expression. This is the Great Work of the alchemists; the supreme virtue of the Bodhisattvas; the final goal of the Adepts; and the ultimate expression and purpose of human spirituality.

Despite all I have said here today, it must be remembered that Love is now and shall always be the greatest mystery for it lies at the very core of existence. It is the essence of co-creative Providence and we should never forsake its brilliance with word or deed. Thus, it is only appropriate to end with the words of the Sufi poet, Rumi:

"Whatever I have said about love, when love comes, I am ashamed to speak."

Further Reading & Bibliography

Bourke, Vernon (Ed.) 1974, *The Essential Augustine*, Hackett Publishing Company, Indianapolis, USA.

Eliade, Mircea 1959, *The Sacred and Profane: The Nature of Religion*, Harcourt Inc., New York, USA.

Eckartshausen, Karl von 1991, *The Cloud Upon the Sanctuary*, Sure Fire Press, USA.

Fortune, Dion 2000, *The Esoteric Philosophy of Love and Marriage*, Weiser Books, Boston, USA.

Hammond, Cally 2007, *Passionate Christianity: A Journey to the Cross*, Society for Promoting Christian Knowledge, London, UK.

Law, William (Trans.) 1991, *The 'Key' of Jacob Boehme*, Phanes Press, Grand Rapids, USA.

Lucka, Emil 1922, *The Evolution of Love*, Translated by Ellie Schleussner, George Allen & Unwin Ltd., London, UK.

Owen-Jones, Peter 2010, *Letters from an Extreme Pilgrim: Reflections on Life, Love and the Soul*, Rider Books, London, UK.

Swedenborg, Emanuel 1768, *Conjugial Love*, http://www.sacred-texts.com/swd/cjl/index.htm (last accessed 15/04/2011).

Vaughan-Lee, Llewellyn 2000, *Love is a Fire: The Sufi's Mystical Journey Home*, The Golden Sufi Center, Inverness, USA.

ON THE CREATION OF SACRED SPACE

In the Name of the Father, and of the Son, and of the Holy Spirit...

Attending a Catholic school in suburban Australia, the church we celebrated mass in each week was a display of open and spacious architecture with plain, light-wood motifs relatively barren of detail and symbolic mystery. Function over form, light and airy in a way that invited community but held back any deep grappling with our own humanity that the gothic cathedrals have at the heart of their shadowed alcoves.

Yet among this display of 1960s Australiana – seen through a 1980s hypercolour lens – was an object that held my attention; that drew me into Church every week and became the focus of a child's obsession. It housed the Body of Christ. The ritual focused intently upon its contents, its intricate gold gilding clearly displaying the importance placed upon it above all else. The tabernacle stood large and imposing, opened and closed in such a reverential way that I had the distinct impression that what lay within was literally beyond mortal kin. It called to me, beckoned me towards it. Then one day after a service I noticed it had been left open. The congregation cleared out and I remained intrigued by the prospect of finally getting to see inside that mystical repository. I climbed a few steps up toward the altar

– a sense of transgression even in that simple act – and rose up as high as I could to see inside. I was prepared for nothing less than to look upon the face of God. And yet, there was nothing at all. The tabernacle had been left opened because its contents were being renewed. All that was there for me to discover was a satin interior. That off-white colour that seemed to belong to another era, a cross-hatching showing through in one corner as it became frayed and brittle from years of use. My heart sank – *for where was my prize?*

I didn't understand it at that age, but I had my first glimpse of our ability to create sacred space. To demarcate a physical, tangible location and set it aside for the intangible. This isn't something that I had done; this was something that I had witnessed. That the community around me had created. It is this experience, that empty satin-filled box, that in a fundamental way brings me here today with this paper *On the Creation of Sacred Space*.

Sacred space is a concept not only universally practiced by groups or communities, but also universally experienced by individuals through a myriad of cultural lenses. Indeed, it is the story of sacred space that teaches us the most about what it means to be human and how we come to formulate great institutions that bind through time and fold an extraordinary amount of complexity and progressive purpose into a seemingly simple term: 'civilisation'. The Gobekli Tepe in Turkey, dating back over 10,000 years, is considered to be the oldest religious site currently known – and its situation within the context of a hunter-gatherer society caused one archaeologist to note: 'First came the temple, then the city'. A large proportion of other ancient sacred sites have been interpreted as burial tombs of one kind or another, dating back to Neolithic and Bronze Age communities. The distinction between the living and the dead lays out a metaphysical understanding of the human being and its relationship to the natural world. This concept is often seen to develop into an understanding that allows sacred space to flourish, with natural places – rivers, forests, mountains – becoming the dwelling place of mythical ancestral beings and needed 'reservoirs of vitality'.

The correlation between sacred space and geometry – bringing with it increasingly impressive architectural feats – is something that we see throughout the historical record. From the Egyptian and Mesoamerican pyramids, through Greek columns to the Temple of Solomon and beyond, the careful construction of technically magnificent buildings to house our worship takes on an almost universal application. To this mindset, sacred spaces require construction and, as they are a celebration of the Divine, often must be adorned in the most splendid materials and wealth-driven offerings. The gothic cathedrals display the notion that beauty was objective and closely related to a sense of celebrating divine order. Sacredness was hidden in corners and behind screens, to be discovered by the worthy pilgrim fostering that sense of mystery within. Here we come back to the church tabernacle as seen through the eyes of a child, that mystery that draws us forward intuitively before we can begin to grasp what it is really speaking of. The sense of awe and humbling grandeur is an important aspect here, interacting with the psychological components of the human condition in a very holistic manner. So too the use of rich and complex symbolic depictions – with a particularly noteworthy example being Hindu temples that have a vibrant tradition of sculpture and colour – that create a complex network of associations and provides ample depth to cater for all levels of religious engagement. Even to a complete outsider:

> *"Entering the temple is entering a world of meanings that are never exhausted, and one could know something of their complexity even without knowing precisely what those meanings might be."*[1]

The notion of such holy places is predicated upon distinctions between sacred and profane. What makes the ancient temple different from the markets that often surrounded them? Where do physical and metaphysical elements come into contact with one another? The distinction between sacred and profane was seen by the sociologist Emile Durkheim as a fundamental component to the nature of religion itself; the 'things set apart and forbidden' that tended to serve as a focus point for unifying identity and embedding cultural value systems. In his pivotal text, *The Elementary Forms of the Religious Life*, Durkheim outlays the basic definition:

> *"...the real characteristic of religious phenomena is that they always suppose a bipartite division of the whole universe, known and knowable, into two classes which embrace all that exists, but which radically exclude each other. Sacred things are those which the interdictions protect and isolate; profane things, those to which these interdictions are applied and which must remain at a distance from the first."*[2]

---

1. Kieckhefer, R. 2004, *Theology in Stone: Church Architecture from Byzantium to Berkely*, Oxford University Press, p164
2. Durkheim, E. 1976, *The Elementary Forms of Religious Life*, George Allen & Unwin Ltd, p40-41

This duality exists in objects and words, in ritualised movements and moments of social distinction. Mircea Eliade develops this concept to argue that it is the sacred centre – those special places often embodied within a physical location – that allows us to consciously participate in the existential experience of being. The majority of examples of sacred space fall into the following breakdown:

> "...(a) a sacred place constitutes a break in the homogeneity of space; (b) this break is symbolised by an opening by which passage from one cosmic region to another is made possible...(c) communication with heaven is expressed by one or another of certain images, all of which refer to the axis mundi: pillar...ladder...mountain, tree, vine, etc. (d) around this cosmic axis lies the world...hence the axis is located 'in the middle,' at the 'navel of the earth'; it is the Center of the World."[3]

The conception occurs across geography and time, as the creative process that allows it forms the basis of human spirituality – the process by which we order the world into a coherent sphere, enabling the individual personality to function in relation to communal identity. This continuous renewal allows the formation of being out of the primordial soup of chaotic potential; and it is around this creative axis point that we most clearly see the microcosmic mirroring of the macrocosmic universe. It is the distinction of things and places as sacred, as set apart from the physical reality of existence and venerated as custodians of a higher, ultimate, reality that has proven to be one of the most unique characteristics of the human evolutionary process.

So, with a clearer understanding of the sacred laid out as a special distinction beyond the profane, alongside an inexhaustible set of examples that we could draw upon, just how is sacred space *created*?

Ritual and ceremony enable the construction of sacred space through a process of 'mystic mechanics' that combines external and internal operations, relying upon an interface between the individual and the wider cultural paradigm they function within. With the sacred posited as an ideal form, the religious structures put in place allow the individual to strive for a higher sense of duty and purpose through communion with them. From a societal perspective, ritual can often be seen to serve a stabilising role – assisting in the

---

3. Eliade, M. 1987, *The Sacred and the Profane: The Nature of Religion*, Harcourt Inc., p37

alleviation of anxiety and the overcoming of social tensions, particularly in periods of upheaval. They 'fuse' the sometimes distant relationship between the world as imagined and the world as experienced, helping us form the concept of 'meaning' through reconciling the conceptualised ideal with the lived reality. As Clifford Geertz states: *"In ritual, the world as lived and the world as imagined, fused under the agency of a single set of symbolic forms, turns out to be the same world."*[4] In a functionalist sense, publicly performed rites and ceremonies become particularly important due to their talismanic capacity to transmit cultural and cosmological information. In the words of A. R. Radcliffe Brown:

> *"Rites can be seen to be the regulated symbolic expressions of certain sentiments...they have for their effect to regulate, maintain and transmit from one generation to another the sentiments on which the constitution of society depends."*[5]

This continues the 'Centre of the World' function, required by society to put forward its ideal form and renew its processes over successive generations. At its core, *"ritualisation is fundamentally a way of doing things to trigger the perception that these practices are distinct and the associations that they engender are special."*[6] Ritual constructs the distinction of Other required for the formation of sacredness and creates performative boundaries that signal that such formation is taking place. In the context of sacred space – of places and locations – ritualisation is an incredibly complex social activity that enables the *"strategic production of expedient schemes that structure an environment in such a way that the environment appears to be the source of the schemes and their values."*[7]

It is not the spaces themselves that have a fixed access point to a transcendental source, but our formulation of them through communal ceremonial activity, shared symbolic receptivity and interpersonal negotiation that works to unlock the door to an experiential connection to numinous reality. The experiences that these environments facilitate influence us at a fundamental level, deeper than a consciously held belief, as:

---

4. Bell, C. 1992, *Ritual Theory, Ritual Practice*, Oxford University Press, p27
5. Radcliffe-Brown, A. R. 1952, *Structure and Function in Primitive Society*, Cohen & West, p157
6. Bell, C. 1992, p220
7. Ibid., p140

"The sense of the infinite or the consciousness of finitude is not apprehended as a theoretical commitment but as an inchoate sense that provides a practical orientation."[8]

In a spiritual context, when we talk about creating sacred space we are talking about the practice of *consecration*. The altar becomes a central point within the localised circle, the centre of community focus and unifying practice. In relation to the performative importance of ritual, it is interesting to note that in almost all cases there is an empty space left in front of the altar. This extends equally across a variety of sacred focal points, where space for ceremonial dance, prayer, movement etc. is catered for and visually accessible to all present. It is traditionally within the consecrated boundaries of such sacred space that key periods of our lives are demarcated – baptism, marriage, funerals – in order to provide a connection between the individual focal point (the Family/Created) and the societal focal point (the Community/Creation), within a greater theological context of our relationship with the formative source of existence itself (the Divine/Creator). It is sacred space that allows the most authentic form of communication between these three spheres – individual, community, and ultimate reality – to occur and thus what we are really talking about with this topic is the binding material that runs throughout existence and solidifies humanity's place within it.

All of this means something quite personal to those of us that are Rosicrucians today. The transformative nature of initiatory ceremonies, for example, relies strongly upon a formative experience that constructs the context of sacredness and a connection to the 'Centre of the World'. The impacting rituals of various Orders quite clearly condense a great deal of thinking on the *axis mundi* and the cardinal points into their structure and content; and the notion of Death and Resurrection runs as a golden thread throughout the mystery traditions more generally. There are also other key factors to consider in the manner in which modern Rosicrucians go about creating sacred space, that are unsurprisingly in-line with how these rites of passage tend to play out across humanity. Here we find that movement becomes important; the embodiment of hierarchy; the submissive state of the candidate who is guided around and dictated what to say and do; the powerful symbolism that, through the language of ritual, is encouraged to take hold; the experience of liminality and the indication of transformation as the candidate is raised from a lower spiritual state to one of higher status

---

8. Proudfoot, W. 1985, *Religious Experience*, University of California Press, p220

with subsequent expectations of behavioural change. All of these factors exist in some way overtly, but they are also present between the spoken words and lessons of the initiation rituals themselves. Speaking to us with forms that circumvent our habitual attempts to intellectually rationalise, or reduce things down to physical form alone. Eliade explores the progression of humanity away from an all-encompassing notion of the sacred – stating that: *"Modern man is incapable of experiencing the sacred in his dealings with matter; at most he can achieve an aesthetic experience."*[9]

We are led to a confrontation with the numinous through the subjugation of our usual modes of practice and understanding, forgoing the individualistic notion of experience for one that uplifts and enhances a truly communal praxis point. Communal not just in the sense of the people or group that are present in that moment, leading the candidate around and focusing the immediate creative attention upon them, but in the archetypal power of a substantive tradition with proven longevity and impact upon the human mind, body and soul. In the words of Victor Turner: *"The wisdom (mana) that is imparted in sacred liminality is not just an aggregation of words and sentences; it has ontological value, it refashions the very being of the neophyte."*[10]

In an alchemical sense the candidate has become the *prima materia*, developing through calcination to coagulation, and it is the duty of group members participating in the ceremony to invoke the elemental forces accordingly while ensuring that the vessel of sacred space remains hermetically sealed. The foundation of the tradition – the 'conquest of matter' – can then be communicated successfully. Within the carefully constructed boundaries of initiatory space, the re-sanctification of the material world through the being of the candidate can begin. This transmutation from base metal to gold requires a dissolution through death and coagulation through resurrection. The candidate is given instructions to work on their behaviour and personality, to become more virtuous, in order to subdue aspects of themselves that are holding back the ability to access heightened states of consciousness. The intention being to remember once again that the sacramental breath flows through all things and our capacity for mastery over matter allows us to assist in bringing about this hidden core of physical existence and ensure it finds fulfilment in its rightful, graceful place. In the

9. Eliade, M. 1978, *The Forge and the Crucible: The Origins and Structures of Alchemy*, University of Chicago Press, p143
10. Turner, V. 1969 (2008), *The Ritual Process: Structure and Anti-Structure*, Transaction Publishers, p103

Qabalistic sense, the role and place of the World of Action – Olam Asiyah – unified in the physical existence of Yesod/Malkuth is the ground upon which our spiritual path must be laid for it is where our current state of Being rests. It is where our delineation as individual personalities and egos finds manifestation. The sacred space and symbolic content formulated for the initiatory process intends to form channels of communication and experience that can help restore knowledge and understanding of the Divine by mimicking the emanation, creation and formation that precedes all physical existence. With the porchway degrees of the Adept traditions we conduct a simulacrum in the physical of that which brought the physical into being; and by doing so guide us toward overcoming the qliphothic influences that work in this sphere and repair the damage done by their functional impurity.

If it is these initiatory *rites of passage* that form the core focal point of personal, social and spiritual transformation, then performative toolkits devoted to the creation of sacred space are required in order for the process to be successful. Not just in the context of initiation, but more generally in the formation of space for a large variety of sacred purposes. These toolkits vary in form, but generally have the same function in mind. They prepare us for the experience of the sacred, developing latent aspects of our consciousness and directing them towards the construction of those 'thin places' that are often necessary to break through to the numinous. They are the methodological language that allows the wisdom established by their practice to be passed on to subsequent generations. For the truly devout, they eventually culminate in a fluency of the spiritual language necessary to communicate (or approach in Silence) with that which lies beyond the conscious veil.

These practices run the gamut of spiritual expression from cleansings and purifications; banishings and divinations; invocations and evocations of forms and entities, rising the practitioner into the realms of praeternatural or supernatural realities that require extraordinary levels of emotional nous and attentive capacity to successfully navigate. Some see the core of these practices as devotion based; others are empowered more by a sense of wilful achievement and psychological training; and others still that seek to render their personal agency entirely as a tool to be offered to higher planes of existence. Often all three of these elements (and more) are incorporated together into a cosmological conception of remarkable complexity. The kaleidoscopic nature of these practices means that there is an essentially infinite number of interpretations about how and why the practices work and what they should be directed toward. Beneath it all, if we wish to define a single component to make things a bit clearer, the central thread is that they are about enveloping ourselves into the positive, creative structures of the cosmos. Helping us to move away from the tendency towards negative – literally, negating – modes of behaviour in order to dedicate our physical, emotional and mental capacities to the formation of a higher spiritual state of being not merely for ourselves but for all Created existence.

This human psychological development for spiritual means is something that saw reinterpretation into understandings palatable to the increasingly secular mindset of the 20th century. One avenue of interpretation was the focus on social structures explored previously, a major component of the field of anthropology in particular. Another response that developed took its inspiration from the burgeoning field of psychoanalysis. The sacred object that lay at the heart of these traditions became less our relationship with the Divine and more about our relationship with the Self. Spiritual and supernatural hierarchies are reduced to aspects of our own minds; and the practices we use to communicate with such cosmic building blocks are redefined as methods for overcoming neuroses or psychological imbalances. Jung, unlike Freud who dismissed religion as wholly illusory, saw the importance of religion as providing a therapeutic 'transcendent function' – a suitable structure that enabled the conscious ego to find relation to the unconscious self and subsequently the 'cooperation of the impersonal images' of the collective unconscious. Of particular interest here is his development of the practice of 'active imagination', a method of objectifying mental images to help guide the practitioner (or patient) to a more mature understanding of the relationship between their conscious and unconscious minds and the archetypal forms they are influenced by. This has clear parallels with ceremonial magic, appreciated by Jung, as highlighted by his description of the technique:

> "The work has a fascination for them [the patient]; it is the fascination which the archetypes always exert upon consciousness. But by objectifying them, the danger of their inundating consciousness is averted and their positive affect is made accessible. It is almost impossible to define this effect in rational terms; it is a sort of 'magical' effect, that is, a suggestive influence which goes out from the images to the individual, and in this way his unconscious is extended and is changed."[11]

---

11. Jung, C.G. 1916 (1968), *Analytical Psychology: Its Theory and Practice*, Vintage Books, p198

The connection to a therapeutic purpose over a metaphysical one becomes increasingly important to a modern society that seeks the mending of personalities and the unlocking of human potential. For example, the system of human development promoted by Gurdjieff that popularised the notion that we must 'wake up' to our true being. In reference to the tendency of our personalities to be reactive and often inconsistent, Gurdjieff argues that:

> "Our task is to die to this personality, which is a false thing, not our own; it may be necessary to melt it down in the fires of great suffering, but when it is done correctly, in its place will grow individuality; a man will become an individual, possessing real will and an "I". He will be himself."[12]

This thread of thinking runs throughout Gurdjieff's practically focused system. While alluding to deeper spiritual purposes – displayed prominently in his concept of Objective Conscience – much of the immediacy of his work is reduced to a notion of personal development. This tendency towards self-improvement rhetoric, detached from any clear theistic framework, runs as a strong influence throughout many modern 'human potential movements' as the desire for an ultimately secular therapeutic activity takes precedence over the theistic notions that might otherwise lie beneath the surface. Indeed it is interesting to note here without further comment, perhaps sardonically, that one of Gurdjieff's closest disciples, Alfred Orage, edited from 1907-1922 the influential British magazine *The New Age*.

Exposure of the esoteric ceremonial toolkit reached a whole new level when the comprehensive system of the Hermetic Order of the Golden Dawn was published for public consumption. With these evocative rituals increasingly available, and subsequent variations thereof rushing forward, the appetite for these practices grew rapidly and publishers searched through history to find grimoires and magical treatises to translate and publish – a path that reached a new voracity as the commercial value of these systems truly became realised throughout the 1960s and 70s counterculture boom. With this newfound explosion of interest, the psychological/therapeutic model of creating sacred space rose in popularity. This was primarily a result of the adoption of Jung's theories, with more than a few shades of Gurdjieff's individual-centred system mixed with Blavatsky's Theosophical Society objective to investigate the 'powers latent in man'. The construction of sacred space that was previously situated around communities, entire

---

12. Nott, C. S. 1961 (1990), *The Teachings of Gurdjieff: A Pupil's Journal*, Arkana, p71

civilisations even, saw a new path outside of mainstream organised religion and became the domain of the individual. The conscious and systematic creation of sacred space for personal use through esoteric practices found one of its greatest proponents and influencers in Israel Regardie – who not only provided the Golden Dawn keys to the magical castle, so to speak, but was also heavily influenced by Jung's psychoanalytic theories. He lays out this framework most clearly in his book *The Middle Pillar*:

> *"Analytical psychology and magic comprise in my estimation two halves or aspects of a single technical system...whose goal is the integration of the human personality. Its aim is to unify the different departments and functions of man's being, to bring into operation those which previously for various reasons were latent. Incidentally, its technique is such that neurotic symptoms which were too insistent upon expression either become eliminated or toned down by a process of equilibration."*[13]

It's important to note that Regardie still holds a clear and overt belief that ceremonial magic has a transcendental foundation, but many overlook the pivot point between the psychological and the transcendent that his work relies upon; preferring, it seems, a focus on the therapeutic aspects which he also promotes. This approach is something that we are all familiar with and one that a large proportion of modern practitioners hold in their minds, perhaps as a kind of backup clause to help justify the amount of time and energy spent with practices that many (partners, family and friends especially) might consider absurd. However, there is a risk that by following this approach we detach these processes from the sanctifying purposes that they have always been intended to serve. As one sociological commentator on the growth in popularity of new religious movements – and particularly so-called human potential movements – in the 20th Century has noted:

> *"The danger here as elsewhere is that post-critical religion can become purely utilitarian. This can happen if one fails to see that any religious symbol or practice, however relative and partial, is an effort to express or attain the truth about ultimate reality. If such symbols and practices become mere techniques for 'self-realisation', then once again we see utilitarian individualism reborn from its own ashes."*[14]

---

13. Regardie, I. 1938 (2000), *The Middle Pillar*, Llewellyn Publications, p5
14. Bellah, R. 1976, New Religious Consciousness and the Crisis in Modernity, in *The New Religious Consciousness* (ed. Glock, C. & Bellah, R.), University of California Press, p348

From the perspective of our modern proclivities, anthropological and psychoanalytic models of the sacred are not only persuasive but wholly compatible with the secular paradigm that forms the modern cultural bedrock. The concept that one might act as an agent or harbinger of Divine Will tends to find itself in conflict with this predominant framework, so it is understandably tempting (not to mention the safest option, socially) to reduce the creation of sacred space to these paradigms alone. Thankfully, even with this pressure, scholarly perspectives still speak directly and unashamedly of the necessity of the religious impulse. The creation of sacred space as a human activity performs a completely necessary utility in the construction of personal identity and the continual formation of social structure. Eliade points out that even the wholly non-religious cannot avoid the need to formulate a relationship with the *axis mundi* – we all need a sacred centre, even if it is defined by the seemingly profane physicality of the four walls (or cardinal points) of our home; the sights and sounds of our children; or the memory of our first love. Indeed, we arguably amount to nothing without these anchoring points. There would be no sense of individual identity or difference from others without them. A beautiful mystery that underpins all of humanity, no matter how we choose to define or relate to it.

Having said this, most Rosicrucians meet today as Christians that have a conception of reality and its relationship with the Divine that does not so readily converge with many of the secular frameworks of academic and scientific understanding. We would be remiss if we did not wholeheartedly embrace what these fields have to teach us about our motivations, agendas and unconscious desires – but it does demand something more. We cannot allow ourselves to feel comfortable with wholly reductive paradigms and resisting the temptation to adhere to them, by holding a sense of their inability to articulate an unbounded, unknowable and infinitely diverse universe, should be seen as a spiritual imperative. In the words of one social theorist who recognised this dissonance: *"A failure to take these matters seriously can only result in a trivialised theology and an ever more superficial study of religion."*[15]

The esoteric traditions we are involved with demand more from us and how we approach the creation of sacred space should be reflected accordingly. If nothing else – if faith proves unobtainable to the practitioner – at the very

---

15. Garrett, W. R.   1989, Theological Reflection and Social Theory: An Emerging Rapprochement, in *Social Consequences of Religious Belief* (ed. Garrett), p224

least one must recognise that a conception of the sacred, that formulates multiple levels of truth, is a prerequisite for the effectiveness of practice and the attainment of experiential results. Jung understood this implicitly in his work with active imagination, stating that:

> *"We depend entirely upon the benevolent co-operation of our unconscious. If it does not cooperate, we are completely lost. Therefore I am convinced that we cannot do much in the way of conscious invention; we over-estimate the power of intention and will. And so when we concentrate on an inner picture and when we are careful not to interrupt the natural flow of events, our unconscious will produce a series of images which make a complete story."*[16]

The tendency to hold firmly to rational, conscious definitions of what is occurring when we participate in sacred ceremonies negates their true efficacy. Yes, there will be results; but the ironic reality is that we are not engaging in the intended psychological process if we hold within our minds a psychological model of our actions while conducting them. The modern esoteric community has responded to this paradox in quite creative ways, embracing scientific understanding alongside an appreciation for the mythological truths that such practices are intending to embody. Chaos magicians are a primary example that toes this line deftly, with the adoption of a postmodern pluralism that, in theory at least, relies upon dynamic and regular cosmological transition. In the words of Phil Hine: *"involvement with magical practice shows that the game rules of Consensus Reality are more flexible, and have more loopholes than one may have originally thought."*[17]

To the Chaos magician, suspension of disbelief is a prerequisite in order to hold back rational frameworks from dispelling the power of creative imagination and playful ecstatic convergence. However, these lofty ambitions still have a tendency to fall back onto consciously reductive frameworks in the minds of practitioners. The psychedelic-like capacity to shatter so-called 'reality tunnels' one after another is an incredibly elusive ideal, that still has at its basis and primary function ideas of developing human potential and the power of the will.

Indeed, by failing to take a theistic path with the still confidence of faith there is a dangerous tendency to remove the creative act away from

---

16. Jung, C. G. 1916 (1968), p193
17. Hine, P. 1999, *Prime Chaos: Adventures in Chaos Magic*, New Falcon Publications, p25

a true notion of the sacred – of something Wholly Other – ensuring that such works tend towards profane acts that increasingly centre around the changing desires of an insatiable ego. If one was looking merely for a path towards psychotherapeutic results, there are far more effective and safely administered approaches over the complex and demanding cosmologies of the esoteric traditions.

When we situate ourselves within these traditions and their associated practices we must work based upon a receptive relationship to the Divine, anchoring our actions to the rhythm of the cosmos with humility toward the authentic source of our creative capacity. However, we must also remember that the physical world is part of the ultimate reality that we are seeking to commune with. There is a danger for the spiritual cosmologies and theistic frameworks of particular systems to render the practitioner of little use to the world within which they currently operate. The desire to commune with archetypal, elemental or supernatural forces can overwhelm the individual and even the protective embrace of the magical circle is little guard against the wide variety of corrupting influences that might intrude. Marjorie Cameron, the second wife of scientific pioneer and infamous occultist Jack Parsons, recalls his obsession with ceremonial magic that often precluded common sense solutions – giving the example of a heavy windstorm: *"It blew the French doors open, and everything was blowing and I was yelling... And can you imagine? I'm running around trying to close the windows, and Jack goes upstairs with his dagger to stop the wind!"*[18]

The ultimate goal of ceremonial work should be understood as allegorical movement that expresses and encourages the manifestation of Divine Will through the form of human dynamism. The beginnings of such practice necessarily work towards mastery over elemental forces and the archetypal influences that enwrap our material being, but they do so in order to prepare us to act as vessels of sanctification; rather than agents of the sinister, negating forces that seek to enslave us. Entered into collectively, with purity of intention, this process-driven expression has the capacity to raise our consciousness outside of its normal mode of being and elevate it to the point of transformation. A point of transformation that balances the psychological tendency towards self-centred egotism and primal instinct, while finding its inspiration from something deeper than the exoteric cosmology or dogma that the external process is often contextualised by. Although particular

---

18. Pendle, G. 2005, *Strange Angel: The Otherworldly Life of Rocket Scientist John Whiteside Parsons*, Harcourt Inc., p275

structures are required to return to the source, upon arriving the universal spring of understanding is rediscovered and becomes the new point of reference and motivation. We must rely upon these structures in order to be liberated from them, but the sacred refreshes itself anew with every pass under its wing.

One of the more revolutionary notions of the Christian tradition (which unfortunately didn't hold too well) was the democratisation of sacred space. The gateway to heaven is removed from closed sanctuaries and proscribed temples as humanity is given a direct proxy by which the sacred can be brought into all places. With the destruction of the temple, we are given a new path to Light through the redemption brought by Jesus Christ. The act of creating sacred space becomes available to all those who are able to open their hearts to this shining presence, as our relationship with the sacred removes itself from the confines of architecturally magnificent buildings and their robed custodians to become immediately relevant in our lives and found in every aspect of our individual experience of existence. Paula Gooder, an eminent Anglican theologian, covers this impeccably in her exploration of heaven, highlighting that:

> "Believing in heaven should not mean that we stand looking upwards all the time (or in whatever direction we think heaven might be), yearning to see it or feel it again. Instead, believing in heaven should mean that we carry with us a vision of the world as God intended it to be and strive with everything that we have to bring about that kind of world in the places where we live and work...It challenges us to recognise that nowhere on earth is the boundary between heaven and earth so thick that God's presence cannot be felt."[19]

This gives us a duty to ensure that we do not reduce our creative power to mere notions of individual gain and psychological potential. These elements of the process are useful and can be important when approached with measured caution, but far too often they become the primary desired result and the surrounding systems inevitably become mired down in petty squabbling and egotistical mind-games that are entirely irrelevant to helping bring about a reality that lives up to the 'vision of the world as God intended'. We must be ever vigilant against the temptations of self-love that draw us away

---

19. Gooder, P. 2011, *Heaven*, SPCK Publishing, p102

from our spiritual responsibilities and cause us to *"mistake for a knowledge of the divine objects that which removes [us] the farthest from them."*[20]

As initiates, particularly so as esoteric Christians, we have promised with the very core of our beings – mind, body and soul – to uplift ourselves and the world around us into the warm embrace of God's grace and merciful glory. We have many symbols by which this is communicated – the Philosopher's Stone; the Holy Grail; the Rose Cross; the Keystone – and we have practices that create the sacred spaces necessary for us to develop understanding that goes beyond knowledge and provides a path for developing the Sacred Vessel that is humanity's birthright and spiritual duty to uphold. This process of sacramental purification culminates in the experiential conversation with the Divine source behind, within, before, and surrounding all. Alan Watts explores this poetic truth throughout his book *Myth and Ritual in Christianity*:

> *"Thus the Tree [of Life] standing at the axis, the cross-roads of the world, at the central point of time and space, is at once the Now out of which time and space, past and future, are exfoliated to the crucifixion of the Self, and the Now into which the Self 'returns' when it 'takes up the Cross' and no longer 'misses the mark' - the 'target' into which the spear of attention is at last thrust, releasing the river of blood and water which cleanses the world."*[21]

This search is fundamentally one that liberates, not enslaves. And it is important to keep that in mind as we traverse the difficult landscape of a multitude of spiritual practices in our own lives. The true path toward God allows us to discover that freedom has been gifted to us, allowing access to a level of reality that sets us free of all confines and enables us to embrace the infinite possibilities of universal co-creation. This freedom is discovered not to be a chaotic desire for irrational or impulsive behaviour, but rather a still confidence that observes and exists alongside the motivations and pressures of daily existence. As Paul states in his letter to the Philippians (4:7): *"And the peace of God, which surpasses all understanding, will guard your hearts and your minds in Christ Jesus."* It is freedom through surety; diligent to avoid hubris; informed by a newfound capacity to communicate with the voice of Providence that emerges from all that is around and within us.

---

20. Lopukhin, I.V. 2009, *Some Characteristics of the Interior Church*, Scriptoria Books, p85
21. Watts, A. 1983, *Myth and Ritual in Christianity*, Thames & Hudson, p165

With all of this in place I can't be the only one who sometimes asks: *why am I doing this?* To have doubt – particularly within a context of faith – and to scrutinise one's path is an important prerequisite to a fruitful and productive spiritual life. The question is misleading to a certain extent, because as we experience sacred space and develop our capability to create it we find that the relationship unfolds in a process of emergent becoming that defies fixed interpretation. Underlying the inherent dynamism of the human personality there is a very real, supremely important, function being served when one enters into these spaces purposefully. We find ourselves within the context of an infinitely creative and unbounded framework of existence, even though our natural mode of interacting with that foundational reality is inherently bounded and almost obsessively inclined to demarcation and classification. Through the creation of spaces that overcome this limitation of everyday human consciousness we strive to connect with a higher frame of reference than our primal desires and sensory input normally allow. Most remarkable is that what is discovered within these spaces is a still voice of inspiration that draws us deeper into the creative bedrock of the cosmos. In more dramatic instances, the participant can be enveloped in an ecstatic or visionary experience of ultimate reality *"where we come upon something which not merely overtops our every concept, but astounds us by its absolute and utter difference from our whole nature."*[22]

Through these codified practices, which have evolved over millennia of human experimentation and revelation, we find ourselves able to unfold into the presence of something Wholly Other that can be described simultaneously as electric thunderclap and gently-hanging summer air. We communicate with a level of reality that exists beyond human comprehension and shows itself as both present and absent, discovered and lost, as movement and stillness. It feeds us and enlivens our capacity to truly be as *"the Dove descends from Heaven carrying the arch-natural Host to renew the virtues of the Stone"*[23]. Embodiment is key here, as we are talking about external places where the internality of our souls, expressed as individuals, integrates with the wider soul expressed through community and ultimately the foundational soul that underpins universal reality. We must 'Know Thyself' before we can begin to truly discover others, but it is through these others – and ultimately through something Wholly Other – that our being can fundamentally begin to exist at all.

---

22. Otto, R. 1917 (1982), *The Idea of the Holy*, translated by John W. Harvey, Oxford University Press, p180
23. Waite, A.E. 1909, *The Hidden Church of the Holy Graal*, Rebman Ltd, p544

These encounters with ultimate authenticity are impacting and transformative and, once encouraged to develop, we begin to crave communion with similarly pointed expressions; learning to recognise the presence of this voice within others. Where at first we felt an intensely personal journey, one begins to open out to a broader understanding of identity and a more multi-faceted experience of reality. We see the flow of information around, within and between us. How it acts upon us and is transubstantiated through us. Where God dwells cannot be adequately described or rationalised, cannot be encapsulated in any combination of words, artworks, sounds or movements – yet some semblance can be encoded in all these things and when one catches a glimpse it is undeniable and never forgotten. The core of our being holds onto the experiential memory of this holy place and develops a new sensory capacity to better recognise it the next time it appears.

Our capacity to create sacred space is in a very real sense the birthright of humanity. As we are born in the image of God, so are we given the capacity to communicate most forthrightly with the Divine. Indeed, it becomes part of our solemn duty as created stewards of being and to give our thanks we should consciously embrace this through all we say and do. Importantly, this ability is only strengthened when we are able to synchronise with others as the nature of our social identities resonates through these spaces and attaches the numinous directly to the social structures we exist within. Sacred space is the talismanic transformation of material existence, allowing us to traverse the crossroads of individual consciousness and rediscover its miraculous relationship with the communal construction of shared existence; resting atop the sanctified purity of ultimate reality.

The creation of sacred space speaks clearly of our ability to learn how to find our way back to this empowering convergence of belief and action. Once experienced we can't help but seek to elongate our time spent within its warm embrace, until finally our path allows us to submit with understanding to the supreme expression of Divine Love. Through the Grace of God that we emerge from we enable the continued elevation of this intangible, collective, eternal soul of humanity toward the resting place within the cosmic order that has been allotted to us.

One part amongst many. In all things, of all things, by all things.

I Am That I Am. The Beginning and the End. *Amen.*

Further Reading & Bibliography

Bell, C. 1992, *Ritual Theory, Ritual Practice*, Oxford University Press, NY

Bellah, R. 1976, New Religious Consciousness and the Crisis in Modernity, p333-353 in *The New Religious Consciousness* (ed. Glock, C. & Bellah, R.), University of California Press, Los Angeles.

Clift, W. 1982, *Jung and Christianity: The Challenge of Reconciliation*, Crossroad, New York.

Durkheim, E. 1976, *The Elementary Forms of Religious Life*, George Allen & Unwin Ltd, London.

Eliade, M. 1978, *The Forge and the Crucible: The Origins and Structures of Alchemy*, The University of Chicago Press, Chicago.

Eliade, M. 1987, *The Sacred and the Profane: The Nature of Religion*, Harcourt Inc., Orlando.

Garrett, W. R. 1989, Theological Reflection and Social Theory: An Emerging Rapprochement, p211-225 in *Social Consequences of Religious Belief* (ed. Garrett, William R.)

Gooder, P. 2011, *Heaven*, SPCK Publishing, London.

Hine, P. 1999, *Prime Chaos: Adventures in Chaos Magic*, New Falcon Publications, USA.

Jung, C.G. 1916 (1968), *Analytical Psychology: Its Theory and Practice*, Vintage Books, New York.

Kieckhefer, R. 2004, *Theology in Stone: Church Architecture from Byzantium to Berkely*, Oxford University Press, New York.

Levi, E. 2004, *Paradoxes of the Highest Science*, Ibis Press, Berwick.

Lopukhin, I.V. 1798 (2009), *Some Characteristics of the Interior Church*, Scriptoria Books, Mesa.

Mathers, S. L. 1887 (1989), *The Kabbalah Unveiled* (1684 trans.), Samuel Weiser, Maine.

North, P. & North, J. (eds.) 2007, *Sacred Space: House of God, Gate of Heaven*, Continuum, London.

Nott, C. S. 1961 (1990), *The Teachings of Gurdjieff: A Pupil's Journal*, Arkana, London.

Otto, R. 1917 (1982), *The Idea of the Holy*, translated by John W. Harvey, Oxford University Press, London.

Papus 1896 (2000), *The Qabalah: Secret Tradition of the West*, Samuel Weiser, York Beach.

Pendle, G. 2005, *Strange Angel: The Otherworldly Life of Rocket Scientist John Whiteside Parsons*, Harcourt Inc., Orlando.

Proudfoot, W. 1985, *Religious Experience*, University of California Press, Los Angeles.

Regardie, I. 1938 (2000), *The Middle Pillar: The Balance Between Mind and Magic*, Llewellyn Publications, USA.

Turner, V. 1969 (2008), *The Ritual Process: Structure and Anti-Structure*, Transaction Publishers, New Jersey.

Waite, A.E. 1909, *The Hidden Church of the Holy Graal*, Rebman Ltd, London.

Watts, A. 1983, *Myth and Ritual in Christianity*, Thames & Hudson.

ON THE SEARCH FOR POWERFUL KNOWLEDGE

This paper is the third in a series, building upon one on the esoteric varieties of Love, and another on the creation of sacred space. In the first paper on *Esoteric Love* I explored some of the processes taking place as we nurture our relationship with the Divine. This internal focus was then explored in the second paper through the communal, pragmatic context of *Sacred Space* – the tangible realities that we create to explore this incredibly rich aspect of our relationship to the cosmos.

With this third paper we return again to the internal world, to the world of our personal motivations and desires, in order to delve deeper into that which drives us to participate in the 'esoteric' or 'occult'. What motivates us to join often secretive and exclusive orders, that conduct their work behind closed doors? What truth lies behind the often lofty aspirations that we aspire to; and how dedicated are we to achieving them? How can we create a space that encourages collaborative mindfulness amongst those dedicated to knowledge of the Self and its relationship to the Divine?

These questions emerge from a phrase heard recently in a talk given by a Benedictine monk, Mark Barrett, who stated that our contemporary spiritual culture has 'a preoccupation with powerful knowledge'. This phrase struck a chord with my experiences in a variety of esoteric orders. Themes of hidden knowledge; of control over metaphysical beings and access to secret chiefs; of becoming involved with the special few, run prominently through the many pathways that fall under the umbrella of the Western Mystery Tradition. Founded so heavily as it is on Gnostic and Neo-platonic cosmology, such focus on a higher, secret plane of existence along with its concordant state of power is a core component of our tradition and its many branches.

By highlighting some of these themes we can create a framework for discussion where the tension between spiritual undertaking and self-serving behaviour can be more directly addressed. I will begin with a brief exploration of the notion of perfection and its historical context; then highlight some of the prevalent themes in the esoteric traditions before showing examples of how the modern, hyper-commercial world has twisted such spiritual undertakings. Finally, I want to explore how these different strands can influence our own approach to self-realisation and mystical attainment in the hopes of encouraging a more open space for communication on how our driving motivations might ultimately be counter-productive. This paper contains few answers and many questions, but the intention is to unpack some of my own experiences to provide something of value for your journey along this often convoluted path towards a more perfected form.

Looking back through history, there is an interesting dynamic in play with those who like to think of perfection. The classical world tended to look back towards a mythical Golden Age. The Greek poet Hesiod, writing in the 8th century BC, states that the gods of Olympus *"made first of mortals a Golden Race...and they lived like gods and no sorrow of heart they felt."*[1] The Roman poet Ovid, writing six hundred years later, longs for a similar distant past: a *"Golden Age [where]...the peoples of the world, untroubled by any fears, enjoyed a leisurely and peaceful existence, and had no use for soldiers."*[2] We see other mythological golden eras in the Epic of Gilgamesh; Plato's Atlantis; and of course the biblical Garden of Eden.

This perfect past is then coupled with a renewed perfection to come. Augustine's juxtaposition of the City of God and the City of Man outlays a constant struggle between good and evil that will find resolve at the close of existence:

---

1. Coverley, M. 2010, *Utopia*, Pocket Essentials, p20
2. Ibid. p22

"In the New Jerusalem, the redeemed will share with angels and ranks of saints a 'house of the New Testament', a lustrous, glorious edifice studded with precious jewels, a permanent haven that will never fall to ruin."[3]

In these modes of thinking, our fallen time exists between the perfected past and the perfected future. We are framed by concepts of purity that lay beyond our grasp.

Leaping ahead, in 1516 Thomas More coined the term 'utopia' in his novel of the same name and a host of similar discourse followed in its wake. This new resurgence of the 'perfection' genre showed a marked difference from the classical approach. Instead of locating the perfect in the mythological past or eschatological future, writers of the early modern period were keen to focus on the here and now. The fictional *Utopia* exists on a map and is situated in the present; Francis Bacon's *New Atlantis* of 1627 is right at hand through scientific advancement. Perfection can be achieved, right now, if only we can discover the collective will to do so.

At this time we also see the rise of the authentic self – Montaigne, Descartes, Rousseau and others strongly push the need for self-exploration and the perfection of free will as directed towards a virtuous pinnacle. All of this following a time when the Reformation declares forthrightly that the road to God lies not with those institutions who hold the most power but through the path of faith alone – that each can find their own way into the perfected salvation enabled through Grace. If you will forgive this shockingly lax overview of history, it is among all of this that we see the emergence of Rosicrucianism as a force in Europe – a movement that combines a deep appreciation for millennial goals of redemption, with a call for a utopian now via a hidden collective of individuals that shall help realise it.

Whilst public discourse was finding new levels of expressive freedom and blossoming in many previously censored areas, we see in our forebears a narrative focusing on hidden secrets held by an unseen force. An invisible group of adepts that beckons to the aspirant, telling: *"all learned who will make themselves known unto us, and come into our brotherhood, shall find more wonderful secrets by us than heretofore they did attain unto, and did know, or are able to believe or utter."*[4]

---

3. Ibid. p32
4. *Confessio Fraternitatis*

Even during this time of great opening, when the *Fama* and *Confessio* are spread far and wide, there is the explicit statement that *"wherefore we neither can be seen or known by anybody, except he had the eyes of an eagle."*[5] Thus our illustrious tradition has at its very beginnings the notion of a publicly known body, whom at the same time are hidden from view and possess a secret knowledge that shall 'enrich the whole world'. This is all heavily steeped in mystical allegory – *"small is the gate and narrow the road that leads to life, and only a few find it"*[6] – but nonetheless the enticement of powerful knowledge is clearly present. To be directed towards the supreme cause of Good, of course, but powerful nonetheless and beyond the ken of the average person.

This all comes with a rejection of the corrupt ways of false practitioners – those less spiritual than thou – whether in the form of deceptive alchemists and astrologists, spiritual dilettantes or the numerous hypocritical people of the Church, all the way up to the 'tyrannical' Pope himself. We are powerful, but you should trust us because we are pure...

Purity of this kind emerges from a spiritual connection to the source of all that is Holy, an inner spark that enables the true Adept to work according to divine motivation. This inherently Gnostic concept remains with us today and runs throughout most of the modern esoteric vision. A search for perfect wisdom that shall bring with it the capacity to turn dross into gold(en age) and dissolve the finite ego into the boundless eternity of the Almighty – aligning our own motivations with that of the Divine Will in the fulfilment of the Great Work. These enticing aspects – the perfected world, the hidden group, the powerful knowledge, the purest wisdom –come together in countless orders with exotically charged symbolic motifs that claim to offer their adherents a proven path to illumination. Combined with this, we also see prominent narratives of connection to higher beings; a communion of saints directing the course of history for the betterment of humanity.

Think here of the 'Great White Brotherhood' of Eckartshausen, the 'Hidden Masters' of Blavatsky or 'Secret Chiefs' of the Golden Dawn, a deep sense of spiritual hierarchy that runs back to Zoroaster's 'blessed immortals' and beyond. On the material side of this equation, the notion of the Magus runs as a strong thread through a mix of mythology, literature and history – Moses and Solomon, Pythagoras and Simon, Merlin and Faust, through

---

5. Ibid
6. Matthew 7:14

to John Dee and those closer to us in time for whom the mythologising processes have not (yet) taken hold. We have a very clear model of the individual brought to immense spiritual power through the utilisation of secret knowledge – and it is something that, at least to some degree, motivates many of us at some point along our journey. When considering such gatherings of the spiritual Elect, I've always been torn by the thought: *Is the desire to arrive humbly at the feet of the Masters, or is the attainment of powerful knowledge seen as the means to <u>become</u> one of the Elect?*

A question worth considering carefully.

When all of these enticing elements hit the advertising-fuelled, commercial drives of the twentieth century they take on an altogether more blatant and telling tone. The locked doors are blown open by the likes of Aleister Crowley and Israel Regardie, who sought to subvert the notion of secret knowledge through the publication of the Golden Dawn curriculum. Helena Blavatsky serves the same purpose in many ways for the esoteric and occult counterparts of the East, cataloguing with great (albeit stereotyped) detail the many capabilities supplied through the world of occult practice.

However, as the secretive factor is marginalised and information becomes increasingly widespread, the notion of powerful knowledge only seems to become even more prominent. Blavatsky's reliance on Hidden Masters and attempts to prove her own occult ability lead her increasingly down the path of confidence trickster and fraudulent guru, undermining the gems that can be found in her large corpus of work. Crowley's texts, while embedded with a sense of cosmic humility and duty to the Divine, combine an erudite study of mystical and ceremonial practice with an overpowering notion of self-actualisation and a me-centred framework that has led countless astray including 'the Great Beast' himself.

The development of such self-centred lines of enquiry promulgates throughout the twentieth century, arriving at examples such as advertisements from the AMORC in the 1950s proclaiming that through them one can unlock 'The Greatest Power on Earth' or that showcase an image of Benjamin Franklin with the alluring question: *What secret power did this man possess?* The focus here is unashamedly on the individual and what they can obtain for themselves through the search for powerful knowledge. This kind of use of astral or occult powers for their own sake was described by Regardie, for one, as a 'pathological morbidity' – one that forgets entirely the position of servitude to the Divine that should be adopted.[7]

---

7. Regardie, I. 1932 (2003), *The Tree of Life: An Illustrated Study in Magic*, Llewellyn

The Mask by Louis Welden Hawkins (1905)

Bring this strand of me-centered esotericism through to the image-obsessed 1960s and you have examples such as the ruthless humanism of Anton LaVey's Church of Satan which lays out ceremonial practices to find sexual partners, achieve material success, and destroy one's enemies. Covers of *Witchcraft* magazine in the 1970s were showcasing tabloid stories of the occult alongside nude models; and from the 1980s on we see a boom in packaging grand spiritual undertakings into bite-sized, consumer products. Think here of the brazenly titled *The Secret* and its massive popularity as a tool for personal attainment. Thus a stylised, sexualised, hyper-commercial form of esotericism found itself combined with a utilitarian notion of occult powers that could be used for personal gain without detriment. Black magic had become a fashion icon, book stores were filled with me-first spirituality, and rockstars played the occult piper all over the globe.

Tom Wolfe, counterculture commentator extraordinaire, described this new landscape of modern spirituality in a 1976 essay for New York magazine. Observing that: *"The new alchemical dream is changing one's personality - remaking, remodeling, elevating, and polishing one's very self...and observing, studying, and doting on it. (Me!)"*[8]

These *Me* movements continue to have significant influence on the spiritual zeitgeist of our modern era. Magical practices, originally intended for primarily theurgic means, have in many areas become thoroughly debased – forgoing God for Mammon and succumbing to the auspices of the untamed ego rather than holding onto a finely honed intuition of the common good. In such cases we seek not for the restoration of all humanity, and act not as disciples of the cosmos, but rather search for powerful knowledge and ecstatic personal experiences so that we might attain for *ourselves* a higher state of spiritual perfection:

Hi God, it's Me!

So why have I raced through this thoroughly simplistic, incomplete and cherry-picked view of esoteric history? Mostly because we find ourselves here today through the shared experience of being drawn to the Light, a calling that beckons us nearer to something intangible and provides enticing and all-too-fleeting glimpses of a better way to be. Yet, if I may indulge myself and talk about me (!), when I compare such ideals of pure motivation and theurgic intent to my own experience I find myself wholly lacking in the discipline required of anybody who would aspire to be an Adept. My base

---

8. Wolfe, T. 1976, The "Me" Decade and the Third Great Awakening, *New York Magazine* (August 23 issue)

nature overwhelms my thoughts and motivations easily – anger, jealousy, lust, envy, pride, apathy...a whole list of shortcomings that I have to admit are felt on what seems like a daily basis (sometimes even all at the same time!).

I have been guilty of using my involvement with the esoteric traditions as means to build a kind of social cachet – an unpleasantly boastful tone that refers only obliquely to things known or understood 'behind the veil' of secrecy. A knowing wink or nod that places those who are not in the know as somehow outside or beneath my current 'illustrious' state of attainment and recognition. This is not a sign of spiritual development but rather one of regression, a succumbing to the temptations that those who seek to develop their spiritual connection to God must endure. To appropriate a turn of phrase from Lewis Carroll: *Uncharitable Thoughts? Why, sometimes I've had as many as six uncharitable thoughts before breakfast!*

And yet, despite all this I can recognise the development of that core component that speaks of a higher goodness; that directs an increasing number of actions and undertakings and beckons the soul toward it. Among all the failings there is progress, a deeper understanding of the wide variety of roles present throughout this sacred dance of cosmic proportions. Not so much an ecstatic awakening, with all the projected status that such might bring, but an emergent becoming. Unfolding away the darker parts of the human condition and replacing them with something more truly compassionate and understanding. Of course, usually any feelings of progress are once again met with a swift and immediate failing – the reminder that I am not as enlightened as I may feel; still motivated by power, arrogance and ownership to too great a degree. But there is some solace found in recognising the failing, if nothing else.

This might just sound like self-indulgent tripe, but I don't feel alone in experiencing this tension. To be tormented by the stark shortcomings that playfully tease the soul while the external personality presents a far more balanced and exalted form to others. This tension is one that ultimately is only answered at the very threshold of one's being. *Who are you, and why are you here? What do you hope to find, and why do you want to find it?*

It's not as easy as merely stating that we are pure, that we understand what it's all about and do it for exactly the right reasons. The history and failings of some of our most praised forebears is clear evidence of the difficulties faced. Even among the Great and the Good, chaos reigned supreme and the destructive force of unfettered egos lusting for political power runs as a thick, bloody stain on the white albs of those we are guided and inspired by. The line between divinely-inspired motivation and self-serving narcissism is very thin indeed, so it is vitally important to foster a permissive environment where we can be open about our shortcomings and encouraged to present something other than our most finely crafted masks. A safe space within which we can name the demons and discover a new communal reassurance in the vulnerability of our own flaws. Knowing that we are accepted by the Grace of God for *who we are*, not just who we pretend to be.

The search for powerful knowledge – encoded in a hidden past – means that we often become too concerned with relatively narrow notions of truth, of definite answers to be figured out if only we had the right key. The esoteric traditions have come about specifically because the knowledge they are trying to transmit cannot be readily articulated – and therefore the manner in which they must be communicated is less about knowing and more about recognising the humility brought to us by relationship with the unknowable.

One thing seems certain, looking back at those who have trod this path before us: the more we feel a sense of powerful attainment, the further away we have journeyed from the source of our spiritual growth and development. This might lead to unfortunate personality traits, but it can also lead to devastating consequences for those we come into contact with. On a larger scale there are many notable instances where entire spiritual communities have imploded through the quest for powerful knowledge. At its darkest hour we have seen the cataclysmic results of this imbalance manifest in mass murder/suicide, brutal crusades and racial genocide. All guided by a search for something pure, a righteous desire for power or exaltation. When we pause to consider this fact of human history and the degree to which spiritual mysteries can be perverted as such, we start to understand how vigilant we must be right down to the level of our individual identity and internal honesty on what motivates us. We need to discover a new level of authenticity in our discourse, one that allows for failure without shame and acknowledges the need to constantly strive against our primal impulses.

If we can be honest to ourselves that we are often motivated by elusive phantasms of power, status or perfect knowledge then we can begin a relationship with a deeper Truth. One that energises our traditions and enables them to renew over and again from the desolation of those who have misused their cosmic momentum. It is our ongoing duty to try and shed the negative influences that our own profane desires bring to the egregore of the groups we become part of. Remembering, also, that the failings of our fellow travellers are at least in some part to be carried on our own shoulders. As John Donne famously laid out:

"No man is an Iland, intire of it selfe; every man is a peece of the Continent, a part of the maine...Any man's death diminishes me, because I am involved in mankind, and therefore never send to know for whom the bell tolls; It tolls for thee."[9]

Our path demands that we confront our own karmic echoes and arrive at an understanding of how they unwittingly radiate out into existence. The realisation then emerges that this undertaking isn't done merely for our own attainment, but because our flaws are negatively influencing the modality of those around us – and through them even those we will never have direct contact with. We have the opportunity to work as proxy for the Divine in many specific, fleeting moments in time. The more we seek attentiveness and compassionate understanding, the more we are capable of acting as dutiful servant to that source of Light when and where it might be needed most. Our motivation moves from that which is internally focused and works for the gains of narrow interests, to one which can productively use the energy harnessed in sealed spaces to help restore the co-created world to its rightful place enveloped in the boundless love of God.

There is a beautiful paradox involved in treading the esoteric path: to rediscover the hidden treasures that lie at its heart we cannot seek ownership of them. To attain we must forgo the desire for attainment. Of course, even to discuss such matters in a paper such as this desire is still evident, a yearning for achievement and exaltation that cannot – and should not – be denied as present and influential. The important thing is that we remind ourselves to continue moving in the right direction. So that the path continues to be walked, *"trodden out in the wind and darkness of the barren places of the soul"* as Dion Fortune so eloquently put it[10].

When we are motivated by the search for powerful knowledge it is true that we are being drawn towards something miraculous, but if we succumb too readily to the temptations surrounding such a jewel then our actions only add to the quagmire of destructive thought-forms that have kept humanity distant from the fountain of life. Our fundamental approach must not be one that seeks to attain to power, but rather that which recognises the humble role of the Servants of Light and joyfully embraces the vulnerability of our place in the cosmic order:

---

9. Donne, J. 1623, *Meditation XVII*
10. Fortune, D. 1928 (2000), *Esoteric Orders and Their Work*, Samuel Weiser Inc, p112

"...yea, it shall be so far from him whosoever thinks to get the benefit and be partaker of our riches and knowledge, without and against the will of God, that he shall sooner lose his life in seeking and searching for us, than to find us, and attain to come to the wished happiness of the Fraternity of the Rosy Cross."[11]

With this paper I've taken a rapid tour through the more self-indulgent side of esoteric history and opened up to my own shortcomings in the hopes that they might resonate with some of yours. By trying to unpick some of the corrupting influence of the ego the aim is not to stand in judgement, but to become more comfortable with the fact that we are all flawed. We know the warnings about the impact of the ego on the path that we tread, yet it is far too easy to continuously point to flaws in others while settling into a complacency that blinds us to our own. To help overcome this tendency, we should aim to encourage a more permissive environment in which such drawbacks can be named and openly discussed. Through doing so we come to a deeper understanding of how these aspects influence us, dispelling the fear that by showing weakness we will be abandoned by our fellow seekers.

As a community who aim to bring Light to the world around us, it is when our collective efforts are aligned that we shall always see the most success in our important work of cosmic healing. Which makes it essential that we develop the common language and conversational space to openly co-operate and exist comfortably within one another's sphere of influence. Our strengths are varied; the lessons to be learned from one another are many; and the spaces we create are extremely effective in helping us hear that still voice within that seeks to guide us back to its source. This journey is not undertaken merely for our own accomplishment or salvation, but for the betterment of all. Rather than searching for the powerful we seek to embrace vulnerability; rather than ownership we yearn to be more attentive; instead of entitlement we renew our sense of humility – all for a single purpose: *Thy* kingdom come, *Thy* will be done.

At every step along the way there is the opportunity to do harm, sometimes minor sometimes great, to the spiritual wellbeing of humanity. Which is why we must regularly stop to ask of ourselves and one another, always with compassionate understanding to whatever answers might emerge, those perennial questions for seekers on the path: *For what are you looking, and for whom are you looking for?*

---

11. *Confessio Fraternitatis*

S. O. S. by Evelyn De Morgan (1916)

ON THE TRANSFORMATION OF GLAMOUR

"If you want me to cry, you cry first." - Karl von Eckhartshausen

It is once again an honour and privilege to have the opportunity to share with you some musings along the way. This is the fourth entry in a series related to the well-rehearsed notion that it is our spiritual duty and perennial quest to lay down the firm foundations required to be pillars of Light, acting as humble servants of Divine Providence and agents of ever-loving Grace.

The series has explored some of the internal processes that establish an authentic connection with the Divine, alongside the practices that enable us to experience, communicate and embed this most important relationship. The previous paper, *On the Search for Powerful Knowledge*, then encouraged an open recognition that the esoteric path is a constant struggle between understanding our highest selves and the pitfalls of daily existence that lead us towards excessive self-regard and a preponderance to succumb to our lower, more primal natures. By finding a renewed sense of solidarity with one another's weaknesses, we can move toward a more honest and genuine expression of cosmic co-creation. It should therefore be a defining feature of organised spiritual groups to effectively create the spaces required to overcome personal and collective shortcomings.

In this paper I would like to extend the focus onto modern society as a whole, in the hope that we might better articulate what it means to be a Rosicrucian today and consider the role that we can play in helping to *cure the sick, and that gratis*. What are some of the core social maladies facing the world and how can our search for illumination be put towards healing them? What does Rosicrucianism look like when interacting with the world and how can we think of our journey as something more than just a personal quest for communication with the Divine?

In particular, I want to take a closer look at the impact of *glamour* on our lives and spiritual being. This is an evocative term, one that emerges out of esoteric tradition and yet has in most instances been inverted in its modern usage. By deconstructing the impact of glamour in our lives today, and its relationship to ideological hegemony, we can then begin to formulate a response to its influence. One that brings the ancient wisdom of spiritual illumination into direct contact with the unique and rapidly evolving circumstances of the modern era, doing so in a way that fulfils the edicts of the *Fama Fraternitatis* and adheres to the assertion that our purpose is to cure the sick, while following the custom of the country; meeting in the Sancti Spiritus in a sacramental communion that unfolds the incorruptible body here and now.

The origin of the term 'glamour' brings us immediately into familiar territory. A phrase of early 18th century Scottish origin (*to cast the glamor*) it is a variant of the term *gramarye* (enchantment, spell) which in itself comes from the well-known English phrase *grammar*. A phrase that carries a commonly-held interpretation of scholarship, but also holds a particular sense of occult learning and hidden signification in its early use[1]. Sir Walter Scott used the term in his 1805 poem, *The Lay of the Last Minstrel*:

> *And one short spell therein he read:*
> *it had much of glamour might;*
> *Could make a ladye seem a knight;*
> *The cobwebs on a dungeon wall*
> *Seem tapestry in lordly hall.*

This was part of a rapid popularisation of the phrase as referring to a spell or enchantment that charms the eye. Making things seem to appear other than

---

1. *Online Etymology Dictionary*, etymonline.com

they are; more beautiful and enticing; of higher status and worthy of praise.

We will discuss the illusory impact of glamour more in a moment, but of interest to us at this point is the transformation of glamour into a less recognisable form of psychological obfuscation. A move into the realms of public spectacle and aristocratic luxury that begins to manipulate on a much larger scale and draws people into the political mythologies of Europe and, later, the forthcoming landscape of the new 'American Dream'. The emergence of new modes of entertainment – such as the collective escapism of cinema – begins to commodify glamour as something desirable, to be sought after and attained rather than afflicted by. Here we see the widening influence of glamour into a force that begins to underpin (and mesmerise) society as a whole. Indeed, celebrities take on a mythological quality at the turn of the 20th century: *"suspended between the ordinary and the extraordinary, the real and the ideal, the stars were the gods and goddesses of a modern Olympus."*[2]

Depictions that hark back to a more literal and traditional view of glamour (consider the enchantments present in modern Vampire tales) are steeped in submissive sexuality (the term 'glamour model' is another example). It is primarily within the new, image-led entertainment mediums that glamour transforms from an act of enchantment into a medium of cultural expression in and of itself; representative of the conflicted identities of a post-industrial world. Society begins to increasingly embrace an alluring combination of forever yearning for the unattainable. Overt depictions of glamorous figures emerging as *"a loosely aesthetic category in response to cultural change, and consequently [acting] as a medium of such change. [Arising] as an intelligible quality at the very moment when time seems to quicken, turning the everyday world into an anxious experience for metropolitan citizens."*[3]

However, depicting glamour as an important functional pivot-point for modern culture often overlooks the corrosive ideological paradigms that this social mechanism is ultimately serving. Accelerating from the 1950s onward, the process of manufacturing desire and the construction of glamorous facades becomes deeply embedded in society through the advertising industry and its rapid take-up of a new field known at the time as 'Motivational Research'. Proving highly successful in persuading people

---

2. Gundle, S. 2008, *Glamour: A History*, Oxford University Press, p172
3. Parkins, I. 2012, *Poiret, Dior and Schiaparelli: Fashion, Femininity and Modernity*, Berg Publishers, p87

to spend more as consumers, this approach quickly jumped out of the realm of product sales into the core of our social institutions as a systematically researched, psychodynamic approach to political persuasion. As the journalist Vance Packard noted with alarm in 1957:

> *"No longer is the aim just to play on our subconscious to persuade us to buy a refrigerator or new motorboat that we may or may not need. The aim now is nothing less than to influence the state of our mind and to channel our behaviour as citizens."*[4]

As Kalle Lasn, founder of the Canadian publication *Ad Busters*, articulated, the core problem of glamour (i.e. persuasion through illusory facades) comes from its relation to ideological hegemony:

> *"Dreams, by definition, are supposed to be unique and imaginative. Yet the bulk of the population is dreaming the same dream. It's a dream of wealth, power, fame, plenty of sex and exciting recreational opportunities. What does it mean when a whole culture dreams the same dream?"*[5]

The core of the issue that we face today is that what was once a descriptor of a one-to-one enchantment has transformed over the centuries to something so pervasive that it not only has the ability to control our hearts and minds like never before, but has in many ways become almost unstoppable. Woven so comprehensively into the fabric of society as to become seen as part of its basic cultural functionality:

> *"as a form of nonverbal rhetoric, which moves and persuades not through words but through images, concepts and totems...By binding image and desire, glamour gives us pleasure, even as it heightens our yearning. It leads us to feel that the life we dream of exists, and to desire it even more."*[6]

At the same time, the fog of contemporary facades that we collectively find ourselves under promotes an increasing sense of spiritual and emotional

---

4. Packard, V. 1957, *The Hidden Persuaders*, Penguin Books, p148
5. Lasn, K. 2000, *Culture Jam*, HarperCollins, p57
6. Postrel, V. 2013, *The Power of Glamour*, Simon & Shuster, p6

malaise that rests underneath the surface of recreational luxury, frivolous consumer choice and the illusion of social progress. We continue to be drawn into this cycle of yearning for the items of our own existential discontent because our true vision is clouded by the impact of glamour, to the extent that we often cannot even define the source of our unrest and instead allow it to be channelled down unproductive and hostile avenues. The negative consequences of allowing glamour to act as a cultural focal point – fear, loathing, degradation, greed etc. – are *themselves* used as fuel for the continued utilisation of glamour towards the embedding of ruthlessly self-serving ideologies. The cycle perpetuates and we find ourselves deeper down the hole, further away from a true connection with one another and the world around us. As an iconographic cultural medium, glamour might *"[reveal] the truth about what we desire and, sometimes, what we can become"*[7] but it is also the all-encompassing mechanism through which destructive ideologies, manifesting violence and suffering across the globe, are finding a foothold at the very threshold of our souls.

Which brings us with urgency to a discussion on what can we, as Rosicrucians, do about this? What role can we play in helping to cure the sickness of this age-old, yet particularly modern spiritual affliction? In his famous Letter from Birmingham Jail, Martin Luther King Jr. put out an important call for faith-based resistance to the racial injustices of the day – looking back to the courage of the early Christians: *"In those days the church was not merely a thermometer that recorded the ideas and principles of popular opinion; it was a thermostat that transformed the mores of society."*[8]

It is part of our duty, he posits, to actively transform society through our connection to a higher vision of universal justice. Civil-rights activist and Harvard Law Professor, Derrick Bell, explored this in relation to our modern global society and the structures that maintain it:

> *"The gravitational pulls of our 'free enterprise' society urge acceptance of the social system as it is. It counsels us to compete and win by any available means. As needed, we can pretend we are ethical and humane. Our posturing will look like spirit and it will appear sufficient. The challenge for those with ethical ambition is to transform the symbolically sufficient into the substantively real."*[9]

---

7. Ibid. p23
8. King Jr., M. L. 1963, *Letter from a Birmingham Jail*, Stanford University
9. Bell, D. 2002, *Ethical Ambition*, Bloomsbury, p93

What he is talking of when using phrases such as 'gravitational pulls', 'urge acceptance', and 'counsels us' are manifestations of the glamour mechanisms that afflict the world today. Our response to this affliction as Rosicrucians, therefore, must be seen in the light of the substantively real. We have an abundance of symbolic sufficiency, but we must question and challenge our practices against a notion of true impact in order to ascertain whether or not our activities are merely self-regarding posturing. In my previous paper, I discussed some of the unproductive motivations that often bring us together into a variety of organisations – where we are often motivated by a sense of powerful knowledge, of exclusive secrets and personal masteries.

Our first step towards the substantively real, then, is to recognise these motivations when we come across them and place ourselves in open communication with one another; standing together in a posture of purposeful submission and humble servitude over the allure of personal gain. Aware that we have been entranced by the ideological glamours of the world and that, unless we can discover a new narrative of solidarity and duty to societal reconstruction, our actions to uplift ourselves will tend towards a replication of the same self-serving structures we are trying to free ourselves from. This purposeful submission begins by seeing the path we walk not as an individualistic striving for ecstatic experience, but rather as an activity that is undertaken collectively in order to provide a transformative mechanism for the world as a whole. We must understand our journey as ultimately one that is not done for personal liberation, but acts as a counterbalance to the 'glamours which hold humanity in thrall'.

Alice Bailey, a key leader of the Theosophical Society, gives a detailed exploration of this transformative process in her book *Glamour: A World Problem* and places great importance on the struggle with individualistic motivations:

> "*Any emphasis upon the personality can distort most easily the pure light of the soul as it seeks to pur through the lower self. Any effort to call attention to the mission or task which the personality has undertaken detracts from that mission and handicaps the man in his task; it leads to the deferring of its fulfillment until such time when the disciple can be naught but a channel through which love can pour, and light can shine. This pouring through and shining forth has to be a spontaneous happening, and contain no self-reference.*"[10]

---

10. Bailey, A. 1950 (1988), *Glamour: A World Problem*, Lucis Press Ltd, p53

The task of overcoming the allure of the personality thus makes up the bulk of the Initiate's journey, allowing for the spontaneous happening of Love and Light to occur in ever more frequent (and challenging) circumstances. Franz Hartmann conveyed this as an ability to still the waters of the passionate mind, a common and useful metaphor, poetically positing that:

> "*The divine principle in man remains in itself unaltered and undisturbed, like the image of a star reflected in water, but unless its dwelling is rendered clear and transparent, it cannot send its rays through the surrounding walls.*"[11]

The process of stilling the waters is an ongoing and difficult one, but it has an immediately noticeable effect after only a few genuine steps upon the path. Thus, in order to begin to undertake our duty to transform the mores of society, it is the obligation of every Initiate to undertake this journey with pure intention. For positive results will inevitably follow such faithfulness, as our intuitive capacity blooms in its yearning *"to be united with the beauty we see, to pass into it, to receive it into ourselves, to bathe in it, to become part of it."*[12]

Providing a channel for the shining forth of Light and Love to interact with the ideological foundations of society is then the work of the Adept – who has made such progress as to become (at times) an active and fruitful agent for Divine Providence. The *transformation* of glamour now becomes viewed as an alchemical process taking place within the internal sphere of the Adept themselves. A totemic consummation of the enchantments that mesmerise us in order to understand the manner in which they function, enabling us to clearly articulate the deceptions surrounding modern identity and returning to the world a newly illuminated form. A process of microcosmic transubstantiation that enables us, as *a* point within *a* circle, to influence wider and more collective modes of existence and to do so without the projection of our own personal structures of power – *to cure the sick, and that gratis.*

This is absolutely not a call to push a particular political or material outcome, one self-serving ideology over another, but rather to develop the ability to deconstruct the deceptive nature of our motivating passions,

---

11. Hartmann, F. 1890 (1969), *Magic White and Black*, The Aquarian Press, p155
12. Lewis, C.S. 1942, *The Weight of Glory*, SPCK, p8

framing a more harmonious vision of humanity that understands the true nature of the illusions we face. Here, the second article of the *Fama* – *None of the posterity should be constrained to wear one kind of habit, but to follow the custom of the country* – comes into view. The transformative mystery at the heart of Rosicrucianism requires a universal praxis, done without grand gestures that draw undue attention to the Work. It is not our role to proselytise as Christians, but rather to transform through the ever-loving Grace and the fellowship of the Holy Spirit. Each working within our area of knowledge, expertise and belief to develop the spiritual expression of our particular focal point toward harmony and away from discord.

In practice, this means different things to all of us – we are not constrained to wear one kind of habit – and varies from the most simple of friendly gestures to the most complex, long-running efforts of societal change. We can then see how, in their multitude, our efforts as a group of spiritual healers are able to have an exponential effect. Finding leverage within all avenues of social creation and working through numerous spheres of influence simultaneously. The importance of our coming together into spiritual organisations of various kinds is then to provide both the tools needed to overcome our own personal spiritual pitfalls, but also to allow the multiplying effect of working through alignment to have the greatest impact. We know when our work is pointed true because it springs from the still voice of inspiration that lies at the heart of Creation; that calls us to strive for a unified and holistic view of our place in the cosmos, our reliance upon the natural world, and our dignified relationship to one another. Dion Fortune puts this by stating: *"We may safely say that whatever brings harmony where there was disharmony leads to a legitimate end"*[13]; and Mouni Sadhu, in his treatise on theurgy, puts simply that *"everything which unites and does not divide always has some spiritual aspect."*[14]

The difficult part, of course, comes from the fact that our perceptions of harmony and unity are themselves constructed and directed by the glamours that surround us. It is in this immense challenge of defining universal foundations for salvation *without* replicating self-serving ideologies that we can discover our perennial role as Rosicrucians: a duty to act as cultural interlocutors tied closely to the spiritual evolution of humanity. Through placing ourselves in an intermediary role, based upon deeply met

---

13. Fortune, D. 1935 (1985), *Practical Occultism in Daily Life*, The Aquarian Press, p47
14. Sadhu, M. 1965, *Theurgy: The Art of Effective Worship*, George Allen & Unwin, p66

spiritual alignment, the Adept can help define the space that exists *between* subjectively restricted world views. Discovering the interpretive mindset required to overcome the infatuating powers of glamour and doing so with a presence that allows them to dissipate, without immediately being replaced by similar forces drawn into what would otherwise be an ideological vacuum. In this way, we can unify where once there was discord; reconciling conflicting perspectives that find themselves in opposition not because of any fundamental truth of incompatibility, but because they are working on the basis of shallow understandings of the Other forged by the glamours of the day. Conflicts that arise out of an aversion to manufactured facades of difference, rather than a clear view of the dignity of experiential emergence that lies beneath. As Alice Bailey states: *"It is mediating interpreters of ideas that are needed and not mediums."*[15]

The process of glamour is something that relates to the core of the human condition. It is not a construction of the modern era, but lies at the heart of our shortcoming as material beings. However, what is of great importance is to realise the extent to which we have subsumed ourselves (and others) to the influence of this primal aspect of existence. The bedrock of consumer culture depends upon the effects of glamour; our political systems are founded upon its mechanisms; and we unconsciously interact with highly-charged symbolism thousands of times a day.

This problem is of particular concern in areas of greater urban density, but with the emergence of an ever-present and increasingly accessible global internet the structural agents of glamour are able to approach us at all times and in almost any location. The path to individualism has provided us with the illusion of freedom, while ensuring our enslavement to structures and psychosocial entities that are no longer, and possibly never were, under our control. This is an issue that lies at the core of our relationship to material existence, but it is one that we must now face with a renewed sense of urgency. Not only because the expression of glamour has become so all-encompassing in modern global society, but because we have developed the technological and scientific capacity for our collective thoughts to manifest like never before. Rudolf Steiner understood the potential that such twisted thought-forms have to misguide us, stating that:

"What humanity thinks to-day, that will it be in the future. A humanity that thinks materialistically will produce frightful beings in the future,

---

15. Bailey, A. 1950 (1988), p31

and a humanity that thinks spiritual thoughts, so works upon and transforms the future organism that beautiful bodies will proceed from it."[16]

The affliction of glamour is fundamentally an issue about control over imaginative will. The ability to conceive forms and bring them to material reality lies at the heart of humanity's birthright in the cosmic order, but it is an ability that can be utilised for positive or negative outcomes. For the tyranny of vice or the liberation of virtue. By allowing our creative capacity to fall under the control of external entities that want not for the betterment of humankind and the natural world, but rather seek to satisfy depraved and insatiable cravings driven by power and greed, we forsake the divine gift that lies at the core of our spiritual being.

It is our duty not only to recognise this in and of ourselves, but to accept and facilitate such recognition in others in a manner that removes our own immediate sense of self-fixated outcome. Uplifting one another to the status of our divine potentiality, that we share in our role as stewards of material creation. As C.S. Lewis implored:

> *"It is a serious thing to live in a society of possible gods and goddesses, to remember that the dullest and most uninteresting person you talk to may one day be a creature which, if you saw it now, you would be strongly tempted to worship, or else a horror and a corruption such as you now meet, if at all, only in a nightmare. All day long we are, in some degree, helping each other to one or other of these destinations. It is in the light of these overwhelming possibilities, it is with the awe and the circumspection proper to them, that we should conduct all our dealings with one another, all friendships, all loves, all play, all politics. There are no ordinary people. You have never talked to a mere mortal."*[17]

The relevance of Rosicrucianism comes directly from our ability to transform glamour within the molten forge of our souls, returning to the world a more just and illuminated perspective that seeks to undo the harmful effects of humanity's journey through material existence. In a very practical sense, Rosicrucians should seek to mediate between vastly different ideas and ideologies; standing as repairers and facilitators of the gateways

---

16. Steiner, R. 1907 (1981), *Theosophy of the Rosicrucian*, Rudolf Steiner Press, p150
17. Lewis, C. S. 1942, p9

between disparate viewpoints. The ability to encourage reconciliation, mutual understanding and the cessation of conflict of all kinds should be considered the curative vocation of the Adept. Each according to the station and circumstances of their life and ultimately beholden to the generative source of movement within All that Is.

This should be understood as a primary spiritual duty of the Great Work, allowing humanity to freely embody the liberating life-breath that emerges from unity with our divine purpose and cosmic nature. The glamour we so readily consume seeks to distract us from this duty – from our Love and exaltation of one another in Grace – and our esotericism is most relevant to humanity when directed toward developing the metaphysical organs required to clear the fog that hangs over our collective consciousness.

We must lead by example, acting as a shining beacon that lights the path not only for ourselves but for all those with whom we share existence. Breaking the spell that binds us to the dross and releasing the luminous gold that is our cosmic inheritance. Allowing others to see, through our works, a reflection of the Divine within themselves.

Further Reading & Bibliography

Bailey, A. 1988 (1950), *Glamour: A World Problem*, Lucis Press Ltd, London.

Bell, D. 2002, *Ethical Ambition*, Bloomsbury, New York and London.

Fortune, D. 1985 (1935), *Practical Occultism in Daily Life*, The Aquarian Press, UK

Gundle, S. 2008, *Glamour: A History*, Oxford University Press, Oxford.

Hartmann, F. 1890 (1969), *Magic White and Black*, The Aquarian Press.

King Jr., M.L. 1963, *Letter from a Birmingham Jail*, Stanford University.

Lasn, K. 2000, *Culture Jam: How to Reverse America's Suicidal Consumer Binge - And Why We Must*, HarperCollins, New York.

Lewis, C.S. 1942, *The Weight of Glory*, SPCK, London

Packard, V. 1957, *The Hidden Persuaders*, Penguin Books, Middlesex.

Parkins, I. 2012, *Poiret, Dior and Schiaparelli: Fashion, Femininity and Modernity*, Berg Publishers, Oxford.

Postrel, V. 2013, *The Power of Glamour: Longing and the Art of Visual Persuasion*, Simon & Shuster, New York.

Sadhu, M. 1965, *Theurgy: The Art of Effective Worship*, George Allen & Unwin, London.

Steiner, R. 1981 (1907), *Theosophy of the Rosicrucian*, Rudolf Steiner Press, London.

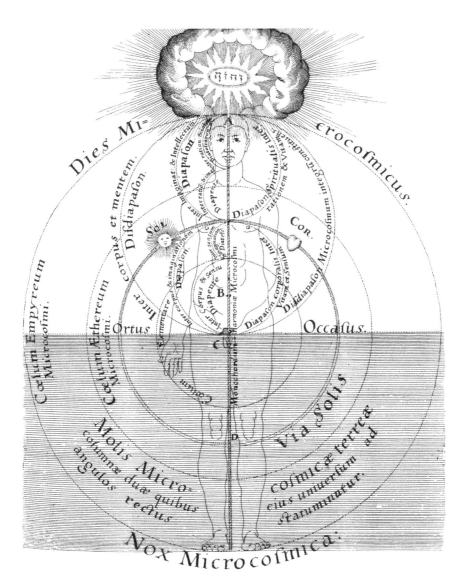

Dies Microcosmicus from *Utriusque cosmi...* by Robert Fludd (1617)

The Great Wheel illustration from *A Vision* by W. B. Yeats (1925)

ON THE NATURE OF TRUTH

"...the fixing of the Volatile, and volatilization of the Fixed."

We hear these words as we Opened in the Grade of Practicus today[1]. They speak of transmutation and remind us of the impermanence of form. The focus of the grade is Alchemy and so, in place of the formal lecture, I want to take a few moments to consider the mechanism of transformation that lies behind this term. More specifically, I want to talk for a few minutes about the nature of Truth.

To begin, we can say that the most recognisable form of Truth are facts. Empirical observations that are objective and finite, that can be replicated and repeated continuously until attaining a trusted status as being intrinsically real. The alchemists of the past were certainly as interested in the facts of natural science as they were more lofty, spiritual ideals. We have modern chemistry, botany and genetics as a result of their empirically-led endeavours.

It's important to acknowledge, though, that while facts are treated as

---

1. This address was presented to the London College of Adepts, SRIA, during my year as Celebrant of the college

inherently true, they are not in and of themselves the totality of Truth. They can be manipulated and filled with errors in methodology that only come to light at a much later date, sometimes decades, centuries or even millennia after being first established. Facts give us a glimmer of Truth bounded by time and material existence, but they are often replaced and updated.

From the facts that we have accumulated over time comes a greater and more substantial part of the human condition, which is *reason*. Reason ties itself to facts and repeatable observations, but it abstracts them into forms of logic and deeper understanding that provide a rich tapestry of thought, intuition and inspiration. Importantly, reason enables us to debate and transform; to give structure to the many different elements of existence and derive ways of thinking beyond the material physicality represented by facts alone. It is thus the source of much invention both philosophical and technological; enabling new forms to emerge based on contemplation, deduction and experimentation.

Of course, reason isn't the only creative force that we have access to. It is the birthplace of invention, but not the wellspring of imagination itself. Our imaginative lives have access to a different relationship with Truth that thrives on the subjective, amorphous nature of the universe. This inner life is communicated through mythology; that poetic medium of storytelling, ritual and prophetic transmission that doesn't require things to be factually correct – nor necessarily adhere to strict notions of logic and reason – but still teaches us how to traverse through life in a meaningful, fulfilling and successful manner. In many ways, Truth is more present in the mythological than it is the factual; because mythology inherently understands the imaginative force behind creation and has a deep appreciation for experiences of transition and transformation central to our shared humanity.

Reason and facts are thus an initial form of communication with Truth – they are beginnings, allowing us to educate and purify ourselves of baseless passions and the folly of ignorant action. Once this relationship is understood, through the study of the Theoricus and embedded within our lives through the work of the Practicus, we move beyond rational thought and material practice toward the mythological, prophetic voice that allows Truth to manifest. These expressions of Truth are timeless and eternal, yet immeasurable because they exist primarily in non-physical forms. Through this path from Facts to Reason to Myth we move from the Physical to the Spiritual Alchemy referred to in our ceremony today and become *'possessed of the Key to the Constitution of Malkuth'*.

Yet, there still seems to be something missing. Ultimately these three manifestations of Truth – facts, reason and myth – are reducible down to human experiences and perception. They bring us towards Truth as experienced by our material forms but, at the same time, aren't able to sum up its entire nature. Perhaps this is because we tend to think of Truth as something fixed and immutable, true or false, when it is something much more dynamic and responsive than that.

The esoteric philosopher Manly Palmer Hall, in his lecture on *The Love of Truth*, stated this poignantly when he said:

> "*Truth is not a word; truth is not a doctrine; truth is not essentially a system or a school, but – as all the ancients realised – truth is a living thing. It is a creature itself. It is something that has its own being. It has its own life and its own death. Its own beginnings and its own ends, and an infinitude beyond our comprehension. Truth is a conscious being...*"[2]

Truth is not merely fact; the sum total of our reason or mythologies; nor is it just another word used to help define the ineffable. Truth is a living thing – a creature itself – a conscious being discrete from human existence. Which means that, if we choose to and know how, we can commune with Truth;. We can work; serve; create in tandem with and in relation to the actions of this being; this Angel of Truth as it interacts with the material world.

Within the Christian context, this concept of Truth as a living, spiritual being brings us to conceptions of the Holy Spirit's role within the Trinity. An active spiritual force that combines, bridges and translates between the infinite power, knowledge and presence of God with the incarnate, sacrificial, painful finiteness of Christ. As Pico della Mirandola stated, humanity is *"the interval between fixed eternity and fleeting time...the marriage song of the world."*[3]

Truth is an entity that connects the timeless with each present moment in time, operating through the nexus of humanity and guiding the actions of those who seek to serve Love and Light above all other instincts and purposes. Importantly, Truth is not flawless or perfect – the relationship that we have with Truth is different to an awe-inspiring dissolution with the Godhead. Truth is not static, but rather an energetic form of dynamic integration with

---

2. Audio recordings of this talk were produced by The Philosophical Research Society, 1989
3. Mirandola, P. 1496, *Oration on the Dignity of Man*

emergent being. It guides us towards the most secret of esoteric experiences, such as alchemical transformation and the Beatific Vision, but is equally to be found communicated universally through aphorisms that bind through time, such as the Golden Rule (*Love Thy Neighbour As Thyself*). Truth is the regenerative force that repairs the decay of material existence by submerging us into the baptismal font of pure creative generation, so we shouldn't seek to 'read' or 'learn" or 'possess' Truth. Rather, we should seek to open ourselves to a communication with the being that is Truth; to become its friend, colleague, lover and companion to use just a few familiar examples of being in relationship with something conscious, beautiful and actively real.

Humanity has the capacity to be the agents of Truth in a universally significant sense, but equally we can find ourselves trapped into the prisms of our own egos. By starting with the rigorous outlooks of reason and natural science, we can then build solid structures of moral philosophy based upon the connectivity that Truth encourages. With such a deepened understanding of the natural world and the responsibilities we owe to one another, we can be guided to higher planes rather than into the broken recesses of our own psyches.

With these genuinely inspirational experiences, held within stable minds and wrapped in virtuous pursuits, we become channels of the prophetic voice that speaks Truth into fixed moments in time. The hope is that this channeling can become more present and common in our lives, as we are guided towards that ultimate dissolution into the boundless perfection from which everything derives:

Faith becomes Knowledge.
Grace consumes Sin.
The Angel of Truth whispers in our ear;
and Eternity is seen through a moment in Time.

My message today is that the practice of Alchemy is an act of friendship with and observance to Truth – the bridge that leads us from the physical, material worlds of reason and empirical facts to the subjective realities of moral virtue, mythological transmission and co-creation with the Divine. By understanding that Truth is a conscious being we can begin to actively collaborate and assist the mechanisms of its manifestations; and in turn Truth itself can benefit from having agents of material existence that are increasingly adept at forging the physical into new and minutely detailed, highly technical forms of creation. This can appear a daunting task if we only have in mind the end result, but the steps of observing and acknowledging empirical facts; of developing our critical thinking; of engaging with the passages and rituals of mythology; working on our own creative and moral virtues; or interacting with that which exists beyond the confines of the material world – these are all achievable with results experienced both immediately and progressively over time.

Alchemy is a language that teaches us how to commune with and create alongside the Angel of Truth. Our duty as Rosicrucians is to learn this language, so that when we meet this being in one of its many forms we know how to recognise its presence and respect its role as messenger of the Divine. To seek companionship, rather than arrogantly deem to control its course.

The path towards the Divine is a long and arduous one, but it is Truth that walks alongside and wants to see us attain to the summits of esoteric experience. For what more is Alchemy than a relationship and communion with Truth?

The Sower, James Tissot (c.1894)

CHRIST AND THE PERENNIAL TRADITION

There are many different people drawn to modern forms of Rosicrucianism, whether that be the Masonic variety or others in the wide umbrella of activity that now exists under the term. As we know, the key element that runs throughout these groups and orders is that they are fundamentally Christian. However, there is undeniably a wider range of traditions, practices and beliefs now present within modern Rosicrucianism then its original purpose and historical context expressed. The extent to which we feel this is appropriate leads to numerous debates on the boundaries of Rosicrucianism and we shouldn't shy away from seeing our tradition as dynamic and evolving, so it is important to try and discern the details of where the core of our tradition might lie.

With this paper I want to explore two specific areas that seem to be increasingly common within Rosicrucian circles and how they relate to the necessity of including a Christian perspective that accepts the role of Christ as the material incarnation of the Godhead and Redeemer of humanity.

The two areas that I want to explore are often conflated and different people use the terms in different ways (some of them highly negative), but for the sake of this paper they will be put forward as:

Traditionalism – the notion that most all religious traditions harken back to a primordial source of ancient Wisdom (that we have, in many areas of modernity, lost contact with);

Universalism – the idea that all religions point towards one ultimate source of Truth, experienced though it may be through many different cultural and psychological lenses around the world, and therefore share a common esoteric understanding at their core.

To simplify what would otherwise be a deeply academic discussion (well beyond my personal capability): the first idea is that there is an ancient source of metaphysical Wisdom that we should try to reconnect with; the second is that all religions inherently have the same teachings and experiences of Truth once you remove their exoteric trappings.

It's important to say from the outset that I do not claim any kind of detailed knowledge of the Perennial Tradition, nor is this paper presented from the perspective of an expert. I am far from either of those things, so my intention today is to present a more intuitive view. Hopefully one that will be helpful in reconciling some of the core theological issues that I believe our Society of Rosicrucians (in its varied forms) faces today. As humanity's level of scientific and academic knowledge, as well as cross-cultural influence, advances, we are reassessing the role and foundations of religion in our lives and social institutions. Esoteric orders such as those found in modern Rosicrucianism are not immune from this evolution of thinking, nor should they be as the historical roots from which they emerge were themselves involved in the kind of broad changes of zeitgeist found throughout Europe at the time; albeit one held within a more strictly Christian perspective. Which is what makes this question about the influence of the Perennial Tradition in modern esotericism an important one to consider, because it is particularly relevant as Rosicrucians that we are comfortable that it can be properly reconciled with Christianity in broad terms and the role of Jesus Christ as Messiah more specifically.

There are three things to explore here to see how they might relate to one another. First, if there is one ancient source tradition then what is its content and form? Secondly, from a metaphysical perspective is it accurate to state that all religions hold essentially the same *esoteric* understandings of the Divine? Finally, can these ideas – often displayed in practice as a kind of pseudo-pluralist approach – be fully reconciled within a form of esoteric

Christianity? I'm sure that many other questions will arise in our discussion also and I'm keen to hear how everyone else might approach the topic.

What is the Perennial Tradition?

The concept of the Perennial Tradition really emerges in response to the conflicts seen in modernity between different exoteric forms of religion, with a call to reassert their esoteric purpose beyond the political machinery that many religions in large part represent. There is also a deep criticism of the growing secular individualism of the 20th century, with Rene Guenon as the most prominent figure in forming this line of thinking; and it is his work that others, such as Frithjof Schuon, Mircea Eliade and Joseph Campbell seem to be strongly influenced by as the idea eventually emerges out of mystical circles and into the social sciences[1]. An important element in this line of thought is that our knowledge traditions have lost contact with the spiritual methods required to respectfully assimilate them into the cosmos, causing a great deal of violence and upheaval that finds root in a growing sense of individualism.

There's a lot of discussion about what the perennial tradition, or wisdom, might consist of – but a few of the elements that are put forward will be familiar to all of us. There is a clear conception of the importance of spiritual over temporal, that the divine realms are to be considered to have power over material existence (hence a fundamental issue with individualism). This is coupled with a deep sense of primordial perfection that preceded a kind of cataclysmic, human-driven Fall from Grace that requires a redemptive Path of Return (often based on slowly revealed knowledge and experience through initiation). The point of this Return being to enable humanity to reintegrate with the cosmic order and restore a proper relationship with the Divine. Death and Resurrection feature strongly, as do the practices of invoking the name/s of God and becoming the embodiment of the conjunction of God and humanity writ in material form – often through a form of *theosis* and experiential Divine Union.

Interestingly, Guenon argues that one of the key symbols of this

---

1. We also need to acknowledge Julius Evola, whose thoughts on Traditionalism have become influential in far-right circles today and brought about a highly negative form of spiritually-justified supremicism; similar to those we've seen in the recent past to destructive and violent result. Suffice to say, this is certainly not the kind explored in this paper, although it exists within its sphere and needs to be recognised for its corrupting influence today

primordial tradition is the sign of the cross – which he related to Abrahamic traditions, Hinduism and Taoism among others – and its representation of the 'Universal Man' with the focal point of equilibrium in space/time, spirit and matter, lying at the centre of all traditions. This leads to the notion that humankind has control over its own destiny; which Mircea Eliade outlines in his book *The Forge and the Crucible,* arguing that the alchemical tradition *"prolongs and consummates a very old dream of homo faber [Man the Maker]: collaboration in the perfecting of matter while at the same time securing perfection for himself."*[2]

One of the interesting elements of the Perennial Tradition therefore, seen in avenues such as Gnosticism, is that it moves beyond a sense of submissive Faith and toward an active confidence in Knowledge and Experience of the Godhead. One does not have to just state that *'I Believe'*, but rather the goal is to confidently assert that *'I Know'*. That one has been transformed through direct experience of Grace and dissolution into Divine Love and will now act upon it. This seems to run contrary to a number of points in Christian scripture that highlight the importance and humility of Faith as an act of willful submission, but this kind of Knowledge does link closely to the layers of understanding found in many ancient initiatory traditions. Within the modern context, it can be seen as an attempt to re-tether the collective academic and scientific efforts of humanity to a sacred core that guides direction rather than randomly marching forward into an unknown future.

What is Universalism?

Closely related to the concept of a root tradition, lost to 'time immemorial' but vital to rediscover, is the Universalist approach that seeks to validate all religious traditions as essentially equal because they all relate to the one, universal Absolute. Every culture and time-period will see different forms emerge out of changing contexts, but all are legitimate ways of interacting with something that is, ultimately, beyond human conception. In addition to this, there is an inherent commonality of religious experience in the shared physiology and psychological foundations of the human condition. We all share the same material form, within the same universe, and thus all religious experiences are inherently going to trend towards the same thing. Joseph Campbell is perhaps the most influential in this approach, with his

---

2. Eliade, M. 1978, *The Forge and the Crucible*, Chicago Press, p169

widely quoted view that *'all religions are true but none are literal'*. However, Universalism often goes further by stating that the inner core of the world's religions are all unified in their teachings; and that the external trappings of ritual and institutions are cultural and political conveniences that begin to dissolve as one gets closer to their esoteric centre.

The Universalist perspective makes good theoretical sense, appealing to our desire to be inclusive and egalitarian, however in practice it is also recognised within Perennialism that not everything self-identifying as religious in nature is of equal standing or authenticity. We only need to think of the damaging environments that religious cults are guilty of fostering (plenty of them under the banner of esoteric traditions, even Rosicrucianism) to see numerous examples where the Universalist urge to inclusivity should only go so far. At some point a judgment call needs to be made in order to identify authentic versus misguided, or outright fraudulent and abusive, forms of religious practice – the boundaries of this judgement being amorphous, because it is so heavily dependent on context. This doesn't mean that we should abandon the idea of universal Truth, and indeed any concept of an absolute Godhead ultimately relies upon such an understanding, but it does mean that we should be discerning and not afraid to call out or stand against destructive or unproductive forms of spirituality that exist upon a vast spectrum of human experience and expression. More generally, authenticity was a great and challenging concern of the likes of Guenon and others.

It's also important to consider that there are significant theological differences to be found throughout the world's religions, not least of which in the different conceptions of the Divine to be found in monotheistic, dualist and polytheistic viewpoints. The Universalist perspective draws everything back to a single, unified conception of the Absolute, which is not necessarily the case, particularly in polytheistic theologies but also with the opposing deities outlined by Dualism, and therefore stops us from accepting the idea being as self-evident as it might at first seem. Although it is true that many polytheistic religions often revert back to an Absolute source, it is not always the case. Many modern polytheistic religions, for example neopagan traditions and some forms of Hinduism, define themselves as contrary to the other forms of 'soft polytheism' that reduce their theology to an ultimate unified source. So, although it seems self-evident to say that we are all experiencing the same reality, through the same biology, and therefore there must be some objective universality to authentic religious experience, there are often striking differences in theology between different traditions as to what this objective reality truly entails. In numerous cases, reality is seen as separate and distinct from the Divine and so defining any particular elements as being universal begins to appear overly reductionist. It's entirely possible, for example, that different religions are accessing different gods that emerge from entirely different multiverses in competition for human attention and worship. I'm not sure that's something any widely practiced traditions believe – sounding more like something cooked up in the depths of an uncaring Lovecraftian cosmos – but we have to at least acknowledge the possibility of distinctly separated theological foundations, even if this made-up example might be an extreme one.

But I digress… Beyond theological differences, there is also an important tension to acknowledge between Traditionalist, Universalist and Christian perspectives in regards to the authenticity of different religious traditions. What authenticity even means depends on the perspective that you take here. Traditionalists would see authenticity as relating to how closely something is connected to and reflects the original primordial tradition, found through experiential knowledge. Universalists work on the connection with the Absolute (itself a difficult thing to define) from which all authentic religious experience derives (Frithjof Schuon states this simply as *"God is in the truth of every truth"*[3]). While the Christian perspective upholds that authenticity comes through a participation in the Sacraments, that assign and embody the path of salvation and symbolise our acceptance of redemption and Christ's physical role as Messiah. These are all interrelated and share many points of contact, both historically and experientially, but they are not identical and so require further consideration before holding them all together in unison.

Reconciling with Esoteric Christianity

One of the ways to begin reconciling this from an esoteric Christian perspective is to take the understanding that a universalist approach should be seen as more about the act of Christ's redemption and how that applies to all humanity – regardless of culture or belief. This helps to answer the criticism that salvation should not be dependent on where one was born and therefore on geographical access to Christianity as an organised religion. The alternative, that salvation depends on receiving the knowledge of Christ's redemption – meaning that the Holy Spirit for mysterious reasons bypasses billions of people – is a callous approach lacking the Mercy and

---

3. Cutsinger, J. 2004, *The Fullness of God: Frithjof Schuon on Christianity*, World Wisdom Inc, p49

Grace we might expect from a benevolent God. Importantly, the distinction between universal redemption and the ability to consciously choose to walk the path of salvation provided by this redemption (which could theoretically manifest through different internal and vocational forms) still highlights the importance of free will and the path of righteousness. As Schuon goes on to state:

> "The possibility of our return to God – wherein are different degrees – is universal and timeless; it is inscribed in the very nature of our existence and our intelligence; our powerlessness can only be accidental, not essential."[4]

When considering how Christ can be reconciled with these viewpoints, it seems clear that the more institutional forms of Christianity become too constrictive. Many dogmatic understandings of Christian theology and practice readily exclude other traditions as inauthentic, based solely on non-participation in accepting Christ as Messiah (or even more granular examples of belief). There are plenty of Rosicrucians who are quite happy to take this more exclusionary approach, with arguments to consider this as necessary (*Jesus Mihi Omnia*), but in practice it seems that most fratres and sorors at home within Rosicrucianism today are doing so under a more esoteric approach to Christianity that incorporates a universal understanding of redemption and accepts the wide range of paths to salvation. It is important to see a strong link and bond with Christianity as vital to the Rosicrucian tradition, however it is also inherently true that an ecumenical and non-dogmatic approach (often found in many forms of esoteric Christianity) goes back to the original manifestos and their position in the Christian landscape of Europe at the time. Frances Yates outlines this in her pivotal history of the movement, when she states that:

> "The common basis [in Rosicrucian thinking] would be a common Christianity, interpreted mystically, and a philosophy of nature which sought the divine meaning of the hieroglyphic characters written by God in the universe, and interpreted microcosm and macrocosm through mathematical-magical systems of universal harmony."[5]

---

4. Ibid. p66
5. Yates, F. 1972 (2007), *The Rosicrucian Enlightenment*, Routledge, p134-135

We can therefore state that by working with an esoteric interpretation of Jesus Christ as manifested in more mystical and personal ways, in particular a communication and reintegration with the Christ Within, there emerges an understanding of the macro/microcosmic act of universal harmony; redemption from sin; and access to eternal salvation. This links with Perennial Wisdom through the mystical conception of the Trinity, which is available to be experienced and known (rather than just believed) via the ecstatic illumination of the Beatific Vision; understood as the culminating experience of the path to salvation and our Return from the Fall.

Similar to the Perennial Tradition, esoteric Christianity recognises that the Beatific Vision can be obtained in this life and is the fundamental goal of spiritual pursuits. Our efforts should be channelled into an active process that is not just understood intellectually, or believed solely through the strength of Faith, but can be received experientially through Grace and direct contact with the infinite presence and illumination of God. An experience that occurs via a loving relationship with the resurrected Christ Within; guided by the still Truth of the Holy Spirit that lies at the central Rose of the Cross. This is not just a mechanical process, a recipe of steps that can be followed while ignoring the context of the world around us. Practice and prayer must be combined with the actions of moral virtue and Love, remembering, as Charles Williams states, that:

> "[Our] acts are only from the fullness of the treasury of the all-meritorious love of God...[but] no one and nothing can produce them except you; unless you do, they will be everlastingly and eternally lost… all the sacraments are communications of love to all – through you."[6]

By consciously combining these strands of Faith and Works we create the environment necessary to realise Heaven on Earth. Not just within the cosmic focal point of Christ born, but in the eternal manifestation of reintegrating material existence into the divine conception of Creation – the collaboration in the perfecting of matter that Eliade references. This is the central truth found in the sacrament of the Eucharist that embodies the Trinity in form and function: invoking the name of God; reconciling ourselves with the body of Christ; and filling participants with the blood and inspiration of the Holy Spirit. Importantly, Christ is the turning point

---

6. Williams, C. 1939, *The Descent of the Dove*, Longmans, Green & Co, p169

where perennial truths of Divine Wisdom become manifest throughout all of humanity. Not just reserved for single priests in the Holy of Holies or initiates who have access to secret teachings, but weaved throughout the fabric of human existence to become available to all who genuinely seek salvation – and providing redemption even to those who don't.

In this way, we can consider Christ as the antithesis of the idea that the spiritual always has power over the temporal – because it is through Christ that the Divine sublimates its own omnipotence in order to fully, utterly and entirely become flesh. The reconciliation, or reintegration, through Christ that takes place is therefore not just the linking of humanity to the Divine, but simultaneously of the Divine to humanity – *As Below, So Above; As Above, So Below* – in a cohabitation and shared experience that speaks irrevocably of the participation of the Creator within Creation. As Christ, the Divine viscerally feels the restrictions and corrupted forms of the material sphere; detached from the omnipotence and power of the Godhead but aware fully of the gap now experienced between God and humankind that comes as a result of the Fall. Through the suffering and sacrifice of Jesus Christ this gap is bridged and the mystical formulation at the heart of all Creation is restored – not just for one or a select few, but for all humanity; eternally.

This brings us closer to the Perennial Tradition in esoteric form, while accepting Christ as the pinnacle of the primordial tradition's expression in recent cosmic history (the perfect form). It also facilitates breaking down boundaries between Christian denominations and other traditions in order to allow a more harmonious vision of religious peace and mystical dynamism that the Universalist viewpoint strives for.

Having said all of this – and acknowledging the shared experience of the human condition – we still need to return to the idea that Christ cannot be completely reconciled with the Perennial Tradition, which in many ways can undermine the act of Divine Incarnation by mythologising it down to a form of archetypal human psychology. As Rosicrucians, there is a moment of commitment that arises to recognise the reality of Christ as Messiah in both material and metaphysical form. This does not mean accepting a particular institutional form of Christianity, but we do acknowledge our personal commitment to the universal application of redemption that Christ embodies and releases throughout time at the point of the supreme sacrifice – at the point of God's death as a human, at the hands of humanity, and yet entirely for humankind.

As an esoteric form of Christianity we cannot, therefore, inherently be a pluralist organisation (as the Universalist perspective encourages) because the role of Christ's relationship to humanity needs to be recognised. For many, the rigid structures of institutional churches run contrary to Christ as a direct incarnation of the Divine; requiring no structure and inherently surpassing the established Law. Yet it is this same context of Holy Law, with its ceremonial focal points, that foreshadows and allows the Incarnation to be recognised for what it is. Infinite to finite; cosmic to atomic; Christ is the meeting point of reality where divine consciousness bursts forth, restricting itself in order to fully enable the regeneration of its formative force and imaginative ability to Create.

By acknowledging that divine incarnation exists outside the realms of dogma and institutional power – as it absolutely must by definition and humble deference to the Almighty – we unravel the corrupting influences of human deceit in order to restore direct access to the Divine through the reincarnated Christ Within. This is the powerful message found in Rosicrucianism (and radicalism of Christianity in its most pure form), but it requires the acknowledgement of each person drawn into the particular sphere of practice that we have inherited.

Thus the nature of Christ dovetails (pun intended), through the influence of the Holy Spirit, with the perspectives taken by those who argue for the importance of the Perennial Tradition. However, it requires a more forthright adherence to make it tangible. For the most part these ideas can be seen in harmony, but ultimately they are also not entirely possible to reconcile without risk of losing important elements of the esoteric truths of Christ's Sacrifice and the Redemption of Humanity as a fixed moment in time that echoes throughout eternity – both before and after the act.

Because it is within the act of Incarnation itself that everything else of importance resides.

Illustration from the alchemical text *Thesaurus thesaurorum et secretum...* (c.1725)
used under CC 4.0 license, provided by Wellcome Trust

Illustration from *Coronatio Naturae* (c.1600)
by permission of University of Glasgow Archives & Special Collections, MS Ferguson 208

PART III:

FINDING VOCATION

WRITINGS FOR ST PAUL'S INSTITUTE (2010 - 2017)

The articles in this section were written during my time as Manager of St Paul's Institute (2010-2017), a think tank run at St Paul's Cathedral, London, from 2002-2020 that focused on ethics and social reform. Mostly released as columnist-style pieces online, a few were also written as addresses for events both public and private.

Written at the same time as the esoteric papers included in Part II of this book, they show the relationship between the esoteric and exoteric life of a Rosicrucian in the 21st century. This was my personal form of social engagement and you can see how my own esoteric experiences were emerging as thought pieces for public consumption, with increasing convergence. You can also see throughout a desire to integrate our personal and professional lives, something that I was still coming to terms with; being for the most part 'sub rosa' during my period of working for the Church of England.

The themes outlined are still of central importance to the challenges that our world faces. In a small way, these pieces contain elements of a new utopian vision. Something we certainly need more of today...

TO BETTER THE BOARDROOM, WE MUST BETTER OURSELVES

It has almost become a cliché these days – ethics. Ever since the financial crisis people have been throwing around the term (and others such as values, integrity, sustainability) like rice at a wedding. 'Corporate Ethics' is the catchphrase on everyone's lips at the moment.

This is partly because we have been forced to discuss it. Through scathing media attacks on bankers' bonuses and ethically questionable dealings; to simple, practical little things such as losing billions of dollars – the corporate and financial sectors were suddenly pressed to become much more aware of the 'common good'. Such an approach is often touted as a way to improve success and help lift us all out of the quagmire, particularly in these difficult times when consumer and public opinion is so fragile and centrally influential.

Managers at all levels are being asked to instil corporate values and ethics 'from the top down'. Assessments should contain an examination of how well employees are meeting a specific Code of Conduct; corporations should consider investing more openly in philanthropic programmes; sustainability initiatives should be put into place. These are but a few of the varied and direct references to 'corporate ethics' that are being made here in the City of London.

To the less sceptical, all of this can only be a good thing. We're moving in the right direction if managing directors and CEOs are considering such things, surely? In many ways, that is correct. It's better that terms such as 'values' and 'ethics' are bandied around with real worth attached to them than the alternative ghost-town of social responsibility that led us directly into this mess.

The question we must be asking, though, is whether or not this approach is the most effective one; the one that allows us to evolve most quickly in the direction that we need to develop in. In other words, how much truth is there behind the sentiment – how deep does the feeling of compassion really go?

One problem is that this new focus often removes personal responsibility from the equation. The discussions are not about 'my ethics' – they are about 'corporate ethics'. The language used continues to build up the corporation as an entity in its own right, one that can have its own internal values and compassion. And yet, all corporations are made up of individuals – all actions and movements made in a businesses' name are conducted by people. Without people, there is nothing real behind the corporate facade.

It sounds obvious, and indeed it is, but the global economy is also made up of individual people. Each transaction has a reality behind it that exists well beyond the numbers on paper; beyond the bottom line for an amorphous group of 'shareholders'. Corporate ethics means individual ethics – or at least that's what we should be talking about in addition to the current discussions surrounding regulations, tax plans and corporate responsibility.

We should be discussing not merely corporate improvements; social improvements; or regulatory improvements – but personal improvements. This is the foundation that we must build upon. The whole might be greater than the sum of its parts, but its entire basis is dependent on the nature of those parts. *To better the boardroom, we must better ourselves.*

Perhaps a practical example might help bring all of this out of the lofty clouds of idealism. A few weeks ago I attended a lecture conducted by a high-level director of one of the largest corporations in the world, talking specifically about ethical values in business. There were a number of panel members responding to the initial lecture and one of them, another leader of a large multi-national, proclaimed proudly that this year – for the first time – his company would be specifically assessing how closely individual employees met the corporate Code of Conduct. The room as a whole seemed to think it was a great idea and a wonderful way to build ethics into the fabric of any corporate structure (judging by the number of nodding heads). I wasn't so impressed.

Assessing our professional behaviour purely through such means takes us down a path that, ironically, removes personal accountability – replacing responsibility of action instead onto 'the Code'. If it's alright by the Code, it must be proper and ethical. Keep in mind that, for the most part, these codes are not of the spiritual variety. These aren't 'love thy neighbour' aphorisms. They are often made up of statements such as 'strictly adhere to Intellectual Property rights' or 'be transparent and honest in reporting your financial figures'. These are corporate Codes of Conduct, after-all.

One could easily adhere to such a code and still make decisions that are fundamentally damaging to a large number of people in our wider, global society. You could pass with flying colours your assessment and yet still have sold out a large portion of agricultural land, that services many thousands of people, to be demolished in the search for precious minerals (possibly a trite example, but one that has and does occur nonetheless).

It's not that the increased, and seemingly sustained, focus on ethical and moral matters within the corporate sector is not encouraging or beneficial. It's surely better than nothing at all. It's also a very good idea that corporations have Codes of Conduct; and that financial regulators and overseers exist and are given some degree of authority. The creation of a culture of ethics within large organisations and governments is something that should definitely be applauded and encouraged.

However, we must question whether such actions alone are the most efficient and effective way to bring about the change that we desire. Some also even need to ask whether they truly desire such change, or are merely paying lip-service to it in the hope of later circumventing any rules or regulations put into place.

For if it truly is change that we want, change on a global economic level, then we must also focus some of our efforts upon the individual. We must make a call for each of us to progress ideologically and spiritually, so that when the time comes to make decisions with ethical consequences we have the best tool for the job: a true and developed moral compass.

We must move away from merely looking externally for corporate ethics; away from shedding our personal responsibility in favour of blaming group ideology. Each of us has to make decisions every single day of our lives that have ethical and moral consequences – and each of us can strive to improve how we make those decisions.

We must ask ourselves, on a regular basis, what we have done that has had an impact – however small or seemingly insignificant – and whether or not our actions were ethical or could have been improved upon.

For it is only when we begin to answer that introspection truthfully, and consciously act upon that answer, that the corporate and financial world really will begin to change for the better.

A TALE OF TWO OCCUPIES

With the eviction of the Occupy camp outside of St Paul's, I thought it would be useful to put forward some reflections on my experience of the last few months. It's worth noting from the outset that this is not an official response to the Cathedral's engagement with the recent protests, but represents some thoughts that I hope might be useful when contemplating recent events.

October 15ᵗʰ 2011 represented a moment in time marked globally, inspired by the Occupy Wall Street protests that had occurred a month earlier. This new movement identified itself with the surge of popular unrest throughout the Middle East and parts of Europe, highlighting that even in the seemingly most comfortable and democratic of societies there were deep grievances that needed to be addressed. It is undeniable that, both as a global and local movement, Occupy has helped keep the focus firmly on questions of economic justice in recent months; displaying a tangible manifestation of the growing public mandate to deal with issues of social equality. In addition, the overall peaceful and dialogue-based nature of the protest is to be highly commended when we consider the outbursts of anger and violence that marked the student protests of 2010 and the London riots of 2011.

The often chaotic nature of the relationship between the camp and St

Paul's Cathedral has been well – if not always accurately – documented and there continue to be voices of opinion that seek to place blame at the feet of one group or another. It is no surprise that the Cathedral and the wider Church have come under scrutiny; the questions put forward are valid ones worthy of deep contemplation and thoughtful response. This article is not going to cover many of those challenges, but one of the questions that I have faced both personally and professionally is how can the social and economic justice work of St Paul's Institute be reconciled with a perceived 'betrayal' of the Occupy encampment? In the wake of our Director's resignation over this issue, surely the two are not mutually exclusive. Aren't our actions a sign of institutional hypocrisy, or at the very least narrow-mindedness?

In articulating a response to this particular question, I am immediately drawn to one of the lessons personally learned throughout this period. When reading articles and speaking with people across the pro/anti-Occupy spectrum it was clear that all of us were relating to a projected form of Occupy, often based on preconceived ideas and informed by varying levels of engagement with the movement throughout the UK and abroad. The more vehement anti-Occupy views could often be readily dismissed as not recognising the genuine depth of thought and inspiring passion that many of the protestors embodied. To claim that the movement was made up merely of 'the Great Unwashed'; junkies; benefit scroungers; and middle class dilettantes is a lazy analysis that says more of the person speaking than it ever does of the Occupy movement itself.

Equally so, but in a different way, the more utopian visions of many pro-Occupy commentators were often in denial – or not aware – of aspects that were failing to live up to the lofty ideals of the movement. For one, there are some real issues with the model of direct democracy that Occupy has experimented with. A process that, although on paper uncomplicated and inclusive, has proven difficult to maintain consistency with and has developed barriers for entry that are not immediately apparent but are contributing to the apathy that the wider public has increasingly presented. Ultimately, on either end of this for/against divide, we see people's egos playing out the narrative that they are emotionally most invested in. Identity is formed in great part through how we articulate our relationship to other human beings and Occupy is one of the more acute examples of this that we have playing out in public consciousness in the UK today.

Through this process, we come to have what can be seen as 'A Tale of Two Occupies' – our projected vision versus the dynamic reality. Some of the most introspectively critical pieces on Occupy come from people closely involved themselves, who have more of an understanding of where the movement might need care and attention. Here we see people trying to reconcile their personal ideal with the pragmatic reality in an attempt to bring the two closer together; and the issues being faced are similar regardless of geographical location. Others seek to focus on the shortfalls of external bodies that interface directly with the identity formation of Occupy: be it the Church, State, City or Media. There are also a number of critical pieces emerging out of the ranks of the Church itself, displaying the same attempt to reconcile apparently disparate positions. Some of the varied grievances on all sides are entirely valid; others based on various levels of misinformation; others still are overstated or overlook the high degree of nuance and compromise that makes up human interaction and decision-making.

One thing that is common amongst all of us is that we tend to relate to Occupy as an allegory that plays out our own particular views, focusing intently on aspects that reinforce our beliefs and either overlooking or dismissing the importance of other factors that play just as valid a part. Clarity often exists in the unclaimed areas between different viewpoints, so the hard part is being able to adjust our own perception of things by openly listening to and empathising with opposing positions.

'*We are the 99%!*' is one of the greatest slogans of empowerment in living memory. It allows everybody to feel like they belong to the movement, that they can claim some form of ownership of it and be motivated into action. However, as inspiring a device as it is, it sets up a remarkably difficult vision of inclusivity to follow through with under a single banner. This is an issue that, despite a great deal of hard work and good intentions, is proving contentious as general assemblies around the globe struggle to define behavioural boundaries and have even more difficulty in enforcing them. Related to this, many people are finding it hard to identify themselves with Occupy as, although there are no stated barriers for entry, human nature itself and the way we formulate our personal identity and social groups ensures that barriers arise nonetheless. Affinity groups form around both personal and professional lines and often play off of one another, perceiving the detrimental aspects of others without examining closely where their own actions might fall short.

What is important now, in this period of reflection for us all, is to try and recognise the role that we each played in creating these barriers and implicitly – if often unconsciously – enforcing them. One of the most alluring aspects of the 99% slogan is the sense that genuine, positive change is coming and the popular masses will soon stand together. But, for now at least, the masses have yet to arrive and we often see ourselves in opposition. We must consider carefully why this is the case. Not just under the umbrella of Occupy, but for the universal message of justice and wellbeing that has long been championed by countless organisations and movements.

When I hear the accusations placed against St Paul's Cathedral and the wider Church for failing to properly embrace Occupy, I am struck that these accusations immediately presume that to not wholeheartedly embrace an amorphous movement is equivalent to ignoring an agenda of social and economic justice in general. From the local perspective of St Paul's, departments that focus specifically on justice issues have been ongoing in various incarnations for over a decade and have succeeded in facilitating important and penetrating dialogue, debate and action across all levels of society. The relevance is not lost when I consider that in 2009 we hosted Gordon Brown and Kevin Rudd, both active Prime Ministers at the time, who openly promoted to a full cathedral the need for a more moral and virtuous form of capitalism that served the people rather than exploited them. The arrival of the Occupy London camp rightly brought home the point that words are cheap and that nowhere near enough progress has been made over the last few years toward the practical, systemic changes necessary to right the balance between people and markets. But beyond these systemic issues, we should not be too quick to overlook the fact that the infrastructure of the Church has proven time and again its ability to mobilise large numbers of people to bring about measurable change. We need only look to the involvement of the cathedral and church coalitions in Fairtrade; the Living Wage; microfinance; climate change and ethical investment to name but a few key examples where the Church has been at the forefront of innovation and engagement with justice issues of paramount importance.

This is not to say that we cannot renew our efforts and improve upon them, as this is always the case. However, when much of the current rhetoric begins from a standpoint of antagonism it not only overlooks the truly impacting work already done, but also creates an air of hostility that could hamper future collaborations at a time when widespread cooperation is needed most. There might have been an opportunity lost in how the camp at St Paul's played out, but if so it was one lost by all parties involved and not only through the actions of the Cathedral. In more ways than one, the physical gravitas of Occupy was both its greatest strength and its most difficult challenge. The encampments (and subsequent squatted buildings) became a primary agenda and topic of discussion in and of themselves. They were an important safety net for some; an inspiring community-building exercise for others; a free educational facility that embraced alternative views; or an ineffective self-indulgence in the eyes of detractors. After a period of time, however, the inward-looking nature of the tactic was one that started to draw away from the inclusive, participatory democracy that created the initial spark of energy in favour of increasingly closed circles and divisive group mentalities that made true engagement difficult.

For all the faults we could see in one another (and ourselves), we should never take our eyes off the fact that we all desire to head in the same direction. Since the financial crisis of 2008, there are a growing number of people who agree that an evolution of the very foundations of society is required to overcome the challenges of coming years. Our own *Value and Values* report showed that this sentiment is held even within the financial sector itself – a sector that quite clearly has a great deal of penitence required, to say the least. Structural changes to our financial systems are occurring, while corporate social responsibility and philanthropic efforts continue to improve and have real effect; as they must do if we are to see progress towards a more unified and compassionate society.

When discussing how we move forward, grievances toward perceived enemies of the common good certainly need to be voiced and addressed, but it is ultimately not productive to presume that there exist evil caricatures that can be conclusively identified and eradicated. A position of ongoing, positive and dynamic collaboration that includes all members of our global society must form the basis of our call for change. The difficulty lies ultimately in agreeing upon what change looks like; what practical steps are required; who might have to make sacrifices for the greater good of others; where and how authority is created; and how we are collectively going to bring it all together. It is the transition from one form of existence to another that often proves the most disruptive and we are clearly in a transitional period. This will require compromise; it will require a position of openness to different driving motivations and ideas; and it will require the humbling process of self-improvement as opposed to the comforting embrace of judgement. It demands that we see past differences in action and opinion and move the message into the heart of our collective being, with the understanding that, while facing in the same direction, it is by walking different paths that we strengthen rather than weaken our overall position.

There are important lessons to be learned in how the Cathedral approached the Occupy movement, but I do not have too much difficulty with the seeming contradictions; because in the end there was an honest attempt at trying to come together in reconciliation based upon common principles. In my extended interactions with many people in both the camp and cathedral, I can sincerely state that the level of resolve and commitment to finding a productive and positive outcome that worked for the greater good of society was displayed in almost everybody I came across. The fact that compromises in key areas were not obtained is a fault less of the people involved and more of the paradigms that we are all subsumed by when going about our daily existence, for it is often difficult to see beyond our personal vision and accept that everybody around us is equally transfixed on their own version of the way things should be.

Looking forward, I am enthused by the knowledge that efforts in addressing the pressing issues of our time will continue to take place at St Paul's Cathedral. That we take seriously the desire to improve and continuously adapt in order to achieve the greatest impact and reach the widest audience possible. Occupy as a movement has already begun to evolve and learn from the lessons of its embryonic period, having been energised by the watershed moment that they embodied, and I look forward to seeing their continued efforts take form over the coming months. In a wider sense, what I find most heartening is the knowledge that countless organisations and initiatives have been emboldened by recent events and will continue the honourable work that has always been done and has brought us to this point. A comprehensive shift toward social and economic justice cannot occur under a single banner, so it will be our diversity acting in parallel with one another that produces lasting results.

It would be a great shame if this time of authentic, ongoing engagement with justice and virtue over the entire cross-spectrum of society is overshadowed by calls for judgement and blame. Down that path lies a whole host of unnecessary conflict that, in the end, will only detract from the core message of justice that we wish to promote. Instead, we must embrace this moment of reflection and renew our appreciation for each other's respective and continued efforts; despite the fact that mistakes might be made along the way. By doing so we remind ourselves that, although our decisions are often motivated by different concerns and responsibilities, we are increasingly facing the same direction across all sectors of society in an attempt to formulate and contribute to the common good.

THE CHURCH AND CAPITALISM: BUILDING FOR SYSTEMIC CHANGE

Recent experiences with the Occupy encampment were outside of our usual comfort zones and ways of operating, representing a different process for formulating a social justice campaign than most were used to. The reality of what was occurring during recent months is incredibly complex and nuanced, but if nothing else it is one that forces us to articulate a response that encapsulates the current socioeconomic context with an updated view of grassroots mobilisation and citizenship.

There are many who feel it is the obligation of faith-based institutions to fully support the popular call for justice that Occupy represented, but in order to do so we must clearly and carefully articulate the manner in which grassroots movements can interface with more traditional structures for change. It is a call that must be heeded, but it is not one that can be taken flippantly or without a proper sense of the responsibility that arises once a course of action is decided upon. What I wanted to discuss with you today was how our Church institutions and related organisations can help people come to terms with some of the anxieties that we are all facing, while actively formulating the new structural paradigms that are required in a manner that is relevant, effective and sustainable.

Among many other things, the 2008 financial crisis has been portrayed as a breakdown of the sense-making narratives that lie at the heart of modernity and, for many, our construction of personal identity. The Occupy movement is the manifestation of a response to this breakdown, so I wanted to begin by examining the fundamental aspects of the movement that are relevant to the way that we as people of faith, belonging to wide-reaching institutions, might seek to respond to this latest call for justice and equality.

If we were to examine the media portrayal, these recent protests are seen as a struggle between rich and poor – the primary issue being one of wealth disparity and the dominant narrative of neoliberal capitalism. Although a fair representation of the motivations of many drawn to Occupy, it should be recognised that these grievances are ultimately referring to a much deeper social issue: which is the distribution of power and the creation of authority. It's important to understand Occupy as an experiment in participatory democracy, rather than merely an anti-capitalist movement with set agendas. An often heard criticism is that the protestors didn't have a clear set of demands that were easily definable, nor did they offer solutions to the ones they did raise. Although valid concerns, it is more valuable to focus on the attempt to set up a process through which society could create consensus-based agendas as opposed to dictating what those agendas would be from the outset and rallying support around them as other organisations do. It is arguable whether or not this initial ethos was observed as things developed, but it is certainly because of this democratic process that Occupy comes across as something unique – and it was this inclusive aspect that drew people to it and created such a sense of passion around its initial stages.

In a pure, ideological sense Occupy is about participation instigated through the concept of general assemblies and the communal authority that they represent. These people's assemblies are an attempt at consensus decision-making that seeks to provide equal footing to all voices involved, regardless of political or financial clout. When they work well, they are empowering things to witness and take part in. The collectivist mentality can allow for outcomes that are far greater than the sum of its parts; and the ability for strangers to come together to discuss deep-seated issues is an avenue of discourse that we have lost in many areas of modern society. The lack of these avenues promotes social disconnection and disenfranchisement, which lead to the sense of betrayal and distrust that many individuals attracted to Occupy feel. It is for this reason that no matter what we might think about the Occupy movement and its effectiveness, we have to take its existence seriously because it is an indication of underlying issues in our social frameworks that *must* be properly addressed rather than rhetorically side-stepped. We must take it seriously, not least of which because it is this disenfranchisement that culminated in the collapse of the social contract witnessed in the devastation of the London riots last year. We cannot allow ourselves to be comforted by dismissing such behaviour as resulting merely from the 'thuggish', 'criminal' or 'lower class' of society and relying upon imprisonment – for to do so causes these problems to become further embedded in our local communities, rather than attempting to navigate away from them. In order to overcome this growing sense of disenfranchisement, we must seek to recreate a sense of participation in society and a feeling of personal investment in the resulting outcomes.

While pursuing this goal, we must also bear in mind the many pitfalls that result from being overly emotive and oppositional – as is often the case in the high-energy environment of a protest movement. We must be careful not to forego civil liberties in the pursuit of an imagined utopia, nor alternatively strive to break down social structures that have proven to be effective means of distributing goods and services to those who need or desire them. In other words, we must temper our idealism with pragmatism; set attainable goals and strategies for achieving them; enter into conversations that have at their core a structure for transformation, rather than merely a platform for disapproval; and engage in a proactive, systemic change that enables us to overcome the challenges of coming years without oppressing or alienating large cross-sections of the population.

So the question becomes: *how can we play our part in achieving this?* The response must be that we further integrate the highly successful and wide-ranging programmes that are already in place and continue to expand the message of social and economic integrity that they champion. Although the events of recent months have provided a catalyst for renewed effort, we mustn't lose sight of the fact that any viable solution requires long-term strategies that work upon iterative thinking. Now is not the time to drastically change course in the hopes that by doing so we will come across some miraculous panacea that will solve the challenges we face. At this stage we must not be afraid of passionate response, but it's also of vital importance to craft well-planned efforts that move beyond emotive patterns and into sustainable, practical implementations.

I would suggest in brief three aspects of our work as faith-based institutions that can assist greatly in this process. First, we must raise the economic literacy of clergy and other church-based positions. Second, we should examine our church infrastructure and renew our appreciation for how it can bring about widespread systemic change. Finally, we must strengthen both local and global collaboration and cohesion in order to ensure that we act together where necessary and use our collective weight to overcome barriers that are otherwise insurmountable. These three overarching aspects do not dictate what changes must occur, but instead focus on the structures needed to achieve change. In most regards, we already have them ready and available; so what is required now is to focus our efforts to ensuring that they act in tandem towards the righteous and ecumenical goals that we seek.

To begin with, raising the economic literacy of clergy should be considered a top priority. They must be able to respond to questions from parishioners and also to challenges put forward by those who think the Church – in a broad sense – should not have anything to say about finance, business or economics. We must articulate and build the bridge between the theology of money and wealth and the modern context of capitalist enterprise, doing so in a manner that is both accessible and inspiring. We can no longer be 'intimidated by expertise' as Archbishop Rowan Williams referred to it, but at the same time should not feel that we need to be technical experts to talk about money and the power that it has in our lives. We already have at our disposal a rich body of thought that deals directly with many of the underlying issues we face today.

By raising the financial literacy of our clergy and through them parishioners and local communities we are equipping ourselves with the tools needed to bring about greater engagement with the direction that society takes. A new language must be created that enables the two spheres of theology and economy to become unified once more in order to navigate what are tricky and sometimes very personal topics of discussion. Otherwise, we face a period of transition based predominately on emotional responses to crisis situations that can have far-reaching negative consequences that are difficult to undo. Ownership of our society's future must be provided to as broad-based a constituency as possible; and it is here that the second suggestion I would like to make comes into play.

Our Church institutions, and the buildings that they inhabit, provide us with an ideal infrastructure for social change predicated on a mandate of equality and we must find a way to take advantage of this possibility with what can often be limited resources. Enabling community conversations in parishes should be seen as an important aspect of how we utilise Church infrastructure to ensure that we become a relevant and effective tool for local empowerment and issues of mutual concern.

By coupling our mission of faith with social justice initiatives, we can mobilise vast cross-sections of society for causes that require critical mass in order to become effective vehicles for social change. Particular examples such as Fairtrade and the Living Wage campaign, to name but two, are examples where faith communities have been at the forefront of innovation in these areas that have brought about proven, measurable results. We must be emboldened by the recent energy around participatory democracy and its direct links with social justice issues, seeing this as an opportunity to renew the participation that our communities are capable of through the infrastructure that we already have in place.

The last suggestion that I would like to put forward is one that has seen a considerable amount of headway over the last few years, which is the level of cross-fertilisation of strategy across numerous faith-based organisations, non-profits and ethical investment enterprises. We need to be aware of each other's efforts and move toward effective dissemination of mission-driven initiatives that work to one another's strengths. These efforts have the greatest impact when done in parallel and the collaborative work of numerous Church-based organisations highlight the power that such co-operation is able to harness. Networks such as these need to be extended; and they need to incorporate a global membership in order to respond to global challenges.

Practically speaking, we should continue to develop cross-institution committees that explore each other's initiatives on a regular basis; reporting back on areas of success, as well as difficulty, and ensuring that we bring to bear the collective wisdom of our respective networks. By co-ordinating our efforts in such a way, through our various channels of influence, we can ensure that the issues we wish to focus on remain at the forefront of agendas across all sectors. In this manner, we can come together to view the larger picture and see areas of mutual concern and possible collaboration; but work as separate bodies with independent workflows in order to promote action over organisational paralysis. We need to promote an approach that looks more closely at the structures we have in place to instigate change, rather than solely focusing on the changes we wish to see. It is important that we take an iterative approach to our efforts. Learn from each other's initiatives, whether successful or not, and develop our modes of action in order to arrive at a sustainable approach. What we mustn't do is fall into the trap of attaching our efforts to each passing campaign that catches our eye without a detailed understanding of how such a campaign would fit into the long-term strategies and structures we have in place.

With the recent example of Occupy, there was a rush by various organisations and institutions to attach themselves to the movement and operate under its banner. Although interfacing with such spontaneous movements is important and should be done with enthusiasm, without adequate due diligence and strategic planning a great deal of time and resources can be spent on laborious projects that are ultimately ineffective. We must not overlook the passion and energy that sparked this movement and reinvigorated the conversation, and we must always find ways to interface with individuals who are seeking positive change, but we also can't allow ourselves to overly romanticise such movements if doing so means that we allow proven and productive relationships to falter.

We must be emboldened by the call for change, while understanding the responsibility that comes from long-term projects with goals that require significant time and effort to embed into modern society. We must strive to build a basis of wide-scale community engagement that incorporates the needs and concerns of local areas, while situating them within a wider national and global context. In order to do this successfully we must take a systemic approach and ensure that a comprehensive, all-inclusive programme for social change arises that meets the high standards demanded by the traditions we take as our inspiration. While there are many who feel that faith-based institutions should be marginalised in discussions surrounding the models of our new, post-financial crisis society, it is actually at this very moment, when action is required that inspires the foundations of human interaction and empathy, that our religious institutions have the greatest role to play. It's important that we do not waste this opportunity.

We must deepen our commitment to these efforts and combine this with an improvement in our ability to mobilise those who are seeking new narratives of social cohesion. We need to integrate this with our models of wealth creation in a manner that gives precedence to the wellbeing of humanity and protects the natural world. When we start to view things in this way, our actions become less about arguing a case for relevance in a society that feels we are increasingly marginalised. Instead, our engagement proves that the needed mechanisms and motivations for systemic change are in place and ready to be called upon.

IN SEARCH OF AUTHENTICITY

As we continue to deconstruct truth narratives and question traditional crucibles of power, many people are searching for new paradigms upon which to base our collective hopes and dreams. Recent failures in our political and economic structures are not a new or unique tale and a common response to such periods of social upheaval lies in the attempt to discover a new level of authenticity. To construct a discourse that speaks directly to the experience of the individual, while encouraging commitment to a shared reality.

The new modes of communication and organisation that modern technology offers are a vital component of this search for authenticity, through our new found capacity to share information, canvas opinion, and subvert media and political narratives. At the same time, they often highlight that we consciously construct our social image in a way that is removed from our own honest understanding of self identity. We compartmentalise our lives and digitally craft an idealised version of ourselves; and we do this with increasing levels of detail and care. Thus, we have simultaneously developed the perfect medium for collectivism but also the ideal tools for narcissism. With no shared commitment to integrating the various components of our lives – indeed, encouragement to do otherwise – we hide parts of ourselves further; we abstract further; we work upon shared ideas of goodness and righteousness often without having a genuine conversation about what these concepts mean to us, where they are generated and how they might be achieved.

When thinking about socio-economic 'progress' it is difficult to approach a sense of objective reality, but we can often do so by examining some pragmatic outcomes. The ongoing financial crisis is the manifestation of deep-seated social trauma. A severance from the imagined social cohesion displayed before the crisis that undermines previously accepted views of how we relate to one another, such as what it means to succeed; how we create value; and the meaning of wealth. The negative outcomes lie in foreclosed homes; unemployment and disenfranchisement; exponentially increasing wealth disparity; in the detrimental impact we are having on the environment; and in a widening of the gap between those who truly have autonomy and those who must submit to a global political reality that they have limited capacity to escape the negative impacts of.

As feelings of disenfranchisement broaden (beginning to envelope what we refer to as the 'middle class') the social malaise suddenly becomes palpable and can no longer be hidden, as the anger and resentment transfers onto those who have more capacity to be heard. The call for authenticity comes from feelings of exploitation; subjection to external pressures; and the conscious realisation of how political and economic structures are manipulated by those displaying predatory behaviour to the detriment of our collective wellbeing. The social contract then begins to fall apart, even in societies perceived as well-off, precisely because there is no shared sense of enjoyment of social output; rather a blatant display of inequality and injustice typified by feelings of cultural and political alienation as well as economic despair. For the London 2012 Olympics, we spectacularly succeeded at recreating this shared enjoyment; finding a modern mythology that enabled us to feel closer to the unified whole that we all subconsciously crave (something that sport, in general, is good at). Yet this enjoyment was underpinned by a high level of fear and mistrust – of security and paranoia – in the sense that at any moment the shared enjoyment could be stripped away and we would be left facing one another; judging one another; hiding from ourselves in the often monstrous, always imagined, images of those we have no authentic relationship with.

We need to ask ourselves how we might formulate a new public discourse that releases this growing social pressure and lack of trust. What structural models do we have that subvert illusory modes of communication and inherently disingenuous or ignorant relationships? Can we build an open and transparent form of policy-making, in order that through wide-scale peer review we come to find a more genuine sense of social reality? Can horizontal movements such as Occupy replace traditional power hierarchies, or by doing so might we actually move further away from a realistic understanding of what it means to relate to other human beings? To live with and trust; to work for or employ; to love and despise; the realities of charisma, persuasion, rhetoric; the realities of the power relationships that exist between us at all times, in often imperceptible ways.

With the human condition in mind, can a structure that encourages public, unashamed honesty successfully promote the common good and allow wellbeing to flourish? Surely not everything can be so forthright and raw, so what do we gain from a reliance on inauthentic discourse and obfuscated agendas? Is the search for this so-called 'authenticity' itself another illusory creation, a utopian vision that is unattainable no matter how desperately we might want to discover it?

In the end, the answer might be that we don't really want to discover it at all. For to do so will force us to make significant sacrifices, requiring us to deal with a more complex and difficult form of dialogue then we are used to having even with ourselves. Maybe we are not ready to truly commit to authenticity in public life, instead utilising the call for cultural change as just another mask that we wear to appear respectable and decent while privately delighted in our personal comforts and narcissistic desires.

It is time to build up the courage to remove these masks. To stop ignoring the oppressive realities of the social order that we create together every time we act; interact; or refuse to act. Can we discover such authenticity? Or are we too afraid of what we might find waiting for us if we do?

The All-Pervading by George Watts (c.1887)

THE LANGUAGE OF REFORMED CAPITALISM

The narrative of global financial reform was ready for another shake-up, and it arrived in the guise of Thomas Piketty and his data-driven polemic on the inherent flaws in modern capitalism. When coupled with the eye-opening research conducted by Oxfam, along with the sustained resonance of public indignation, excessive wealth concentration and the systemic issues that might be facilitating it are firmly on the agenda. Since the 'Great Recession' emerged many have called for viable alternatives, and now we're beginning to see the first true contenders for consideration. When discussing collective modes of being, the language we use tells us a lot about the traction certain ideas are gaining and the rhetorical devices being used to convey them. Amongst all the discussion there are a number of terms that will be familiar to many of us: words such as inequality, trust, purpose, culture and justice.

At the recent conference on *Inclusive Capitalism*, Christine Lagarde[1] continued a linguistic phrasing heard often by highlighting the pressing need to restore trust in the system. Using familiar language, she posits that we *'need to turn our attention to the culture of financial institutions'* and

---

1. Christine Lagarde was at this time Managing Director of the International Monetary Fund, a position she held from 2011-2019

rediscover *'the social purpose of the financial sector'*. In many ways, her speech is a useful synopsis of where the reform debate has settled over recent years.

Mark Carney[2] focused on social wellbeing over private gain – where *'a sense of self must be accompanied by a sense of the systemic'* – and by doing so conveyed the crux of reformed capitalism. He recognised the need for 'distributive justice' that promotes relative equality and encourages investment in social capital alongside economic capital, alongside a call for a genuine answer to the question *'Who does finance serve?'* that draws capitalism away from being 'an end in itself'. The importance of this speech should not be underestimated, as it displays a tonal shift from the top that will hopefully be received loud and clear.

At a different event I attended recently, a senior banking representative (tasked with internal cultural change) laid out clearly that the bank had a duty to meet the needs of *'stakeholders, shareholders, customers, clients and society'*. When an implied hierarchy of priorities can place society last in this manner (even if only unconsciously), it should cause us to ask: *what is currently missing from the language of reformed capitalism?*

As indicative as the *Inclusive Capitalism* conference was of recent dialogue on economic reform, I remain intrigued by the phrases and terms we *don't* hear as much as those we do. There is something all-together too convenient about much of the rhetoric surrounding this debate, primarily because, in order to prove palatable to key audiences, relatively small modifications are favoured over paradigmatic change. Systemic shifts are too daunting or threatening for many, and so we rest upon incremental paths that are easier to convince and implement in the short-term but run the risk of falling foul of some of the same systemic problems in the future. Alongside this, discussions on culture and purpose necessarily rely on broad terms of reference whilst those using such phrases often blame predecessors and defer responsibility onto a loosely defined future period. Antony Jenkins' well-known statement[3] that *'it will take several years – probably five to 10 – to rebuild trust'* is just one such example, with the Archbishop of Canterbury adding that it could take *'a generation'*. Changes of this kind take time, that is certainly true, but as a result it means that those making the promises are able to avoid being held accountable for the end results – particularly in an environment where average CEO tenure rests between 5 to 8 years. Overall, we should be optimistic because it seems like some key messages are being

---

2. Mark Carney was Governor of the Bank of England from 2013-2020
3. Antony Jenkins was the Group Chief Executive of Barclays from 2012-2015

taken seriously and broadly embraced. However, there are terms missing from the reform lexicon that it might be worth seeing whether or not we can realistically introduce...

Can we reinvigorate an understanding of *discernment?* Mark Carney touched on this with ideas of personal vocation and meaning in the workplace. On a systemic level we often rush toward answers that are rhetorically pleasing (*purpose, culture*) without a notion that such terms require a depth of integrated understanding and interdisciplinary thinking that we have not yet mustered. The forms of discernment with the most impact are not those that are only reactionary, but rather showcase a degree of insight that can lead to proactive responses to problems yet to arise.

Can we create space for the exploration of *recompense?* Not merely the kind of forced compensation that follows the PPI scandal, LIBOR rigging, or numerous other regulatory fines – but the notion that the financial sector owes society a very great debt and this must be paid back in non-financial (systemic) capital. Restorative justice that brings a sense of closure to both victim and perpetrator depends on open and attentive dialogue with those who have been wronged, rather than the victim being told what is best by those who committed the injustice in the first place.

Can we acknowledge the need for *sacrifice?* That the financial sector cannot adequately implement true reform without also accepting that it will negatively impact the bottom line. This is not about profitable change. This is about reining in a set of business practices that are unsustainable and inherently anti-social, and to do so will mean a commitment to lower (but perhaps less volatile) financial returns in order to shift cultures and restore trust. It also means, on an individual level, the willingness to forgo many of the excesses of modern consumer society and recognise the extent to which we might ourselves be complicit in facilitating resistance to systemic change.

The language we use to articulate reform is the bridge between abstract principles and real-world practice. We have found momentum recently with inspiring rhetoric, backed by a number of hard-hitting structural and regulatory changes, and we should be optimistic as a result. It's important, though, that at this pivotal moment we consider carefully the use of language and rhetoric and its impact on lasting change.

By ensuring that we link a genuine understanding of the injustice often caused by profit-led ideologies with an acknowledgement that we need a deeper sense of restitution and transformation, we can lay down the foundations that will enable one of the most important phrases to enter into the conversation on reformed capitalism: *forgiveness.*

The Golden Tree (partial) from *The Quest and Achievement of the Holy Grail* by
Edwin A. Abbey (c.1895)

PUBLIC VULNERABILITY IS THE KEY TO SHARED SUCCESS

The communal intake of breath was noticeable at St Paul's when it was announced that the play *Temple* would open up the world of the Dean and Chapter, focusing on the tense period when an Occupy encampment had sprung up outside. From the Cathedral's perspective it was a difficult and challenging time, one that sparked a rediscovery of a higher purpose sometimes clouded by the necessary rigours of daily routine. I have written about our complex relationship with the protestors at the time, so it was with a certain level of curious apprehension that I attended this theatrical rendition of it.

I came away heartened by the sophisticated manner in which the subject was conveyed. There is a deep humanity running through the play and a large degree of truth about a situation that was impossible to resolve to the liking of all parties involved. Ultimately, the message is that there was no correct answer that could emerge from any one person or organisation. This was a moment of global significance, with many different focal points, triggered by issues of widespread inequality and the systemic failures of our economic and political institutions.

What came across most powerfully, though, was the open vulnerability displayed by the characters. The writer, producers and actors managed to attach this exposure of the soul to a committed sense of belonging to something larger than the self; to a shared vision of what it means to embody an experience of community that aims to gracefully uplift us all. It's an immediately recognisable place to be: doubting decisions made; wanting to live up to potential; striving to succeed but falling into pitfalls of our own creation. Depictions of vulnerability such as this, while prevalent throughout many literary forms, are rare in today's society, which may be what made the Occupy encampments around the world so significant.

Instead of allowing one another to speak truth, we have somehow settled upon a public arena that calls for hollow platitudes (and sales pitches); where those who confront the difficulty of trying to reconcile competing motivations are often ridiculed. We have developed an overwhelming addiction to crafting public narratives of ourselves and others that protect our vulnerabilities through deceptive rhetoric. This lies at the heart of much of the disillusionment evident throughout modern society and should be viewed as a primary area of concern.

With the General Election fresh in our minds, the evasive and insubstantive nature of political campaigning is a powerful example of how these facades have replaced substantive debate. Not only have such illusions stifled our ability to discern what might constitute a healthy and flourishing society, but they have actively positioned us against one another through the corrosive effect of preferring stereotypes over nuanced dialogue. We are continuously presented with manicured clichés, because to welcome ideas from opponents or to have to retract in error is perceived as weakness. It is not until faced with demoralising defeat that we see any lasting semblance of deep conviction and honesty from our politicians. Maybe if we could encourage (and allow) an open vulnerability from our political leaders, then we could foster a more productive dialogue that incorporates a broader set of ideological viewpoints.

This same issue runs through the private sector and, in particular, so much of what has occurred following the global financial crisis. The pressures that resulted from linking shareholder value to fluctuating stock prices have promoted short-term facades that hide the long-term viability of business practices and their true impact on the world. We continue to see new examples of a serious lack of financial probity. Senior figures often avoid addressing deep-seated systemic issues, preferring to point out the misconduct of a few 'bad apples' that can be addressed with ambiguous 'culture change'. There is something that rings hollow about a commitment to change that looks at the purpose and culture of business, but will say little on issues of global inequality and the facilitation of structural injustice.

As discussed in my previous piece about trust and the social contract, there is a massive opportunity for organisations that are able to embrace an authentic voice – and a large requirement of this is the courage to be open about areas of weakness and vulnerability. An example of this was Archbishop Justin Welby's well-known 'War on Wonga' that was firmly placed in the media spotlight, before being followed quickly by revelations that Church investments had exposure to the very same company and its predatory lending practices. There were quick calls of hypocrisy, responded to by an equally quick and open admission of error. When taking a longer view, this mistake actually provided credibility to the Archbishop's desire to challenge these injustices of debt. There was a raw humanity to his expression of irritation about the situation, that enabled many to see that his words carried more depth than perhaps first thought. This was indeed a genuine attempt to meaningfully overcome some of the wealth inequality that people face on a day-to-day basis; and the campaign has continued to grow.

This is one small example of why it is important that we encourage public vulnerability, because it is often where our most truthful, compassionate and charitable natures reside. We know how important the emotional experience is to personal change, but we have developed a public discourse that does not allow such a central aspect of ourselves to be expressed on a larger scale. It is telling that when vulnerability is expressed, it is usually as apologies that follow being caught or called out rather than an honest and proactive appraisal that admits where problems might occur in the first place. The recent FIFA scandal has seen numerous high-level sponsors become critical of the organisation, distancing themselves from corruption while at the same time having spent years ignoring a well-documented humanitarian crisis. This is a direct example of a duplicitous and inauthentic discourse allowed to run rife, with the sponsors seeing the resulting backlash across social media as the general public are increasingly challenging these narratives.

Might we, the so-called 'general public', be to blame as we use the services, subscribe to the media and buy the endorsed products? It's important that we don't fully accept the 'complicit consumer' argument, but we do need to find ways to applaud vulnerability rather than immediately holding everyone to strict and unforgiving account. Accountability is vital, of course, but the sharing of self-doubts should be encouraged and the discursive process of discovering new directions should not be fraught with the threat of quick and vicious backlash. To the extent we collectively punish those who admit mistakes, we should not be surprised by obfuscation and cover-up. If we want a more authentic and open discourse, then we have to create a safer space for it to occur and that is where responsibility lies at the feet of the public. We must collectively become less quick to raise judgement; more committed to the process of understanding; and more willing to provide forgiveness for past wrongs once genuinely addressed.

As a result, we will rediscover vital aspects of public life that have been increasingly eroded away – such as trust, empathy and solidarity. Trust has been shattered not simply because of wrong-doing, but through endemic duplicity. Empathy has faded because we constantly see one another in oppositional terms. Solidarity will return when we find a new way to communicate forthrightly and with a commitment to including the views returned in response. Greater respect will be gathered in this way through shared understanding of one another's true positions and thoughts. It is thus vital that we rediscover how to meet with one another face-to-face (both metaphorically and literally) and conduct our dealings with mutual concern for the world we are co-creating with each step.

Can we encourage a new public discourse that is openly vulnerable and ready to discuss our own flaws, so that they might be overcome together? I hope that we have the courage to do so and get to experience the collective results that would emerge if we could.

THE POWER OF MEANINGFUL WORK

Three workers [were] breaking up rocks. When the first was asked what he was doing, he replied, 'Making little ones out of big ones'; the second said, 'Making a living'; and the third, 'Building a cathedral'.[1]

It is surprisingly easy to overlook the importance of work. Throughout much of our lives we don't really consider what it means to us, it's just something we do. On some days we're excited to get stuck in, on others we groan about why we have to do it at all. It pays the bills, introduces us to new friends (sometimes enemies) and helps provide for ourselves and those dear to us. When we do stop to consider more deeply why we work, it can often be accompanied with a great deal of anxiety. What do I really want to do with my life? Am I living up to my potential? What's next and how do I find it?

These kinds of questions revolve around meaning and identity. They centre upon notions of purpose and creativity; of what it truly means to be successful. There are also closely related concerns about working towards

---

1. Ryan, J. J. 1977, Humanistic Work: Its philosophical and cultural implications, in Heisler & Houck (Eds.) *A Matter of Dignity: Inquiries into the Humanization of Work,* pp. 11-22, Notre Dame

common goals, helping others and the nature of community. Most people don't want to merely be a cog in someone else's machine, we yearn for self-empowerment and are most fulfilled when we find a way to do so in collaboration with other people. Think of the contrast between repetitive factory work under harsh conditions, compared to more innovative companies that promote flexible working; allow employees to voice their ideas; concerns; and consider carefully their wider role in the world. The latter is filled with life and connectivity, the former dehumanising and detached from creative fulfilment.

Discovering a deeper sense of purpose and meaning in our work brings with it not only personal fulfilment, but productivity and organisational loyalty. A Gallup Poll in 2013 found that only 13% of employees worldwide were engaged at work, a shocking figure when you consider the implications. There is a growing body of research that clearly shows the benefits of a more engaged workforce – to employees and employers alike – while also helping define just what it is that makes work meaningful. Purpose comes from activities that have personal meaning, while being of consequence to the world beyond the self. Meaning arises from an ongoing process of self-examination about your motivations and what is most important to you. For many, these two things come together most readily when you focus your energy on the needs of others through the achievement of long-term goals. Combining all this, meaningful work could be considered a repackaging of two perennial truths: *Love one another* and *know thyself.* Easy to learn, but can take a lifetime to master.

It's important to note that this doesn't need to be attached to what are seen as traditionally meaningful sectors (such as charity work or health care), but is more dependent on the perspective that the individual brings to whatever it is they are doing. Almost any profession can be pursued with purpose and meaning and to do so is to embrace the power to form new ways of life, inherent within each of us as human beings. A capacity that rests at the core of all human endeavour and achievement, yet one that we often presume we don't have the ability to access within ourselves. By rediscovering the power of meaningful work we can become more effective agents of transformation within the world around us.

I would argue that this is primarily because our work is the mechanism through which we interact with the power dynamics of society writ large. Not just in the sense that the institutional structures of our world exert their influence on how we use our time and energy, but also because we are the agents of structural power on a daily basis. Through our work, both as individuals and groups, we influence the momentum of society and help forge the vision of what it will become. Having a passionate and meaningful relationship to work connects our professional efforts with the social construction of new and collective ways of being. The future is created on the foundations of the present, which are built upon the efforts of the past, so we have a moral obligation to enter into this chain of creation consciously and faithfully. As Pope John Paul II laid out in his 1981 encyclical *Laborem Exercens* (Section 25), it is through *"the knowledge that by means of work man shares in the work of creation [that] constitutes the most profound motive for undertaking it."*

Meaningful work is often powerful because it redirects the impulse of activity towards others, working against the internalising motivators of our increasingly atomised and self-serving lifestyles. By seeing the core of meaningful work as being other-focused, our productivity is directed towards those around us in a form of mutual support that ultimately benefits us all as individuals as well as collectively. This goes against the notion that many people fall back upon when considering how their careers are meaningful, which is to ensure the wellbeing of their immediate family. While providing for our own families is certainly an honourable and worthwhile pursuit, if it becomes the sole purpose of our working lives then we are limiting the potential benefit that society could receive through our efforts. We are also setting ourselves up with a logic that can lead to a mercenary approach, devoid of loyalty or true commitment to the common good.

Restoring work with meaning and purpose returns a more colourful, passionate and fulfilling set of relationships from which to develop a deeper understanding of our lives and role in society. It renews the artistry in our professions and moves them away from a mechanistic and dehumanising approach to activity. It can help us to, as former Archbishop of Canterbury Rowan Williams has stated, *"affirm the solidity of 'intermediate' communities that are neither private nor state-franchised (professional guilds, trade unions, religious associations, volunteer organisations and activist citizens' networks)"*[2]. It challenges an often hierarchical status quo and builds a greater sense of partnership, one that uplifts through community rather than gains status through control.

The power of meaningful work comes in large part from this ability to

---

2. Williams, R. 2016, *Liberalism and capitalism have hollowed out society – so where do we turn now?*, New Statesman, 18th October edition

redefine the authority with which we lead our lives and direct our passions. By working toward a greater vision of what we can achieve together, it allows us to unburden any feelings of powerlessness that the day-to-day realities of our working lives can sometimes bring. Of course, taking such an approach does not guarantee that our actions will always be aligned with the common good (if only it were that easy!). However, it is important to note that the common good is not a fixed subject but rather a process entered upon with good faith and commitment to understanding the needs and experiences of others. As I have heard said at a workshop run by the organisation Good Works: *you don't need a definition of the common good in order to behave as if it exists.* You do your best, make a difference (small or large) and the common good is made more manifest; with each cycle bringing further clarity about your own motivations and reasons for being.

There are many different ways to explore what is meaningful to us, what is most important is that we take the time to actually do so. The process of discerning what is important to you is one that needs to take place on an ongoing basis and can often be a difficult journey to undertake. Each of us will come to different conclusions, but it's highly rewarding to make even a small change on how we approach our working lives and see the immediate influence that can have on our workplaces. This requires both the courage to lead and the humility to serve. In the closing event for our series on meaningful work, held in partnership with the London School of Economics, Prof. Nava Ashraf reminded us that *"work in the spirit of service could be the highest form of worship, and that in fact it could be devotion."* Find some time to consider what it means for your work to be a devotional act and you may be pleasantly surprised by the journey it takes you on.

We often overlook the importance of work in our lives. By doing so we forget that it can be the point at which we integrate our personal, civic and spiritual selves into one complete and powerful whole. Enabling us to not only find a deep sense of fulfilment, but also more fully participate in the chain of creation that we have been graced with as human beings. Through discovering meaningful work we build not just individual character, but strong and resilient communities. Allowing us to stand up to structural injustices and build better alternatives through which we can uplift the dignity of our fellow global citizens.

In the inspiring words of the anthropologist Margaret Mead: *"Never doubt that a small group of thoughtful, committed citizens can change the world; indeed, it is the only thing that ever has."*

LOVE IN ACTION: THE THEOLOGY OF MARTIN LUTHER KING JR.

"In these days of worldwide confusion, there is a dire need for men and women who will courageously do battle for truth."[1]

Today, on Martin Luther King Jr. Day in the United States, we remember the meaning behind this great man's life. He was never a politician, even though his life had great political consequence. He was a citizen and a preacher who wanted the Church to rise above being merely a *"weak and ineffectual trumpet making uncertain sounds"* and redefined for many what it meant to be a Christian. With the world today appearing so uncertain and detached from a sense of mutual responsibility we call the common good, it is worth hearing his message once again.

The legacy of Martin Luther King Jr. is lasting because he reminds us to strive for a lofty ideal of what we could be. His great civil rights successes are an assurance that the prophetic voice carries with it more than just words, that we can speak of truth and love without reservation and by doing so make a real difference. Secure in the knowledge that lasting change can

---

1. King Jr., M. L.   2017, *A Gift of Love: Sermons from Strength to Love and Other Preachings*, Penguin Classics (all quotes taken from this collection of sermons)

result when we invoke the glory of God and walk the path of faith without feeling ashamed. Indeed not just that we *can* do so, but in times of great conflict and exploitation we are duty bound and *must* do so with all the strength and wisdom that we can muster.

His theology is based primarily on the power of truth and love to transform the world around us, particularly when built upon a solid core of peace and forgiveness. Today, we often hear that we have entered a 'post-truth' world. This would be anathema to a man who felt that it was through the light of truth that progress is made and darkness overcome. He was also deeply aware that in a time that appears to hold great wealth, *"our abundance has brought us neither peace of mind nor serenity of spirit."* The structural injustice of poverty and inequality, a struggle that remains as important today as it has ever been, was every bit as much the focus for his attention as segregation.

It's wonderful that he preached at St Paul's Cathedral in 1964, on his way to Oslo to accept the Nobel Peace Prize. A newly reprinted collection of sermons released by Penguin reintroduces us to the words of a man passionate about the role of faith and prayer in creating a better vision of the world. He calls us to an active faith that works in our daily lives to transform the world proactively and courageously, becoming *"open receptacles ... into which God's strength [can] be freely poured."* Such faith can makes us feel truly alive, participating in society rather than accepting a sedated lifestyle of indifference.

King is admired because he assertively stood up to injustice, reminding us that we are not helpless in the face of adversity and have the capacity within our own souls to generate a more equal and just socioeconomic reality. His theology highlights that true power does not rely on government or industry, but can come from an unwavering dedication to truth and love that each and every one of us has the capacity to be transformed by. Even more so, that our redemption cannot merely be dictated by laws and regulations but must come from what he called 'unenforceable obligations':

> *"... unenforceable obligations are beyond the reach of the laws of society. They concern inner attitudes, genuine person-to-person relations, and expressions of compassion which law books cannot regulate and jails cannot rectify. Such obligations are met by one's commitment to an inner law, written on the heart. Man-made laws assure justice, but a higher law produces love."*

Finding a way to continuously renew our commitment to this inner law lies at the core of his theology and, along with many examples of empowered citizens throughout history that he drew upon, inspired the non-violent action that he is known for. Much of his preaching was specifically on the obligation that Christians have to understand that we each take some responsibility for the injustices of the world – that through wrong action, or inaction, we often serve to exacerbate suffering. If we are to live up to his message then we must seek to correct our own flaws even as we rally against the destructive actions of others. We mustn't just loudly preach and pontificate, but should always strive to act with mindful devotion and self-reflection.

The path that King laid out for us combines powerful words with transformative deeds and builds upon forgiveness rather than retribution; upon peace over conflict. His theology emphasises the power of love for what is right and true, as opposed to corrupting hatred for the people responsible for the ills of the world. He strongly believed that by walking the path of love in action we can overcome evil deeds while accepting the inherent goodness of those who mistakenly conducted them, preaching that the lasting way to destroy an enemy is to find friendship with them. His legacy is a living example of how faith can provide the foresight to know that the strength of the soul can overcome violence in all its forms.

While standing up against the injustices we see, we must always remember that *"returning hate for hate multiplies hate, adding deeper darkness to a night already devoid of stars"*. The message that King repeated time and again was that by waving the banner of love we seek a more complete response that undermines the cycles of violence and works towards redirecting them in total, not just in part. He recognised that this was a difficult thing to do, but as the world around him became more chaotic and less certain he knew that it was an increasingly *necessary* thing to do. This is what makes his sermons so timeless and one of the key lessons to be learned is that we must find the humility and compassion to see the totality of those we come into contact with. There is more to a person than the content of their words or the outcomes of their deeds, there is also the potential of their being. Great transformations can result through recognising the best in others and realising that *"forgiveness is not an occasional act; it is a permanent attitude."*

The encouraging fact of today's world is that we do not need to wait for another individual figure as transformative as Martin Luther King Jr. (although there are many out there). Together we can, through technology and global communications, build a collective voice that uplifts the discourse of our time and feeds back into the daily actions of all who hear its call and contribute to its meaning. By actively participating, we can overcome the tendency to merely be *"thermometers that record or register the temperature of majority opinion"* and each play a part in being *"thermostats that transform and regulate the temperature of society."*

As we face a period of rapid and unsettling change, there is no better time to hear this legendary preacher's words spoken passionately as you watch a recording or read them on the page. To feel the universal truth of what is being shared and the unwavering love that it is born of, recognising in our faith an obligation to act for a more just and loving world. Martin Luther King Jr. is revered because he had a dream, a vision of a better existence that could be achieved when we all acted as if it were possible. He believed that there is a role for all of us in creating the future and that our participation should be seen as a duty-bound obligation of the Christian life.

Our world today seems to be desperately lacking in uplifting visions of what we could become, so it is important to remind ourselves of what it looks like when someone truly has one:

> *"Midnight is a confusing hour when it is difficult to be faithful. The most inspiring word that the church may speak is that no midnight long remains. The weary traveller by midnight who asks for bread is really seeking the dawn. Our eternal message of hope is that dawn will come."*

Our eternal message of hope

is that dawn will come.

BV - #0006 - 220822 - C18 - 229/152/14 - PB - 9780853186243 - Gloss Lamination